Cross-Currents

Books by Arnold Forster

Anti-Semitism—1947
A Measure of Freedom
The Troublemakers (with Benjamin R. Epstein)

Books by Benjamin R. Epstein

Cold Pogrom *translated from the German*
Collected Essays on Masaryk *translated from the German*
The Troublemakers (with Arnold Forster)

CROSS-

CURRENTS

by   Arnold Forster

and   Benjamin R. Epstein

Doubleday & Company, Inc.

1956   GARDEN CITY, NEW YORK

Library of Congress Catalog Card Number 56-7657
Copyright ©, 1956, by The Anti-Defamation League of B'nai B'rith
All Rights Reserved
Printed in the United States
First Edition

To May and Ethel

—whose deep convictions and understanding patience permitted us to take from them the endless and irretrievable days and nights which were needed for the writing of this book.

Authors' Note

No nation in our time can remain an island unto itself. In writing a book about the dangerous cross-currents of prejudice disturbing the mainstream of democratic life in the United States, we found, when tracing them to their source, that these currents frequently reach us from distant lands. Tides that rise in Germany and the Middle East seriously affect our political life at home. Thus, while many pages are devoted to the German scene and to the Middle East, this is, in fact, a book about the United States.

The story we tell is constructed from a very large number of memoranda and documents which actually repose in the files of the Anti-Defamation League. To be sure, the book's memoranda are not exact copies. Simplicity suggested that the men and women who were involved in the preparation or receipt of the relevant correspondence be described collectively, in accordance with their departmental responsibilities, as "Research," "Library," "German Correspondent," "New York Correspondent," etc., etc. Information extraneous to the essential story was deleted; descriptive background was added where necessary to make the story intelligible; language was edited for pur-

Authors' Note

poses of clarity and smoothness. In several places the chronology of memoranda was modified—to make clearer the chronology of investigation. In some correspondence, names were changed to protect the sources of information from retaliation or embarrassment. *But no facts have been changed in any way. Nor has the meaning of any memorandum or document been modified in any way.* These are presented to the reader as excerpts or in full, for him to evaluate in his own best judgment.

AF BRE

Authors' Acknowledgment

Only after reading this book from cover to cover can one truly understand the debt its authors owe to the Anti-Defamation League of B'nai B'rith. The work is based upon the files of an agency composed of many men and women whose actual memoranda make up page after page of this document. To each and all of them goes our heartfelt appreciation. To Jack Baker, Jerome Bakst, Milton Ellerin, Morton Kass, and Shirley Feinberg, our deep gratitude for their research on the memoranda which form the backbone of our story. To Nathan C. Belth, Harold Berman, and Harold Braverman, our thanks for their editorial assistance on the entire manuscript.

AF BRE

Foreword

From 1944 until the end of the war, as he saw victory swiftly slipping from his grasp, Adolf Hitler carried on with one great hope. He looked upon the uneasy alliance between the Western democracies and the Soviet Union—an alliance he was responsible for forging by his two-front attack—and judged that there was bound to be a parting of the ways. Hitler himself had made an alliance of convenience with the Soviet Union which he abruptly ended by his attack on Russia in 1940. He knew that neither his nor any other totalitarian regime could long maintain an international partnership, least of all with a democratic ally. So as the tides of war turned against him, he was left with this one great hope: that the East-West wartime alliance would collapse before his Nazi armies did. On the political and propaganda fronts the Nazis worked desperately to bring this about before the military debacle which finally engulfed Hitler and his evil regime.

The subsequent history of the Soviet-Western conflict has shown that Hitler's calculations were not without foundation. Hitler's one miscalculation lay in this: the free world recognized that, while his brutal forces were on the march, nazism was the greater menace; the Soviet Union, with a Nazi army on its soil, found an alliance with the

Foreword

West the only assurance of its own survival. Soviet leaders, therefore, put aside their enmity to the West until Hitler had been dealt with. It was a waiting game Hitler could not win.

This bit of history will help the reader to put the story recounted in the following pages into focus. Hitler, in the crisis of war, could not capitalize on the very real schism between the communist and the democratic worlds, but his spiritual heirs, in this continuing era of cold war, are seeking to take up where their master left off. This is the story which *Cross-Currents* has to tell.

Through the years the Anti-Defamation League of B'nai B'rith, concerned with the strengthening of democracy, has maintained an unceasing vigil on the activities of the backward-looking forces which, spawned in the ferment created by an aggressive and hostile Soviet power, have sought to regain a lost world for fascist ideas and ideals. The activities of these forces have been carefully recorded in the researches which the League maintains: how they seek to divide the counsels of free people, to stir unrest among us, to weaken our resolution; how they have operated in our country, in Germany—once the seat of their power—and now in the Middle East and other areas of the world. Because it is crucially important for Americans to know who these people and what their calculations are, the Civil Rights Committee of the League determined that access to this information be given to all who would read it. *Cross-Currents* is designed to do this.

Cross-Currents was undertaken at the direction of the Civil Rights Committee of which Judge David A. Rose of Boston is chairman, and Judge Jacob Grumet of New York, associate chairman, and a special committee of Judge Rose, Mr. Bernard Nath of Chicago, Mr. Norman Newhouse of New York, and myself.

In some aspects of this book the reader will enter a world he thought no longer existed—one that had seemingly been destroyed with Hitler's armies. It is important for the ultimate success of the free world that he know it does exist.

Henry Edward Schultz
National Chairman,
Anti-Defamation League of B'nai B'rith

Contents

Authors' Note 9
Authors' Acknowledgment 11
Foreword 13

Cross-Currents in America

One   The Anti-Eisenhower Crusade 19
Two   The Fort Monmouth Scandal 67
Three   The Chasanow Story 123
Four   The Reactionaries 143

Contents

Cross-Currents in Germany

One   The Nazi Diehards 177

Two   The New Foundation 235

Cross-Currents in the Middle East

One   The Issue 301

Two   The Side Door 311

Three   The New Director 325

Four   The Front Door 337

Five   The Back Door 351

Six   The Touchstone 363

Conclusion

A Final Word 381

CROSS-CURRENTS
IN AMERICA

One   The Anti-Eisenhower Crusade

SEPTEMBER 6, 1955
Arnold Forster and Benjamin R. Epstein to the Reader

Karl von Clausewitz, German military philosopher of the nineteenth century, propounded the thesis that war is a natural and proper extension of diplomacy. German international relations for the next hundred years, indeed until the end of World War II, were predicated upon that thesis. Only now, in a world that knows the atom bomb, does the ultimate error of Clausewitz's thesis become apparent, for an extension of diplomacy into war today can mean not only the end of diplomacy but the end of the world as we know it.

In the second quarter of the twentieth century another German added a little fillip to the Clausewitz thesis. Hitler, recognizing that war was the ultimate extension of his diplomacy, sought a political weapon that would strengthen him at home and perhaps win for him allies in other countries. He was not the inventor of anti-Semitism—or in its broader terms racial and religious bigotry—as a political weapon, but he did bring it to its most cruel development.

1 Cross-Currents in America

Even as there are nations today unwilling to accept the fact that war in the atomic age is unthinkable, so there are men who will not abjure the uses of anti-Semitism as a political weapon despite the utter defeat of Hitler and the world revulsion toward his policies. This book is about these men who, though on the periphery of our political life, manage to operate upon an international scale and to set up crosscurrents that disturb the mainstreams of human relations.

Their centers of operation are three: the United States, Germany, and the Arab lands, though their activities will also be noted in many other areas of the world. There are former Nazis active in Argentina and in Mexico; there is a most vicious pamphleteer working out of Sweden; there are evidences that political anti-Semitism is active in South Africa and in North Africa. But these are peripheral and they depend for sustenance upon the three centers to which we have devoted our investigations.

Since we are writing upon the uses of anti-Semitism as a political weapon, it is well to note here an important omission from the book—the situation behind the Iron Curtain. It should not be forgotten that political anti-Semitism in modern times was largely a Russian invention. The czars' minions worked up a pogrom every time there was need for diverting the people from the corruption or failures or excesses of the regime. Much of the current anti-Semitic hate literature is still based on Russian sources which have long been exposed as fakes and forgeries.

There is clear evidence that the communist regimes of Europe have hesitated no more than their czarist predecessors to utilize anti-Semitism when it has suited their political purpose. Thus the free world has in recent years been treated to the spectacle of a Slansky trial in Czechoslovakia, to a Jewish doctors' plot against the life of Stalin, and to numerous "spy" trials against Jews in other Iron Curtain countries. The Jew has continued, in the Russian tradition, to be a handy scapegoat for warring communist factions.

Whatever is known about these events has already been reported in the newspapers, the periodical press, and the publications of the Anti-Defamation League and other Jewish organizations. There is little we

1 The Anti-Eisenhower Crusade

could add to the total fund of knowledge at this time. Nor did we find that Iron Curtain anti-Semitism, political in nature though it is, fits into the general pattern of fascist-oriented activity which the following pages develop. The methods and the purposes may be similar, but there is little contact between the two.

Since we are not attempting, in this book, an over-all review of the status and development of anti-Semitism today, the reader will also note other omissions which such a review would need to include. There is no report on developing patterns of discrimination, social or economic. Nor do we touch upon those aspects of anti-Semitism which are rooted in religious prejudice. These areas of interest, too, have been extensively reported upon in recent publications of the Anti-Defamation League.

Now that we have noted what this book does not do, it would be well to describe what it does do. It goes far afield into many corners of the United States; it goes deep into the new Germany; and it reaches into the Middle East. Occasionally there are side tours, touching on Argentina, or Sweden, or France. But the book is nevertheless single-minded in purpose, tracing the activities of those who still seek to wield anti-Semitism as a political weapon, and revealing how the cross-currents and eddies that they create disturb the mainstreams of democratic life in the United States. For after all is said and done this is a book about the United States.

Because it is essentially a book about the United States, at one juncture we took time to trace the course of an important side road in our own country which we ignored in Germany and the Middle East: the path of civil liberties. The two problems—religious bigotry and civil liberties—became so intermingled in the United States during the period from 1950 to 1955 that our survey would have been incomplete if we had not examined this collateral issue.

Incidentally, not every person or organization across whose path we came during the course of our investigations, and whose activities are accordingly described in our memoranda, is anti-Semitic. Where we have found them guilty of such prejudice, we say so in specific terms. Where they have appeared to be involved only peripherally, we have

I Cross-Currents in America

tried to make the fact clear. It should not be taken for granted that the mere inclusion of a name in a memorandum means, ipso facto, a charge of religious bigotry.

Our story is told in the following pages by means of memoranda and correspondence from the files of the Anti-Defamation League. This is not done as a literary device, but as a way of developing the facts for the reader exactly as they developed over the course of time for those working on the problems of political anti-Semitism in the League itself. Thus, it is hoped, the reader will himself get the feeling of participating in the unearthing of the facts herein presented.

In order to keep the story unencumbered by non-essentials, all unrelated information in the memoranda has been eliminated. Furthermore, individual names of correspondents have been eliminated in favor of departmental designations such as "Research," "Library," "German Correspondent," "Middle East Correspondent," and so on. In several instances the consecutive arrangement of memoranda has been changed in order to clarify the chronology of events. Also names appearing in correspondence have at times been changed in order to protect sources of information from retaliation or embarrassment. But no facts have been changed in any way. The reader of these pages will receive his information in exactly the way we received it.

It will soon become evident to the reader of these pages, as it did to us, that despite the destruction of the prewar Hitler movement and of Hitler himself there exists today a real, though elusive, anti-Semitic internationale. The leaders of this cabal have no formal organization; but they manage to maintain close personal contact and continuous working relationships. They are drawn together by a community of interest—anti-Semitism and the political uses thereof. Inevitably, these men are committed to extreme nationalism in whatever country they call home. In Germany they are the remnants of the die-hard Nazis; in Italy, of the old-line fascism; in France, of the extreme rightist movements that turned collaborationist during the war; in the United States, of those nativist groups that are forever subverting our democratic processes.

They crave power, these men, and a world made over to conform

1 The Anti-Eisenhower Crusade

to their own warped and hateful ideas. Anti-Semitism, they hope, despite the history of the past twenty years, is still the weapon that will permit them to come to power.

It should come as no surprise that much of the creative thinking among these men comes from those in countries once dominated by Hitler, especially Germany and France. Notable is the development of a neo-Nazi research center by the Werner Naumann group—Naumann, once Goebbels' lieutenant, who despite prosecution by the West German Government may yet become a political factor in Germany. The old Nazi archives on the "Jewish question" have been destroyed and scattered. Now the Naumann group is working feverishly to soften Nazi misdeeds in world opinion and to rewrite the vanished anti-Semitic propaganda material, some of which has already found its way to the United States.

This is a great boon to the less inventive American anti-Semitic agitators whose wellsprings of new ideas dried up with the coming of World War II. Now they are avidly receiving and readopting new anti-Semitic propaganda from abroad—from German and from Arab sources. Mass mailings, following well-tested mail-order techniques, have replaced mass meetings in purveying hate ideas in the United States. Big rallies of the Madison Square Garden type are in disfavor; they cost too much money and, being too visible, arouse the opposition of decent people. More valuable today for the professional anti-Semitic agitator is the moneyed backer. The well-culled mailing list is, therefore, the most treasured possession of the anti-Semitic propagandist today.

Hate pamphleteering is carried on with little real money changing hands. Instead of dues-paying members, a few well-heeled contributors usually foot the bills for printing and distributing specific items which fit their particular hate. Thus Conde McGinley, the New Jersey hate publisher, gets a special donation to print 300,000 copies of one issue of *Common Sense* and then slips back to his normal 30,000 on the next. Much of today's organized anti-Semitic activity is carried on co-operatively. The anti-Semites lavishly flatter one another's handiwork, distribute each other's diatribes, make all kinds of business deals to keep the stuff rolling through the mails.

Pretty poor stuff, on the whole, the reader will find, but these works of hate manage to create poisoned air in any tension situation that may arise in the country. They become effective at the least expected moment, and because the hatemongers can readily be bought, there are men not averse to using them for political advantage. Indirectly, their work can be felt in such a situation as the security investigation at Fort Monmouth, or more directly in an election campaign for the presidency of the United States.

During the twenty-year period of Democratic Party rule—1932 to 1952—Americans came to understand that a professional network of bigots from border to border regarded the Administration in Washington as an evil. It was an evil that would have to be eliminated, argued the bigots, if the country were to be saved variously from the Jews, the Free Masons, the Negroes, frequently the Catholics, and sometimes the Protestants. The victims of the propaganda network were religious, racial, or other native groups, the announced target was the White House and national political control, but the end goal of the agitators, besides financial profit, was to see the United States run in the fashion of a dictatorship. Franklin D. Roosevelt, Harry S. Truman, the Democratic Party were also the subjects of false attack by these same agitators simply because, having been elected by the majority, their presence blocked this small band of prejudiced tyrants on its path to the goal.

Few Americans understood this at the time—or understand it today. Some of those whose lives have been spent standing guard against the forces of religious hatred in this nation were for a while confused by the tactics of the professional bigots. Everyone *knew* that the bigots, large and small, were anti-Democratic Party, preferring surely the Republicans. Didn't the agitators *say* just that? Everyone *knew* that the only reason the professional bigots abandoned the Republican Party in the Roosevelt-Willkie election was because Wendell Willkie was a Democrat in disguise. Didn't the agitators *say* just that? Everyone *knew* that if the Republicans ever ousted the Democrats the bigots would disappear for lack of a raison d'être. It was *obvious*.

1 The Anti-Eisenhower Crusade

It was no such thing. That it was *not* the fact dawned most quickly on those who had carefully watched the racketeers of prejudice. They were actually opposed to both the Democratic *and* the Republican parties.

The simple proof that the merchants of minority prejudice are, and inevitably must be, opposed to whichever major political group is in the saddle lies in a three-year demonstration of hostility to the Eisenhower Administration. The transfer of their hatred from the Democrats to the Republicans, whipping the minority groups without surcease in the process, furnishes a fascinating insight to the means, the methods, and the nature of the movement.

The permanent files of the Anti-Defamation League, recording day by day the individual fulminations and gyrations of anti-Semites, contain the full narrative, almost to the last detail, of how they changed their target. Even a limited selection of memoranda from these files tells the story.

Anti-Semitic leaders in the United States did not need much more than the barest hint that General Dwight D. Eisenhower might be a presidential candidate to start the attack. They determined to get in their licks quickly; he was not their idea of a leader for the party they hoped to support—and Republican politicians had better learn it quickly. In the spring of 1951 several passing newspaper references to "General Ike" as a possible choice precipitated the bigoted anti-Eisenhower crusade.

Let us delve into the files at this point. . . .

MAY 15, 1951
Research to AF

The current issue of Gerald Smith's monthly magazine, *The Cross and the Flag,* contains a full-page reproduction of the "Swedish Jew" item reprinted from the *Howitzer* yearbook under the caption

Ike Eisenhower (Swedish Jew)

I Cross-Currents in America

Below is an exact photostat of page 80 from the HOWITZER Yearbook, published at the West Point Military Academy in the year 1915. It is the official graduation book for the U. S. Cadet Corps. The original copy of this book may be seen in any important large library, including the Congressional Library in Washington, D.C. Additional copies of this photostat may be had at 25 for $1.00. Address all orders to Patriotic Tract Society, Post Office Box 1031, St. Louis 1, Missouri.

The text of the *Howitzer* article is then reprinted in full with two pictures of Eisenhower as a cadet, as follows:

Dwight David Eisenhower
Abilene, Kansas

Senatorial Appointee, Kansas

"Ike"

Corporal, Sergeant, Color Sergeant; A.B., B.A., Sharpshooter; Football Squad (3, 2), "A" in Football; Baseball Squad (4); Cheer Leader; Indoor Meet (4, 3).

"Now, fellers, it's just like this. I've been asked to say a few words this evening about this business. Now, me and Walter Camp, we think——"

———Himself

This is Señor Dwight David Eisenhower, gentlemen, the terrible Swedish Jew, as big as life and twice as natural. He claims to have the best authority for the statement that he is the handsomest man in the Corps and is ready to back up his claim at any time. At any rate you'll have to give it to him that he's well-developed abdominally—and more graceful in pushing it around than Charles Calvert Benedict. In common with most fat men, he is an enthusiastic and sonorous devotee of the King of Indoor Sports, and roars homage at the shrine of Morpheus on every possible occasion.

However, the memory of man runneth back to the time when the little Dwight was but a slender lad of some 'steen years, full of joy and energy and craving for life and movement and change. 'Twas then that the romantic appeal of West Point's glamour grabbed him by the scruff of the neck and dragged him to his doom. Three weeks of Beast gave him his fill of life and movement and as all the change was locked up at the Cadet Store out of reach, poor Dwight merely consents to exist until graduation shall set him free.

1 The Anti-Eisenhower Crusade

At one time he threatened to get interested in life and won his "A" by being the most promising back in Eastern football—but the Tufts game broke his knee and the promise. Now Ike must content himself with tea, tiddledywinks and talk, at all of which he excels. Said prodigy will now lead us in a long, loud yell for Dare Devil Dwight, the Dauntless Don.

This page from the 1915 issue of West Point's *Howitzer* yearbook was first circulated in 1948 as a reprint by the Patriotic Tract Society of St. Louis, Missouri, the operating headquarters at that time of Gerald Smith. On the basis of this "evidence," the Smith group sought to convince its followers that Eisenhower is a Jew.

When the reprint appeared originally, we submitted it for clarification to the U. S. Military Academy and on September 20, 1948, Lieutenant Colonel W. J. Morton, West Point librarian, replied:

Gentlemen:
I am much obliged to you for having called the flyer on General Eisenhower to my attention. You are undoubtedly correct in surmising that it was put out by some crackpot group. It is nonetheless a vicious attempt to stir up prejudice.

You are also entirely correct in your assumption that the reference to General Eisenhower as a "Swedish-Jew" was simply a gag without any special significance. It was not intended to be derogatory. Cadets with unusual names frequently receive such appellations in fun. When I was a cadet, although my name was not an unusual one, several classmates in the company used to kid me along by calling me a "Virginia-Jew." They knew full well that I was of entirely Gentile extraction, but my peculiarity of dialect, plus an economical disposition inherited from Scottish forebears, sometimes furnished them an amusing topic of conversation. It was all in the spirit of good fun and was so taken. The same applies to Eisenhower. He was, as you know, of German-Swiss extraction on both sides of the family.

Of course, if General Eisenhower were of Jewish extraction I fail to see how that could be regarded as anything against him. There has never been any prejudice against Jews at West Point. Our first class that graduated in 1802 consisted of two men, one a Gentile, the other a Jew. Both were men of character and distinction. Since that time there have been Jews in practically every class, and I can state from personal experience that race, religion and economic status are matters which hold not the slightest interest for cadets. The spirit of the Corps is that each man who enters stands on his own feet and is judged by what he is and what he does rather than by his ancestry, social status or religious affiliation.

I know nothing of the Patriotic Tract Society, but if this is a sample of their efforts, I feel that they are doing our country a very doubtful service in distributing such photostats and to be insinuating that the possession of Jewish blood is something shameful.

Of course we widely circulated Colonel Morton's authoritative comments. But this hardly affected Smith; he republished the item in his magazine and capitalized on the fraud with an editorial warning captioned, "Beware of Eisenhower":

We have tried in vain to find an authentic and complete history of the Eisenhower family background. We have written numerous of his friends and close associates trying to get a statement as to whether the above page, photographed from the graduation book of West Point, was facetious or an attempt at wit or a literal reference to his ancestry. We have been unable to get satisfactory answers to this question. A dispatch out of London reveals that the leading Jewish paper of that city now admits that Eisenhower is Jewish.

It is incomprehensible why the United States Attorney General has not yet added Gerald Smith and his organizations to the Justice Department's published list of subversive organizations. Of the 281 groups now included in the government's enumeration, more than fifty per cent have long been defunct. Posting Smith's organizations—and surely they all come within the Justice Department's definition of "subversive"—would undoubtedly cause a substantial drop in contributions to them. Last January Smith reported an income for the previous year of $106,113.09, a shocking sum, to say the least.

The Attorney General's "subversive list" is prepared without giving those included an opportunity to be heard on the merits of their inclusion. This is bad in principle, due process being denied, and it would be better if the list were abolished altogether rather than continue such an undemocratic practice. But as long as the government maintains an Attorney General's list, if it is to have any value at all it should be complete and accurate.

1 The Anti-Eisenhower Crusade

MAY 17, 1951
Library to AF

To professional bigots the word "Jew" is, in and of itself, derogatory. General Eisenhower is not the only American leader whom they have deliberately labeled Jewish. They have attached the label falsely many times to Americans they had other reasons to oppose. Franklin D. Roosevelt became Rosenvelt to them; they published booklets about FDR's "Jewish Family Tree," meanwhile protesting, "We do not condemn Roosevelt for coming from Jewish stock"; and they quoted alleged newspaper interviews with public officials on the danger of Jewish ancestry. This, from Gerald Smith, was a typical statement resulting from a purported interview with a public official:

> Although a Republican the former Governor has a sincere regard for President Roosevelt and his policies. He referred to the "Jewish ancestry" of the President, explaining how he is a descendant of the Rossacampo family expelled from Spain in 1620. Seeking safety in Germany, Holland and other countries, members of the family, he said, changed their name to Rosenberg, Rosenblum, Rosenbaum and Rosenthal. The Rosenvelts in North Holland finally became Roosevelt, soon becoming apostates with the first generation and others following suit until in the fourth generation, a little storekeeper by the name of Jacobus Roosevelt was the only one who remained true to his Jewish faith. It is because of this Jewish ancestry . . . that President Roosevelt has the trend of economic safety in his veins.

The bigots labeled Harry S. Truman a Jew by the simple but transparent device of supplying him with a false name for his middle initial. It became Harry *Solomon* Truman.

MAY 18, 1951
AF to Research

A full-scale campaign is obviously being launched by the nation's professional hatemongers against General Eisenhower. Smith is merely the starter.

They will work hard to get a candidate they can approve. Let me know what you turn up from their "literature."

JULY 10, 1951
Library to AF

The latest issue of the *Williams Intelligence Summary,* published in Santa Ana, California, by Robert H. Williams, has just arrived. It is entirely devoted to "The Man Most Wanted by the Zionists to Head the Government—General Eisenhower."

Needless to say, his "summary" of the general's career only shows how completely Williams' "intelligence" is devoted to distortion. He is, at least, shrewd enough to report that, though in possession of a photostat of the *Howitzer* excerpt, he rejects it as worthless evidence—he has been assured by an experienced Kansas investigator that "there could not be any Jewish blood in Eisenhower"—*but,* in any case: "Eisenhower does not have to be Jewish to oblige the Zionist machine."

Page 1 of the *Williams Summary* carries a photograph of General Eisenhower whispering into the ear of Soviet General Georgi Zhukov while each holds a cocktail glass. The caption describes it as a telltale picture of Zhukov decorating his "drinking partner," Eisenhower, at Frankfurt, Germany. The obvious implication is that Eisenhower has a genuine sympathy for Soviet communism.

JULY 31, 1951
Research to Library

The Zhukov-Eisenhower photograph in the *Williams Intelligence Summary* is a fraud. It was cropped from a widely published picture of Eisenhower, Zhukov, and Field Marshal Montgomery conferring with their staffs shortly after the German surrender. An examination of the original photograph shows nothing of the conspiratorial implications suggested in the cut-down reprint.

1 The Anti-Eisenhower Crusade

JANUARY 25, 1952
Los Angeles Office to Benjamin R. Epstein

"Eisenhower is a putty-faced individual who will be drafted on both tickets if that haberdasher declares a state of emergency and it won't take long for him to declare a state of emergency. That Swedish Jew was picked as a five-star general by Roosevelt because he knew how to say 'yes sir' even if it was treason." Twenty-two hundred people heard this slanderous political analysis, Gerald L. K. Smith's, at the Embassy Auditorium in Los Angeles last night; the local fire department would not permit the overflow to stand in the aisles or sit on the stairs. There was no report of this Christian Nationalist Crusade rally in the California newspapers this morning. Gerald Smith, of course, will regard the omission as further proof that Jews, controlling the press, have again decreed "the silent treatment."

Smith has been running meetings almost nightly at the Embassy Auditorium. On Wednesday evening an admiring audience of more than two thousand heard the following words of wisdom:

"This afternoon I called the best informed man in Washington on the telephone . . . I'm popular in Washington . . . like Mae West at an Elks Convention . . . he told me that Kefauver is a Jewish world government man, second to Eisenhower. . . . My enemies know I have contacts. . . . The Chicago conventions are very important. . . . I'll have five thousand Christian Nationalists there, fanatic Christian Nationalists with literature, etc. . . . In 1948, Jimmy Roosevelt, Claude Pepper and Walter Reuther were for Eisenhower . . . you know Reuther—he wants nobody in this country to have over $12,000. . . .

"Eisenhower is the ADL candidate . . . so does Marshall Field want him . . . Field, the man who is led by the nose by a New York Jew psychiatrist."

Smith is showing the way to many others; the Rev. Wesley Swift, for one, who maintains an Anglo-Saxon Christian Congregation in Los

Angeles, has been echoing him for months now. In November, part of Swift's Anglo-Saxon Christian message was:

"Eisenhower would be the worst man for the presidency because the Russians like him. Eisenhower says he understands the Russians, and if he understands them he must have a lot in common with them."

And earlier this month, on the eleventh, Swift declared his "hope" that the general would run on both major party tickets. "For then, we will be able to run a hundred per cent American—General MacArthur, on the People's Party ticket." A hundred and fifty men and women applauded violently.

Another Los Angeles figure, Myron C. Fagan, who devotes most of his time to the Cinema Educational Guild, an unsophisticated propaganda movement, told his audience of approximately nine hundred middle-aged, well-dressed people:

"The title of my next bulletin is 'Eisenhower is a Truman trap.' . . . Eisenhower said in 1948 that no military man is fit to be President . . . but he doesn't say that any more. . . . Truman has been growing in ego ever since his re-election. . . . Thank God for his mistake in bringing back MacArthur. . . . Let me give you an idea of Ike's war record . . . never a fighting general . . . closer the fighting came, further back he moved. . . . He removed Patton from command, but Patton was our greatest fighting man. . . . Ike is no genius of war. . . . Stalin decorated him but he never gave back his medal, as Lindbergh was urged to return his to Stalin." (Obviously Fagan meant "Hitler.")

JANUARY 25, 1952
Research to BRE

Here's another on the band wagon. John Hamilton, who some time ago broke away from the leadership of Gerald Smith in St. Louis and formed his own lucrative Citizens Protective Association, has been holding meetings in Turners Hall featuring fellow patriots from different parts of the country. On January 21 the big speech of the evening was that of Peter Xavier's of Dayton, Ohio, a notorious agitator for many years, who created and runs a National Security League in his home town. But the highlight of the evening was not Xavier's speech. The highlight was Hamilton's description of General Eisenhower as "Ike the Kike."

FEBRUARY 26, 1952
Library to AF

In the current *Intelligence Summary,* Major Robert Williams, his busy little mind darting into all corners, has gotten to Eisenhower's mother. Mrs. Eisenhower had been a member of Jehovah's Witnesses in the last few years of her life, declares Williams, adding:

The *Intelligence Summary* has no knowledge of General Eisenhower's own attitude toward the Jehovah Witness cult. . . . However, the fact that his mother was one of that peculiar sect who refused to salute the American Flag, refused to fight for their country, refused to recognize national sovereignty . . . cannot fail to be of extreme interest to every American. . . . It seems not unlikely that General Eisenhower's . . . willingness to swallow the one-world hokum of his Zionist friends and backers may be evidence of an inherited mental deficiency or the result of crackpot parental influence.

Thus Williams is slightly reorchestrating his original theme: Eisenhower is now "a tool of the Jews."

From month to month the Californian has kept up a campaign against Eisenhower. In October, front-paging a tale that the New York *Daily Compass* favored the general for the presidency, he added:

Throughout the nation, the Left Wing Internationalist papers and magazines are praising Eisenhower as the one man for the presidency in 1952. The Anti-Defamation League of B'nai B'rith, the real power behind the Marxist revolution in the Western World, is speeding up its campaign for "Ike."

(Williams never let a fact spoil a good story; the *Compass* was one of the first newspapers, if not the very first, to *oppose* Eisenhower for the presidency. And, of course, the Anti-Defamation League has never in its long history taken a position, one way or the other, respecting a presidential candidate.)

And in November Williams printed a further analysis of what he dared to suggest were the general's leftist tendencies. If elected, the general would surely follow the course "which the extreme liberals or radicals want," Williams wrote, and added that the "only difference would be that Eisenhower would not go as fast as they would like. He would give them the Marxism they want, but not by a sudden stroke, only somewhat more gradually."

MARCH 10, 1952
Research to AF

The Rev. Gerald B. Winrod, the Wichita, Kansas, minister whose Nazi-line pamphleteering got him indicted for sedition in 1942, has some new "evidence" against General Eisenhower. Winrod claims to have discovered irrefutable proof, which he sets forth in a four-page leaflet, that Dwight Eisenhower is the candidate of "Jewish plotters" conspiring to dominate the world. Winrod's concrete evidence is the 1912 novel, *Philip Dru, Administrator,* by the late Colonel E. M. House.

It seems that Woodrow Wilson's aide, Colonel House, wrote a novel embodying in part some Utopian opinions regarding the social and political scene. It seems, too, that Winrod has just read the long-forgotten book.

By "reading between the lines" Winrod has discovered a major conspiracy to seize power in the United States and has produced what he titles *The Philip Dru Conspiracy Exposed*. It is being distributed on a nation-wide scale. "A strange book appeared in 1912 . . . only a few copies were printed," he writes, hoping to convince his readers that House's fiction was meant primarily as a guide for the key promoters of the "conspiracy."

The precise lines of the alleged plot may not be too clear, but they nevertheless bring the Kansas preacher to the conclusion that "Frank-

1 The Anti-Eisenhower Crusade

lin Roosevelt was chosen, groomed and installed in the White House to consummate the conspiracy. This explains why, the day after being nominated the first time, he flew by plane from Chicago to be House's guest in Massachusetts. . . ."

And from this mysterious, peculiar non sequitur, we rattle on to Winrod's conclusion: "Woodrow Wilson failed them; Franklin Roosevelt served them to the end of his days; Harry Truman remains their pawn; Dwight Eisenhower is their choice in this, the catastrophic year of 1952."

The only alternative, he argues in his final paragraph, is to "send a man of the MacArthur, Taft or Russell stature to the White House."

MARCH 10, 1952
Library to Research

Though it is highly unlikely that Winrod's "revelations" will fire the imagination of the country, a substantial ready audience can be reached by him immediately. The *Defender,* an anti-Catholic, anti-Semitic magazine issued monthly by Winrod, with a circulation of more than 100,000, will carry the story to all parts of the country, even outside it. With one of the largest congregations in Wichita, he also maintains missions in Puerto Rico, Cuba, and Liberia; and in 1944, when Winrod mailed out a single letter of solicitation for funds, he received approximately $26,000. Such as they are, his followers are faithful. In a recent annual report his Defenders of the Christian Faith, Inc. revealed a yearly income exceeding a quarter of a million dollars.

Perhaps the nation should be reminded of other facets in the Rev. Mr. Winrod's "career" in religion. He is the minister who, after visiting Hitler's Germany in 1934 at the behest of Otto Vollbehr, then a leading Nazi theoretician, returned to initiate his own pro-Nazi campaign in the United States. He continued his activities, though with some caution, right through three federal indictments for sedition, the last of which, handed down on January 3, 1944, accused him of "unlawfully, wilfully, feloniously, and knowingly conspiring . . . with officials of the government of the German Reich and leaders of the Nazi Party" to wreck the morale of the men in the American armed forces. The Justice Department never pressed the case to final trial. Winrod, still active, has made only slight changes in his propaganda line.

MARCH 11, 1952
Library to BRE

The hate press is in full gallop after Eisenhower.

C. Leon de Aryan, of San Diego, California, asserts in his publication, *The Broom,* that Eisenhower is a Jew, a creature of the Jewish conspiracy to destroy the government and stifle American culture.

Gerald Smith is still arguing in his publication that "no one has explained satisfactorily why the West Point Year Book . . . referred to him as the Swedish Jew." In his current newsletter Smith urges his readers: "Stop Eisenhower . . . the man who has been picked by the Jews to be the world dictator."

From Cedar City, Utah, on February 10, came Stephen Nenoff's *American Commentator.* Its lead story is devoted to proving that Eisenhower is "part of a conspiracy, part of the Morgenthau group, the sworn enemies of Western civilization."

The March issue of John Hoeppel's *National Defense* informed its readers that those who favor Eisenhower are . . . "all internationalists, imperialists, Wall Streeters, me-too Republicans, Communistic Jews and others who [are trying] to foist British and Jewish Internationally-minded Eisenhower on the Republican Party as a candidate for the Presidency." In Chicago, Mrs. Lyrl Clark Van Hyning's anti-Semitic *Women's Voice* made her own modest "factual" contribution to the anti-Eisenhower campaign. On February 28 she reported that Eisenhower's campaign would be financed by "the Rockefeller-Rothschild combination which controls virtually all newspapers, magazine and radio advertising."

In Texas the American Heritage Protective Committee, which has been extravagantly championing the anti-Semitic Professor John Beaty

1 The Anti-Eisenhower Crusade

of Southern Methodist University, took up the cry. In one bulletin editor-publisher Austin Hancock ran a violent piece charging, among other things, that the Anti-Defamation League was among the "notorious left-wingers and/or communist (organizations) supporting Eisenhower for President."

The current issue of Henry S. Sattler's Connecticut sheet, *The Malist,* warns that "Eisenhower is the Zionists' favorite son for president," and urges that "we should take our nation out of Jewish leadership."

The similarity of the distortions shows how closely these propagandists work together.

MARCH 12, 1952
Boston Office to Research

Nearly every Jew-baiting, anti-Eisenhower leaflet, pamphlet, or magazine article which has come to your attention in the last six months was distributed in New Hampshire before the primaries closed last night. (Eisenhower defeated Taft.)

At the height of the campaign Portsmouth voters found the following crudely typewritten postcard, inside envelopes postmarked Philadelphia, in their mailboxes:

```
General Eisenhower is the "Kike's Ike" and the
"JEWS FRONT." He was hand picked and sponsored
by the American Jewish Congress. And the Zionist
International Jewish World Organization. He is
also a "Racial Swine-ologist." During the war
under his Military Command and Orders White Girls
were used exclusively in Europe and Africa in
all U.S.O.'s and Cafe's under M. P. Guards to
Dance with and entertain and Date Negroes. That's
the "Kike's Ike" Version of Romeo & Juliet.
```

This has been air-mailed to civic leaders, veterans' organizations, and manufacturing and business establishments. Within days many other New Hampshire towns were similarly flooded; within weeks Portsmouth, Nashua, Manchester, Concord, Keene, Dover, and other places

37

each reported the distribution of one or another anti-Semitic reprint. Robert Williams' cropped photograph of Eisenhower and Zhukov turned up in many places.

The Gerald Smith leaflet, *Ike Eisenhower, the Swedish Jew,* came to many New Hampshire homes and offices postmarked Chicago, Illinois. One leaflet by Robert H. Williams contained the following paragraph:

> Eisenhower does not have to be Jewish to oblige the Zionist machine. Look at Henry Wallace, Harry Truman, Dean Acheson, Dewey, Warren, Stassen—even Hiss may have had no Jewish blood in his veins. We dare not forgive the arch criminals and morons of our own race merely because they are led by the nose or bribed or driven by the voodoo priests of black magic.

Our office here in New England received hundreds of requests for background information about Williams. We have given them the facts.

MARCH 14, 1952
Library to Research

Robert H. Williams has had a full-time, if unheroic, career as an agitator since his separation from military service.

The anti-Semitic pamphlet, *Know Your Enemy,* one of his major efforts, was written by him in 1950 at his home in Santa Ana, California. Williams claimed it contained "counter-intelligence information" compiled by one [himself] who "organized and directed one of the largest counter-intelligence staffs in the Army Air Forces."

For several years Williams has been accustomed to describe himself in print as "Major Robert H. Williams, Military Intelligence," to give an aura of authority to his ignorant slander of Jews. As far back as 1947 the late Robert Patterson, then Secretary of War, pointed out that Williams' military experience "had to do with weather and air intelligence" rather than counter-intelligence. Despite this, Williams continued to misrepresent his status and to abuse the prestige of his Army

1 The Anti-Eisenhower Crusade

Reserve rank until the Office of the Secretary of Defense was obliged to take action.

A thorough investigation of his fitness to retain his Reserve commission was undertaken; and on January 8, 1951, Major General Edward F. Witsell, the Adjutant General, in an official communication, declared that "the termination of Major Williams' commission would be in the best interest of the Service. He has, accordingly, been discharged from his commission."

This hardly deterred Williams. He had made his debut in 1946 ghost-writing an anti-Semitic pamphlet sponsored by the former radio commentator Upton Close and continued as Close's protégé and employee for about two years. During this time he had good opportunity to absorb the anti-Semitic "material" that he was rehashing as part of his work; and in December 1948 he evidently felt himself ready to strike out on his own. It was then that he broke with Close and began the publication of the newsletter, *Williams Intelligence Summary,* which has been reiterating to this day that Judaism and communism are synonymous. The loss of his Army commission had no restraining effect upon this tireless propagandist.

Williams is always on the lookout for an opening for his particular brand of propaganda. Local California politics have been inflicted with his insistent religious bigotries; the effort to smear former Assistant Secretary of Defense Anna Rosenberg as a communist had his enthusiastic participation; and he has made friendly overtures to the Arab League.

But his success as a molder of public opinion has been minimal. Besides being dropped by the Army, he has achieved listing by the Illinois American Legion as "a dispenser of vitriolic, un-American, anti-Semitic hate literature"; he has been attacked by such California newspapers as the Santa Ana *Independent,* the Los Angeles *Mirror,* and the Santa Barbara *News-Press;* and in February 1949 the chairman of the Los Angeles County Republican Committee warned all party workers against using Williams' literature, labeling it anti-Semitic.

It is plain that Williams' hopes for political influence have not been in any measure achieved—and after so much effort. Still, this sixty-year-old should be watched; disruption is an achievement of sorts.

MARCH 18, 1952

Washington, D.C., Office to Research

This morning California Congressman Samuel W. Yorty, referring to the trick photograph prepared by Williams, argued that it "should serve to focus attention on some of the revolting subversive activity being carried on in this country," and he charged that this activity was being carried on "right under the noses of official investigating agencies and committees which for some reason choose to ignore its vile and evil effects."

Congressman Yorty characterized Williams as a "depraved psychopath . . . the pattern of [whose] attacks indicates that he serves enemies of this nation who desire to divide us from our allies and weaken the free world."

MARCH 19, 1952

Washington, D.C., Office to BRE

Yesterday the Senate Subcommittee on Privileges and Elections issued a severe condemnation of the smear techniques which were used in the New Hampshire campaign. Senator Mike Monroney (D., Okla.) described the material its investigators had uncovered as "scurrilous." However, he made it clear that he and his fellow committee members had no reason to believe that the vilification of the general had been inspired by any of Eisenhower's rival candidates. Senator Taft's office joined the subcommittee in condemning the distribution of the malicious literature. General MacArthur remains aloof.

The subcommittee further pointed out that, while circulation of the anti-Eisenhower literature in New Hampshire "was relatively limited," it nevertheless "anticipates the possibility that efforts to use smear liter-

1 The Anti-Eisenhower Crusade

ature may be made in the coming campaign and intends to focus the spotlight of publicity on this unfair type of political campaign."

Robert Williams' activities were recognized as "misleading and deceptive."

MARCH 20, 1952
West Virginia Office to Research

Forrest C. Sammons[1] of Huntington, West Virginia, has just sent thousands of copies of an Open Letter, written on the stationery of his paper organization, the West Virginia Anti-Communist League, Inc., to all Republican National Committeemen. This wealthy, retired building contractor writes:

> The strong public press that is given to General "Ike" Eisenhower is definite proof that this foreign element feels that their leaders have complete control over him and the record shows that this is the case. For example, General Eisenhower is in Europe "fronting" for Anna Rosenberg, who was the protege of Sidney Hillman with whom Senator Truman had to be "cleared" as Hillman's second choice to Henry Wallace for Vice President in the 1944 campaign.

Having watched Sammons lavishly entertain Gerald L. K. Smith at his home, and invite numerous local friends to come and hear him, this Open Letter is exactly the sort of thing we expected from him. He is an old hand at this game. Back in March 1950, in an Open Letter addressed to Robert A. Taft, Sammons wrote: "Like his father, young Roosevelt has proven that he has 'sold out' to world Judaism. We must have a President who will stand for CHRISTIAN CONSTITUTIONAL GOVERNMENT."

And in a previous mimeographed letter to the Ohio senator, Sammons wrote:

> We know now that Woodrow Wilson and Franklin Roosevelt were hoodwinked by the Marxist Headline Writers to lead the Democratic Party and the American people into two Marxist planned World Wars

---
[1] Forrest Sammons died on October 10, 1954.

for the purpose of establishing Soviet Russia as a step toward World Talmudic Socialism. We also know that our State Department, under the control of Felix Frankfurter, Barney Baruch and the New York Minority Machine, have betrayed our Government and the Laws of Christian Civilization to the World Soviet System.

APRIL 1, 1952
Research to Library

Robert Williams, undaunted, has now issued an 8-page digest of his own previous attacks on the general and his "Jewish backers," culled from past issues of his own publication. This *Special Eisenhower Edition* is available for twenty-five cents a copy with discounts for bulk orders.

APRIL 3, 1952
Library to Research

"The election campaign grows bitter. It may grow desperate on the part of internationalists, socialists, office-holders, the Jewish political machine and certain big financial interests. They feel that they 'have got to have Ike.' They feel that Eisenhower alone can (used by them) prevent their world from crashing about their heads. It's a world of fake, fraud, blood and taxes. But its promoters will resort to any extreme to keep up the pretense that it is successful. Its promoters cling to position and power. They can't bear full exposure."

Thus wrote Upton Close in his monthly newsletter, *Closer-ups*.

This former radio news commentator has now added his (certainly uninvited) support to a different American general. Says Close: "A deadlock of Taft and Ike in the Chicago Convention, followed by a stampede for General MacArthur, would be the blessed miracle of national salvation."

Fifteen years ago Close was respected for his opinions, his judgment, and the several moderately successful books he had written. But his charges that the Administration in Washington was under the complete control of the Marxist movement, his authorship of such tracts as *Treachery in our Government,* and having his material reprinted in publications like Winrod's *Defender,* have resulted in a change of reputation—not for the better. He now performs such comparatively menial chores as writing introductions for Winrod when the Midwestern minister deigns to honor him by reprinting one of his speeches.

Broadcasts, Inc., the corporation which he created to distribute his canned radio programs, virtually closed its doors for business not long after they were opened. Apparently unable to understand that the character and quality of his news comments foredoomed his Broadcasts, Inc., operation, he explained to an inquirer: "Up to last September I had 150 stations that were using our recordings. At that time American Express charged us one dollar more per record package. I canvassed the stations to find out whether they were prepared to carry this extra cost. So many of them turned me down that I decided to suspend production and distribution altogether, even though the company cutting the records, anxious to keep the account alive, made me an attractive proposition. I decided not to go ahead but to take a rest instead."

Undoubtedly a decision of the U. S. Bureau of Internal Revenue helped persuade Upton Close that he needed a rest. When the ex-news analyst created his distributing corporation, he applied for and obtained a tax-exempt status for it on the allegation that Broadcasts, Inc., was an educational, non-profit endeavor. Unfortunately for Close, the government later came to a slightly different conclusion, i.e., the operation was not so educational and seemed, rather, to be a political proposition. Broadcasts, Inc., lost its tax exemption; people stopped making contributions to it; so Close took "a rest instead."

APRIL 7, 1952
Research to AF

Joseph P. Kamp, as the director of the Constitutional Educational League, has just issued a report-to-end-all-reports on the "Jewish control" of Eisenhower. Kamp's irregularly issued publication, *Headlines,* has this time devoted a 16-page special edition to answering the question: "Who's promoting Ike?"

Kamp, who lives like a $15,000-a-year executive in New York City on a reported personal income of far less, has been for years an important propaganda font for a large number of the lunatic fringe groups. Kamp receives financial assistance from many big industrialists and corporations who know nothing of his real activities. They contribute on his plea that his Constitutional Educational League exerts a tremendous impact in the fight against communism and communists. This help enables him to issue his literature on a grand scale.

The federal prison term which he served in 1950 for contempt of Congress when he refused to furnish an investigating committee with significant information about his organizational operations, the repeated exposures of his propaganda efforts in the press and on the radio, the condemnation of his agency and himself by American Legion Americanism commissions and other such groups, have dissuaded neither Kamp nor his wealthy contributors. Even some congressmen in the nation's capital have come to his defense time and again.

In a black-bordered box on the first page of the new pamphlet, written, he says, as a "patriotic duty," Kamp announces it is "not political or partisan; it is not interested in the political fortunes of any party or candidate; it is exclusively dedicated to the preservation of the American way of life." He includes this disclaimer undoubtedly to justify the involvement of his "educational" organization in political matters. Kamp presents his little explanation before going on to present "the truth [that] is being kept from the ordinary channels of public information."

Nevertheless, it is a major development on the *political* scene, he contends, one threatening the destruction of the American system, that compels him to speak. And:

Therefore, an analysis of General Eisenhower's candidacy is presented in this issue (1) because there are unmistakable signs of a conspiracy to prevent the American people from exercising their right to make a ballot-box decision on policies affecting the very existence

1 The Anti-Eisenhower Crusade

of constitutional government: (2) because notorious un-American elements are promoting the Eisenhower candidacy: and (3) because the election of Eisenhower to the Presidency, under his present sponsorship, would insure the continuance in Washington, during the next four years, of the same Socialist, pro-Communist and appease-Russia policies, which have brought the United States to its present precarious position, both throughout the world and at home.

The headlines in Kamp's *Headlines* sufficiently indicate the nature of the 16 pages: RED, NEW DEALERS USE IKE IN PLOT TO HOLD POWER; FINANCIAL ANGELS OF NEW DEAL ARE NOW BOOSTING IKE; NORMAN THOMAS, TOP SOCIALIST, LAUDS IKE; JACOB POTOFSKY HILLMAN'S HEIR BEHIND '52 BOOM; RED RAG FIRST NEWSPAPER TO BALLYHOO FOR IKE; SIDNEY HILLMAN AND ANNA ROSENBERG FATHERED IKE-FOR-PRESIDENT; INTERNATIONALIST LEFT WINGERS PAY TRIBUTE TO IKE; RED PUBLICATION HONORS IKE WITH DUBIOUS AWARD; IKE'S FIRST SPONSOR ACTED FOR POWERFUL SECRET SUBVERSIVE GROUP; IKE CODDLED COMMUNISTS WHILE PRESIDENT OF COLUMBIA UNIVERSITY; EISENHOWER JOINS REDS IN STAND AGAINST LOYALTY OATH FOR TEACHERS, etc., etc.

In the light of the stories offered in support of these headlines, Kamp's lead editorial, captioned "Ike Isn't the Man," is rather an understatement. The only one you'll find, we're afraid.

JUNE 23, 1952
Research to BRE

At a press conference earlier today in Washington, D.C., Senator Robert A. Taft condemned the "smearing tactics" being used against General Dwight Eisenhower.

Senator Taft said he was "particularly disgusted" by Joe Kamp's campaign piece, *Headlines,* and wanted to repudiate political material circulated by Gerald Winrod and other "anti-Semitic sheets" as well. The senator added: "That kind of slander can only hurt the Republican Party." Asked if any Taft organization funds were being used to finance such attacks, the Ohio Republican snapped, "Certainly not."

Other Republican leaders have also repudiated bigotry's support,

Cross-Currents in America

but there has been no similar disavowal from General MacArthur thus far. It is clear, however, that he has not acknowledged their support any more than he has the support which comes from responsible sources.

While MacArthur is not officially a candidate for the presidency, a sizable grass-roots movement is booming him for the job. Unfortunately, though, many of the nation's prominent bigots are also fostering him as "their" candidate. Much of the anti-Semitic literature disseminated throughout the country contains "plugs" for the general. One appeal came from Marilyn Allen, Salt Lake City's irresponsible Jew-baiter, to make "the first move for placing General MacArthur in the White House by deluging his headquarters with signed petition blanks. . . . Please sign and mail the enclosed at once to General Douglas MacArthur."

Douglas MacArthur
90 Church Street, New York 7, NY
Please encourage your friends who wish to see you become President. I hereby promise you my support. Your code of honor is what we need. Your leadership is what your countrymen want.
Sincerely yours,
....

Other promotions for MacArthur's presidency are being mailed from the office of Henry H. Klein,[2] that indefatigable contributor to the lunatic fringe press, and from several others, all using the same "postal-card petition."

JULY 3, 1952

Chicago Office to AF

Chicago is getting ready for its twentieth national political convention in ninety years. Hotel lobbies are stacked high with assorted parade paraphernalia; several small parades have already occurred. The men and women participating are authorized Republican delegates and their supporters.

[2] Henry H. Klein died July 16, 1955.

1 The Anti-Eisenhower Crusade

Also moving into town, quietly however, is another group, intent upon contributing a jarring note to the Republican Convention festivities and its order of business. A motley aggregation of the nation's rabble-rousers is here for a three-day conference to set in motion a propaganda campaign aimed at converting Republican Convention delegates from their choice of candidates. They start tomorrow.

Two days ago the first arrival, malcontent Gerald Smith, immediately rented a downtown office. There, with a full quota of desks and typewriters, he put his entourage. Before leaving his home in Tulsa, Oklahoma, he had written to his "precious friends and compatriots" an urgent letter which included this:

As your representative I am establishing temporary headquarters for the Christian Nationalist Crusade in Chicago. This headquarters will be maintained prior to the Republican convention and until after the Democratic convention. Each day during my stay in Chicago, I shall write a letter to my mother, telling her all the interesting unpublished details concerning what is going on. If you respond to this letter . . . [by sending money] I will put you on a list to receive a copy of this daily report.

Mr. Smith undoubtedly has the only mother in America who requires an office staff to hear from her wandering boy. But the money seems to have come in. Smith has also written his friends:

Between now and the convention, we must bring pressure upon every delegate and every influential Republican in America to cast his influence against Eisenhower. Men in whose wisdom I have great confidence are convinced that Eisenhower and Taft will be deadlocked in the early ballots and that with the generation of the proper sentiment General MacArthur can be nominated as a dark horse. This could be the miracle that would redeem America. . . . I will be in Chicago with a staff of workers, prepared to do this work for you and America. Please, please help us do it.

Whether Smith is willing to share with other organizations the efforts of his followers, the dubious honors, and the proceeds of his coming Chicago shindig remains to be seen. Our information is that his flock is rushing around, talking up a MacArthur Rally for July 6 in the Gold Room of the Congress Hotel, while others in the smear set are concentrating on the three-day conference scheduled for the Atlantic Hotel in the morning. This one, labeled the "Nationalist Convention," was called by Mrs. Lyrl Van Hyning, Chicago's own We, the Mothers, leader.

Van Hyning, whose monthly publication *Women's Voice* has won her an excited local following of elderly housewives, will probably draw even less responsible customers than visitor Smith; she has the edge, as a permanent resident. Besides, she has other old pros on her roster including Bill Hendrix, the recently defeated gubernatorial candidate in Florida and chief of the state's Ku Klux Klan; Kenneth Goff, a former Smith lieutenant; George Foster of the Constitutional Americans of Chicago; Austin Hancock, of San Antonio, Texas, representing the American Heritage Protective Committee; Peter Xavier; and John Hamilton.

There is still a third "movement" in town—one certainly destined for oblivion—planning a "political convention." Called the White Circle League and headed by a native Chicagoan, Joseph Beauharnais, its efforts will be directed mostly against Negroes, and its convention program will unquestionably be rooted in "white supremacy" and "hate Eisenhower" themes.

It is on "stop Ike" that the three movements agree, no matter which of them rallies the most dissidents.

JULY 6, 1952
Chicago Office to AF

The three-day Nationalist Convention is over.

George Foster presided at all the sessions; the attendance consisted mostly of women, never more than a hundred and fifty. Mr. Eisenhower, as hand-picked candidate of Barney Baruch, and Senator Taft, as a tool of Wall Street, took the principal punishment handed out by the different speakers. One speaker took a moment left-handedly to compliment Truman for returning MacArthur to his friends in the United States. Standing ovations with wild horn-blowing and applause

1 The Anti-Eisenhower Crusade

greeted every mention of the general's name. He was nominated for the presidency.

Though no one suggested it would be necessary, Foster assured his listeners there would be "no thought control" at this convention. And for those with qualms, he explained: "Because we fight Communists, we are called anti-Semitic ... This country was founded as a Christian nation and no others should be admitted."

In the three days the group did manage to pass a number of resolutions: about the Anti-Defamation League (which it wants outlawed); about the McCarran-Walter immigration law (which it wants more stringent); about a congressional investigation of neo-fascism in Germany (which it wants discontinued); and about income tax (which it wants abolished).

There was an abundance of printed material on hand at all times.

Attendees were constantly entering and leaving the assembly hall; this probably accounts for the discovery of the "literature" under the doors of the regular Republican delegates, in hotel lobbies, and on streetcars, busses, elevated trains, and other public places throughout the city.

While all of it was repetitious enough, the most recurrent agenda item was, naturally, the solicitation of funds.

JULY 6, 1952
Chicago Office to AF

Today Gerald Smith held *his* convention for General MacArthur. Smith himself was not there. Most of his top lieutenants spent the major part of the morning denying to the Congress Hotel operators that they even knew him.

Smith had been so busy with his staff unloading huge quantities of pro-MacArthur and anti-Eisenhower printed matter, he apparently forgot security measures; and word leaked out that the meeting room rented in the Congress Hotel in other names was really for him. When the management learned the truth, rancher Fred Coogan, of

49

❙ Cross-Currents in America

Sayre, Oklahoma, and Dan Madrano, of Tulsa, Oklahoma, whose names had been used, were called in and questioned. Assured that neither "had the slightest association with Smith" and that he would be barred as the "kiss of death" to General MacArthur if he tried to attend the convention, the hotel allowed the doors to be opened.

About five hundred men and women appeared. Smith's St. Louis office manager, Opal Tanner, introduced convention chairman Madrano, who in turn introduced the keynoter—Don Lohbeck, editor of Smith's *The Cross and the Flag*. Lohbeck pilloried "Christ-hating" elements in Washington; envelopes filled with Smith propaganda were distributed throughout the hall; and General MacArthur, for the second time today, was awarded the presidential nomination.

The nomination was as unanimous as the denials that Smith had anything to do with the convention.

JULY 10, 1952
Library to AF

Gerald Smith's statement in a circular letter headed *History in the Balance,* which he dated today and mailed to all his "Dear Loyal Friends":

In the past 72 hours my staff, in cooperation with approximately 300 volunteers, have distributed by hand in Chicago about 150,000 pieces of literature. We rented the big ballroom in the Congress Hotel. . . . At the last minute, even after we paid the rent and spent a total of more than $1,000.00 on the meeting, the Jew management demanded a letter from the committee assuring them that Gerald L. K. Smith would not speak. We had the choice of cancelling our meeting or fulfilling their Jew-designed demands. Mr. Don Lohbeck, the brilliant editor of the Daily Bulletin and "The Cross and The Flag," spoke in my place. The great audience that filled the Grand Ballroom . . . cheered and leaped to their feet as he paid glowing tribute to General MacArthur and called for his nomination.

The weekly bills on our office total more than $10,000.00 per month. We are alerting millions of people, thanks to your contributions of money. . . . Put the largest gift of money within your ability in the

1 The Anti-Eisenhower Crusade

enclosed self-addressed envelope . . . and rush it into the mail. . . . The humble contribution you make may be the gift that will tip the scale in this dramatic moment. . . .

JULY 11, 1952
Chicago Office to BRE

The day before yesterday, in front of the Chicago headquarters of the Republican National Convention, cards were handed out to all who passed. On each card was a picture of General Eisenhower, a Jewish star, and a caricature of a Jew; under the picture was one word—"IKIE."

Tonight, with Eisenhower's nomination by the convention, the nation's professional hatemongers have abandoned their twenty-year effort to align themselves with the Republicans against the Democrats.

JULY 25, 1952
Library to BRE

Joe Kamp seems particularly vexed over the attitude of the nation's press. His newest issue of *Headlines* declared: "The New York Times, Herald Tribune, Hearst and Scripps-Howard Newspapers Deceive the Public." They "have used every foul trick of crooked journalism to distort the plain facts . . . They have resorted to fact-twisting, news suppression, phony headlining and even outright lying."

This, from Kamp, no less.

JULY 25, 1952
Library to AF

Conde McGinley, the Union, New Jersey, publisher of *Common Sense,* is in the mail today with his post-primary campaign issue.

I Cross-Currents in America

A "staff correspondent" reports the July 4–6 Nationalist Convention in Chicago at length. But McGinley is more concerned with the "lessons" to be drawn from this convention. MacArthur, he reports, was not nominated, and he proposes his alternative in a banner headline: "Start Third Party Now." Underneath the headline is this suggestion: "To Hell with Business until We Clean Out the Conspirators."

Reading through McGinley's description of the resolutions passed at the July 4–6 Nationalist Convention, one understands for the first time George Foster's preoccupation with disclaiming "thought control." It seems that the group wants the United States taken completely out of the United Nations because of UNESCO. Charging that the United Nations Educational, Scientific and Cultural Organization "has planned the collapse of the minds and morals of the present and future generations of American children," McGinley labels it the "thought-control" branch of the world agency.

JULY 25, 1952
Library to AF

McGinley's anti-Semitism appears to be one component of an emotional instability that also shows itself in streaks of violence. Certainly his frequent statements, to confidants, on the need of exterminating all Jews do not precisely argue a balanced outlook for this earnest and self-styled "authority on Communism and Marxism."

Before becoming a professional anti-Semite, McGinley operated a roadside stand in Texas and later emigrated to New Jersey to work in a war plant. The first issue of *Common Sense* was published by him on June 29, 1947, after a year of experimenting with a similar sheet called *Think Weekly*. Initial press runs were small, and McGinley remained another obscure pin on the bigotry map until he was befriended by Benjamin Freedman, the wealthy retired businessman and renegade Jew who devotes himself to the Arab cause. The first fruits of this alliance were two anti-Zionist issues of *Common Sense* in 1948, subsidized by Freedman.

1 The Anti-Eisenhower Crusade

This led to an expansion of *Common Sense's* headquarters and to more Freedman-sponsored editions. Prominent among these was the November 1, 1950, issue (150,000 copies), devoted to smearing Anna Rosenberg. The October 1950 issue of his publication, which contained attacks upon incumbent Senator Brien McMahon, was paid for by a wealthy contributor and 200,000 copies were shipped to Connecticut a few days before the election that year.

Common Sense, issued from Union, New Jersey, and subtitled *The Nation's Anti-Communist Newspaper,* began with a press run of 7000 and now fluctuates between 25,000 and 300,000 copies per edition. The difference is between routine circulation and those issues for which McGinley has gotten special backing. In sworn statements to postal authorities he had declared the paid circulation to be slightly over 20,000 mailed second class from the Union post office. What remains is generally shipped in bulk to distribution contacts throughout the country, among them: Bill Hendrix; Texas millionaire George W. Armstrong,[3] writer and financer of hate pamphlets; Forrest C. Sammons, of Huntington, West Virginia; and Edgar W. Waybright, Sr., of Jacksonville, Florida, county Democratic leader. The St. Louis *Post-Dispatch* has charged Waybright with being a behind-the-scenes adviser to the KKK; he has denied the charge.

McGinley's newspaper can best be described as an anti-Communist sheet that has rarely published a legitimate, factual anti-Communist article. The usual McGinley piece is a shrill hodgepodge of anti-Semitic canards in which communism is less a political actuality than an emotional scare word. But *Common Sense,* besides giving space to its editor's attempts at self-expression, also prints the works of many sympathizers. These are some of the favored guests: Upton Close, whom McGinley described as "simply pro-American . . . no more fascist or anti-Semitic than George Washington"; John J. Fleck, who writes anti-Semitic crank letters as well; Dr. Austin J. App, a pro-Nazi apologist; Joseph P. Kamp; Merwin K. Hart, who runs the National Economic Council; Robert H. Williams; Marilyn Allen; Ron Gostick,

[3] George W. Armstrong died on October 1, 1954.

publisher of the anti-Semitic *Canadian Intelligence Service* and ex-Social Credit theoretician; Colonel Eugene N. Sanctuary, who holds himself out as an "expert" on the Talmud; and Elizabeth Dilling, the Chicago professional anti-Semite.

The foregoing is a bare outline of McGinley and his newspaper.[4]

AUGUST 7, 1952
Press Department to BRE

This morning General Eisenhower repudiated appeals to religious or racial prejudice whether designed to help or hurt his candidacy.

He made a formal statement after Mrs. F. P. Heffelfinger, Minnesota National Committeewoman, had told him that the mail was being flooded with anti-Semitic attacks by Gerald Smith and Joe Kamp among others, aimed at both the Truman Administration and General Eisenhower himself.

"Appeals to prejudice and bigotry have no place in America," Eisenhower said. "Those were the tactics of the Nazis and Fascists. That was why the freedom-loving people of the world destroyed them. Those are the tactics of the Communists today."

AUGUST 8, 1952
Chicago Office to AF

A closely linked crowd from all parts of the nation met yesterday and today in a caucus at the Hotel Sherman; and all is confusion.

They came, weeks after the two big political conventions, to voice their dissatisfaction with the major-party candidates, and to discuss

---

[4] McGinley has added to his long record since the above memorandum was written; he has made himself notorious in anti-Semitic circles: state legislatures and veteran groups have initiated resolutions condemning this biggest (in volume) hate publisher in the East. One of his recent efforts, guaranteed to keep him at least in the official eye, has been the distribution of about 300,000 copies of a special issue devoted to *The Coming Red Dictatorship*. They were sent to county sheriffs, police chiefs, commanders of local veterans' posts, and legislators in every state; the issue, consistent with everything McGinley turns out, was nakedly anti-Semitic.

1 The Anti-Eisenhower Crusade

the formation of a third party. Though the country's hatemongers are making one of their strongest bids for public attention in recent years, there seems to be no unity on what the best possible course for them is now that they have ruled themselves out of the Democratic and Republican parties.

There were 179 delegates, representing 80 organizations, registered at the sessions; a strange mixture of well-mannered nationalists and pillar-of-the-community conservatives with rabble-rousers, racists, and bigots. Prominently participating were Merwin K. Hart, Upton Close, George Foster, Kenneth Goff, and W. Henry MacFarland, Jr., leader in Philadelphia of the Nationalist Action League. The actual sponsor of the two-day meeting was the Minute Women of Maryland, but the work of organizing the convention was conducted by a group called Operation America, Inc.

Also in attendance were Allen Zoll and Jessica Payne, president and vice-president respectively of the National Council for American Education; Lucille Cardin Crain, editor of the *Educational Reviewer;* Suzanne S. Stevenson, national chairman and founder of the Minute Women of America; and Congressmen Ralph Gwinn (R., N.Y.) and Howard Buffett (R., Neb.)

The binding themes of this so-called political convention—rancor over the presidential nominees and the internationalist attitudes of both major parties—were insufficient to maintain cohesion. The convention split quickly and violently into two opposing factions over whether there should be a third party. One group—middle-of-the-road isolationists—looked upon a third party as impractical so close to November; they preferred to concentrate their major efforts on the election of national legislators sympathetic to the convention's views. The other faction advocated formation of a new party immediately. The controversy generated so much heat that the chairman, George Washington Robnett, president of the Church League of America, was unable to prevent pandemonium. At this the "moderates" decamped; and Upton Close, having spoken in their favor, folded his papers and left too.

But the third-partyists remained, immediately formed a rump group,

I Cross-Currents in America

and took over. Mrs. Stevenson announced that she was personally reconvening the convention, and designated Percy Greaves, onetime associate research director of the Republican National Committee, temporary chairman.

Taking the gavel, Greaves called for the names of two persons from each state represented, to be placed on a national committee. Foster, Goff, and MacFarland were among those chosen, and the hundred die-hards dubbed their new movement the Constitution Party of the United States.

When it became clear that the reconstituted organization would actually go forward with a program, Upton Close slipped back into camp. As a token of forgiveness and appreciation, he was chosen the publicity director.

AUGUST 20, 1952
Los Angeles Office to Research

At a Christian Nationalist Crusade meeting in Los Angeles last week, Gerald Smith declared: "We are going to put MacArthur's name on the ballot in every state."

This morning the Associated Press reported that "petitioning by the Christian Nationalist Party has been successful in Texas, and that Gen. Douglas MacArthur will be assigned a spot on the ballot as Presidential candidate of the Party." Listed as vice-presidential candidate is Jack B. Tenney, California state senator.

Back in 1946, Jack B. Tenney, a member of the California State Senate, and until 1949 chairman of its Committee on Un-American Activities, had some harsh things to say about Gerald Smith. Tenney said then: "Smith and his type of rabble-rousing crusader do more good for the Communist cause in one week than the Communists would be able to accomplish in one year. . . . Gerald L. K. Smith merits the most severe public criticism and condemnation for his contribution to racial agitation."

But nothing has a shorter memory than ambition, and Tenney, who

1 The Anti-Eisenhower Crusade

actively campaigned for his own nomination, enthusiastically shares platforms now with veteran anti-Semites like Wesley Swift and Smith himself, to further the Smith ticket. At the moment it is his ticket as well.

Tenney began his adult life as a professional musician. At the age of thirty-seven he started in the practice of law and moved into politics. In 1936, the year of his admission to the bar, he was elected to the California Assembly. In 1938, considered something of a liberal, he spoke at rallies of such agencies as the Hollywood Anti-Nazi League. In the same year he was named in an affidavit before the Dies Committee as having been an active member of the Communist Party. However, it is likely that Tenney was never a Communist Party member; he's not that incautious.

Tenney chaired the Un-American Activities Committee for eight years, and in the course of his investigations and exposures created his own definition of subversion. One did not have to be a communist, fellow traveler, or ideological Marxist, Tenney decided, to be un-American. A man is a "practical communist" if he believes in civil rights, FEPC, and the equality of man, Tenney said, even though he is otherwise a dedicated member of the Republican Party.

His reactionary concept of democracy, his bullying and harsh name-calling of witnesses, earned him a barrage of press criticism in these years. Tenney claimed he thrived on such criticism; but there is no question that the California newspapers helped force his retirement from the committee in 1949.

At one time in his life Tenney was an articulate champion of FEPC. Doubtless, today, he regrets it. Last year he became national chairman of America Plus, Inc., which proposed a "Freedom of Choice" amendment to the California Constitution. The amendment, which never got on the ballot, was designed to "make illegal any further state or municipal FEPC ordinance" and to repeal existing anti-discrimination ordinances. America Plus materials were distributed by both Gerald Smith and Robert Williams.

Tenney has no clear anti-Semitic record up to this time but he has baited minority groups. An editorial in the April 3, 1948, *Pacific Citi-*

| Cross-Currents in America

zen, publication of the Japanese-American Citizens League, said that Tenney and his committee "were responsible in considerable measure for the shameful racist hysteria generated against persons of Japanese ancestry during World War II. . . . Senator Tenney has shown himself to be a man of hate and unreasoning prejudice."

All of which goes a long way toward explaining Tenney's candidacy for Vice-President on Gerald Smith's Christian Nationalist Party.

Tenney comes up for re-election as a state senator in 1954, two years from now. His defeat on the preposterous Smith ticket we take for granted; more important will be his defeat as a major party candidate when he runs for re-election as a state senator.

AUGUST 22, 1952
Press Department to BRE

From yesterday's St. Louis *Post-Dispatch,* commenting on the Christian Nationalist Party's success in winning a place on the Missouri ballot:

Gen. MacArthur's name has been appropriated by St. Louis leaders of Gerald L. K. Smith's race-hating Christian Nationalist crowd and listed as the party's candidate for President. . . . Under Missouri law, consent of the candidate is not required. The Christian Nationalists attempted to launch a "Draft MacArthur" movement at the Republican convention. . . . Gen. MacArthur may not have known of the Chicago shenanigans, but the group's current efforts cannot escape his notice. He ought to disassociate himself from that bunch, completely and immediately.

AUGUST 31, 1952
Chicago Office to AF

Several days after the major conventions, Lar Daly of this city announced the formation of a new political party which he named America First, naming himself at the same time national chairman.

1   The Anti-Eisenhower Crusade

The new party's platform calls for the use of atomic bombs to end the Korean War and for U.S. withdrawal from the United Nations.

In his initial bid to get on the ballot in Illinois, Lar Daly was unsuccessful. The State Electoral Board turned down his nominating petitions containing the names of General MacArthur, Senator Harry Byrd, of Virginia, and John Morse, of Chicago, for the presidency, vice-presidency, and Illinois governorship respectively.

In Missouri, however, Daly's party won a place on the ballot, just as Gerald Smith's group did, filing a slate of electors and the names of MacArthur and Byrd as its presidential and vice-presidential candidates.

Senator Byrd, on learning that he had been honored by the Christian Nationalist Party in Texas as its vice-presidential nominee, promptly wired the Texas chairman of the party to remove his name from the ballot there. Our guess is that the Virginia Democrat will send a similar wire to Missouri.

AUGUST 31, 1952
Research to AF

Yesterday the Constitution Party, offspring of the August 7–8 Chicago schism, met at the Adelphia Hotel, Philadelphia, Pennsylvania, and topped the original structure with a new permanent organization. Apparently there has been yet another split since Chicago; Mrs. Stevenson and Percy Greaves, the supposed permanent co-chairmen of the party, were in Philadelphia but did not attend the sessions. The new splinter group seems at this time to be headed by the pure professionals—Upton Close, Kenneth Goff, W. Henry MacFarland, Jr., and George Foster.

Haliburton Fales, a New York City broker who declared that he had been a heavy contributor to the Republican Party for years and hoped to contribute to the new Constitution Party, was made its "permanent chairman." G. I. Whitmer, of Baltimore, praised highly for his role in distributing Joe Kamp's *Headlines,* was made treasurer.

I Cross-Currents in America

George Foster, the morning session windup speaker, said, "We realize we cannot do much in this election, but we aim for 1954 and 1956. We advocate write-ins and loyal aims whenever we find them. We hope for MacArthur to be our candidate but as yet we have no definite word from him."

A subcommittee drafted the Constitution Party's set of principles; this is the preamble: "Whereas all three branches of the Government have strayed from the Constitution, we have formed a political party dedicated to the basic principles of the Constitution."

Mrs. Stevenson, from the Adelphia Hotel, charged that the meeting was illegal and that all arrangements for it were made without her sanction: "When we saw the people attending this meeting, we decided we wanted no part of it. We are resigning from any connection with the Constitution Party that is organizing in Philadelphia."

Here's the AP dispatch this morning on the political "event":

The Constitution Party, proclaiming itself as opposed to "international conspirators who derided and defied our Constitution for more than a decade," set out today on a campaign to win Electoral College Votes for General of the Army Douglas MacArthur for President and Senator Harry F. Byrd . . . for Vice-President.

Announcement of the party formation, its ticket and its plans was made here last night after a closed meeting. Upton Close . . . spokesman for the group, said thirteen states were represented . . . and a number of candidates endorsed. . . . Mr. Close said the statement of party principles called for: free enterprise and an uncontrolled economy; unalterable opposition to Universal Military Training; withdrawal from "any international spending and boondoggling" . . . the list of candidates named by Mr. Close as having been endorsed at the meeting was headed by Senator Joseph R. McCarthy, Republican of Wisconsin . . . Senator William E. Jenner, Republican of Indiana; Senator John W. Bricker, Republican of Ohio; Price Daniel for United States Senator from Texas; "probably" Gov. Allan Shivers, Democrat, for reelection in Texas; and Representative John F. Kennedy, Democrat of Massachusetts, for United States Senator. . . . General MacArthur could not be reached for comment.

1 The Anti-Eisenhower Crusade

NOVEMBER 12, 1952
Research Department to AF

In no state in which a third party was officially on the ballot did it poll enough votes even to be considered an also-ran.

Although MacArthur gave no consent, his name was used to head three "national" tickets. California State Senator Tenney willingly accepted the number two spot on Smith's slate, Vivian Kellems was named as vice-presidential candidate by the Constitution Party, and Senator Harry Byrd was the general's involuntary running mate on the America First ticket.

Despite Smith's boast that MacArthur would carry "22 states," the dissidents secured less than 18,000 of the 60,000,000 votes cast. This is the tabulation to date—and we believe it to be virtually complete—of the MacArthur vote garnered by the three parties in those states in which they were on the ballot. This tabulation does not account for the write-in votes that General MacArthur and other candidates of these parties may have received in the other thirty-nine states.

MARCH 1, 1953
Library to BRE

It is now four months since General Eisenhower was elected President of the United States and six weeks since he assumed office. A review of the hate press on the subject of the new Administration reveals that the majority insist that "nothing has changed," that the Republican Administration, like the Fair and New Deals, is controlled by the Jews.

In his November 10 newsletter, Gerald Smith professed to "have shed some tears in the past few hours and days" because "the election of Eisenhower means that Baruch and his gang of powerful international Jews have captured the White House again." With a warning

| Cross-Currents in America

that "this vicious international Jew machine . . . is as powerful among Republicans as it is among Democrats," Smith prophesied that:

The first step . . . of Baruch and his ruthless ilk of international manipulators . . . will be complete conscription of all human beings from 17 to 70. Their second gesture of tyranny will be to repeal the McCarran Immigration Act so that 20 million Jews and colored will be dumped on American shores. They propose to see to it that never again will the great white Christian population of America be able to express majority power. . . .

After the inauguration Smith continued his attacks. In an editorial in *The Cross and the Flag,* January 1953, he wrote:

It is unbelievable that mature-minded citizens could think that there has been any serious change in the Administration of our Government. . . . Eisenhower is a creature of Marshall, Roosevelt, Baruch and Truman. Truman's quarrel with Eisenhower was . . . a family quarrel . . . behind the Truman machine and behind the Eisenhower machine stands a Baruch.

Smith also wrote: "It is well for us to refresh ourselves on the magnificent research job done on Eisenhower by the great patriot Mr. Joseph P. Kamp." Smith then tried to bolster his preposterous charge by providing his readers with a summary of the Kamp brochure which "proved" that "the Jews" were backing Eisenhower for President.

C. Leon de Aryan's *The Broom* also felt that the man who really "won the election" was "Bernard Mannes Baruch"; and in an editorial headed "Ike's New Deal Cabinet" maintained that "The Elders of Zion are [again] riding high and driving the nation to slavery."

McGinley's *Common Sense* viewed the election results as, on the whole, "very encouraging" to those "who have been fighting . . . the pro-Communist, anti-Christian plan of the masterminds of the New Deal." Nevertheless, it was constrained to report that "this is not a 100 per cent victory against Marxism" because "the same powerful Zionist International group which has been in complete control of the New Deal for twenty years also has used Eisenhower to do an important part in this plan to break down European countries for Communism."

1 The Anti-Eisenhower Crusade

In a later issue (January 1) McGinley ran a front-page story captioned "Baruch Appoints Eisenhower Cabinet," in which he discussed the "significance" of the impending appointment of C. Douglas Dillon as Ambassador to France. After claiming that Ambassador Dillon's father's real name was Lapowski, *Common Sense* concluded:

The overall picture gives the impression that Eisenhower is knowingly or unknowingly acting as a front for Baruch whom we have always known was the spokesman for World Jewry, for Churchill who now boasts of being a Zionist and for other One-Worlders.

The preinaugural conference of Bernard Baruch, Prime Minister Churchill, and President-elect Eisenhower brought forth a storm of invective from all sections of the malcontent press, which saw it as heralding "another Zionist war." The most pungent comment was Henry H. Klein's article on "King Barney and his Satellites" in the January 29 issue of *Women's Voice:*

King Barney and his satellites gathered in his royal suite . . . and discussed the next steps in zionist rulership. . . . They all got orders from their royal patron. Barney is enthroned not in Palestine, but in New York City, capital of Zionism. He rules as a direct descendant of ancient King David . . . [and] says he is a zionist.

Stephen Nenoff's irregularly published sheet, the *American Commentator* (November 25), likewise expressed concern over the "forces . . . with which Iike seems [to be] in alliance . . ." taking up the theme that "The Zionists which form the Invisible Government are known to wreck every nation they enter." The *Commentator* went on to say that:

Ike was their candidate, and if Bernard Baruch—the Prince of Zionists—engineered his election and voted for him the sad truth is that he will help with their plans. . . .

Robert H. Williams, in the November issue of his *Williams Intelligence Summary,* also voiced alarmed speculation at the possibility that President Eisenhower might be unduly influenced by his "Jewish" advisers:

Will he listen to his campaign backer Felix Frankfurter, who has built inside the government agencies a powerful Marxist machine . . . ?

| Cross-Currents in America

Will he listen to the trio of Jewish nationalists, Frankfurter, Sen. Herbert Lehman and Henry Morgenthau, Jr., described . . . as constituting "the secret government of the United States"?

Then, of course, there was Upton Close, who in the November 17 issue of his *Closer-up* newsletter first congratulated the voters who had "turned out of office the collection of trough-feeding morons and bloody conspirators that manned the Marx-worshipping New Deal," but recommended caution:

. . . Since November 4 the President-elect has been surrounded almost solely by men whom constitutional Americans cannot trust. Foreshadowed Cabinet appointments offend them. . . . Influences which enslaved Truman are reaching for Eisenhower . . . [including] the hypocritical Jewish political gang which has corrupted American politics. . . .

Later, in a speech at Minneapolis on January 22, Close made additional comments in the same vein: after hailing President Eisenhower as "a truly God-fearing man who wants to serve his country," he warned that "Ike has fallen under the influence of international financiers interested only in protecting their world-wide holdings," and added that the new Congress might be torn apart by the "tolerance racketeers who have made vile and vicious attacks on me. . . ."

Evidently Ike did not heed Close's warnings, for the new Administration came under fresh attack in the February 5 issue of his *Closer-up*:

. . . the President has declared drastic pursuit of New Deal social policy [and thus] put both feet into the Marxist trap. . . . In Eisenhower's mistaken labelling of the McCarran-Walter Immigration Act as "unfair" . . . our new President backs the fanatic pressure groups out to change the economy, philosophy of government and texture of our nation. . . .

While most of the attacks so far have been directed against President Eisenhower, Vice-President Nixon is beginning to come in for his share of "criticism." In its February 9 issue *The Broom* ran an article, "Nixon and the Jews," which stated:

It is well known here that Little Dick from Whittier, who is now rattling about in a Vice-Presidential chair that is much too big for him,

1 The Anti-Eisenhower Crusade

was put there by the connivance of the Jewish cabal . . . because he was a small and weak man who could easily be wheedled and otherwise influenced to play the Jewish game. This is clearly shown in his voting and talking record in the House of Representatives and later in the Senate. . . .

Further evidence that Nixon is little better than a Jew-kissing sentimentalist appears in the fact that he was the chief guest and speaker here the other night to honor the Jew contingent in the present Congress. He expressed great concern over the outbreak of anti-Jewism in Russia and the satellite communistic countries.

It would have been naïve to expect a different reaction from the troublemakers. The philosophy and principles of President Eisenhower and of his political party are not the real reasons for their antagonism; the bigots' opposition is no more than an expression of their resentment for failing to win power or influence.

It took the agitators almost two years to broaden their twenty-year war upon the New Deal, the Fair Deal, FDR, and Harry Truman, and to include Mr. Eisenhower and the Republican Party. Now caught in the uncomfortable position of fighting both major political groups, the Smiths, the Upton Closes, the Joe Kamps, and the others must seek a real third party—one that is isolationist, politically and socially reactionary, and jingoist. In the meantime, and until such new political alignments show signs of development, they will be busy with their war upon the minorities, the Administration in Washington, the Democratic Party, the United Nations. All of this is done under the heading of fighting communism.

Until now they have never willingly given power or title to one over-all leader in the United States. Even their attempt to rally around the public prestige of MacArthur did not unify them. MacArthur, though he refused to dignify them even by bothering to disclaim their nomination, may have unwittingly, and probably unwillingly, given them a respectability in the very use of his name. It might have been better had he repudiated them completely. What little success they had was largely due to his name.

These troublemakers rarely learn from experience. Their dismal failure in the 1952 presidential election may, however, be the exception

| Cross-Currents in America

—a bitter defeat from which they departed with perhaps a keener understanding of the elements required for political success. One prime requirement would be a national figure who would permit the use of his name and give his active leadership. If they have learned this lesson, citizens will have to pay even more attention to their activities in the future.

Two   The Fort Monmouth Scandal

In May 1953, the National Executive Committee of the Anti-Defamation League, meeting in Chicago, passed this resolution:

> The communist conspiracy to destroy democracy in the United States compels our nation to mobilize its strength to defeat this subversive weapon of a hostile foreign power.
>
> To this end, increased government vigilance and prosecution, and aroused public understanding of the menace of communism and its devious tactics of infiltration, are necessary if this nation is to preserve its traditions and its liberties. But these necessary measures can and must be taken without trespassing upon our traditional civil liberties and without needlessly imposing upon the American people a climate of blanket suspicion, anxiety and fear.
>
> In the main, the American government, many voluntary organizations and countless individuals have mobilized in the traditional democratic way against the communist menace and have achieved noteworthy success in uprooting subversion in our land. In recent years, however, there has also developed a tendency which has brushed aside the classic American safeguards of human liberty—painstaking investigation, fair and impartial hearing, the right to confront and cross-examine one's accusers, and the presumption of innocence until guilt is

| Cross-Currents in America

proven. This tendency has substituted for these safeguards the destruction of reputation by rumor, defamation and the intimidation of critics. This tendency has injured those institutions which have made America strong and great.

Freedom of thought enshrined in our Bill of Rights has been imperiled and dissent has become confused with disloyalty. Thus preservation of the delicate balance between security and freedom is in jeopardy. A soil has been provided in which the professional bigot flourishes. A nation so divided and confused weakens its defenses and may become easier prey to communism.

Those voices which have been raised in protest against this evil tendency have thus far been too few and, unfortunately, have not been heeded. The Anti-Defamation League of B'nai B'rith adds its voice to those who seek to defend America's great democratic tradition. We plead for a return to the precious political and religious ideals of our nation. We urge that Congress and its committees engaged in their important tasks re-examine the techniques and procedures currently employed to insure the preservation of traditional safeguards of individual freedom and liberties.

These grave responsibilities can be discharged only by the united efforts of the National Administration, by the Congress of the United States, by a press rededicated to its own traditions and by the people themselves. To the achievement of this goal, we pledge our energies and our resources.

Aversion to basic change can be a decent conservative tenet. Opposition to communism (our struggle for survival) can be a reasoned political belief. But when these principles are perverted by an irrational fear of all that seems different, the principles become passions and the result is political hysteria. This hysteria is fertile ground for bigotry, fertile ground for demagoguery. We have seen too much of this in recent years; and it is much more dangerous to the fabric of our society than the hysteria we have illustrated in the preceding chapter.

What have been some of the recent symptoms of this political hysteria?

A prominent American career woman proudly accepts a nomination by the President to be an Assistant Secretary of Defense and, because she is Jewish, foreign-born, and a New Dealer, is attacked and must clear herself of false charges of communist affiliation. A Midwestern

2 The Fort Monmouth Scandal

woman, discovering Robin Hood, concludes that it is communist propaganda and storms at the local school system for keeping copies on its bookshelves; the United States Naval Academy at Annapolis orders its students to engage in no intercollegiate debate which would require them to present even theoretical arguments favoring the admission of Red China to the United Nations; a twenty-three-year career diplomat, cleared by eight full-scale loyalty investigations and hearings, is dismissed despite no substantial case of disloyalty; a leading American public servant, respected as one of the country's most talented immigration experts, is summarily discharged from his post in the Department of State in order to appease a dubious charge of questionable political affiliations.

The atmosphere has been one in which dissent and non-conformism may be maintained only at the cost of a man's livelihood and the risk of his reputation for patriotism. And the security of minority groups, largely dependent upon the strength of our democratic institutions, is imperiled.

On October 9, 1953, the press reported that Senator Joseph R. McCarthy was suddenly interrupting his British West Indies wedding trip and flying back to this country to participate in an investigation of security leaks at the Fort Monmouth Army installation in New Jersey. The news had come from Francis P. Carr, staff director of the Senate Permanent Subcommittee on Investigations.

In the excitement of visualizing the next day's headline, Carr had apparently forgotten the position of subcommittee counsel Roy Cohn twenty-four hours before. Cohn, too, had called in reporters. Telling them he had just privately examined six Monmouth radar research employees and would question twelve more on the morrow, Cohn had added: "In the absence of any Senator members of the subcommittee, we have agreed that it would be proper not to comment on what occurs here now. I want to stress that these are essentially preliminary interviews and that none of these witnesses is under oath."

The "closed" hearings lasted five weeks. Let us jump ahead and examine the files from that point onward.

I Cross-Currents in America

NOVEMBER 16, 1953
BRE to AF

I find it difficult to reconcile the headlines and dispatches of the last five weeks, reporting the Fort Monmouth espionage findings of Senator McCarthy's Permanent Investigations Subcommittee, with today's news story that the subcommittee will only *now* start open hearings. Certainly the public hearings will be anticlimactic unless the senator has additional data not yet revealed by him; since his return from Spanish Cay he has been front-page news with his so-called closed sessions. Even the Army got into the swing of things with daily announcements of civilian suspensions at the Fort.

I am troubled that nearly every Fort Monmouth employee removed as a security risk by the Army or subpoenaed by the subcommittee and publicly labeled a suspected communist or Soviet spy is, judging from names, a Jew. If these men are actually guilty, there is no basis for a charge of anti-Semitism; in that case the number of suspended Jews itself would prove nothing. Thus far, they are only unproved non-legal accusations. The arithmetic of the situation—the large number of Jews —probably accounts for the increasing rumors that suspensions at Monmouth are prompted by anti-Semitism. If the charges are without basis, are rooted in prejudice, the harm being done by the adverse publicity is immeasurable.

Perhaps we will learn some answers in the Senate Subcommittee's now scheduled public hearings. In the meantime, I would appreciate a complete analysis of the suspensions and hearings reported so far.

NOVEMBER 17, 1953
AF to BRE

Here is an analysis of what happened in the last five weeks:—
At the close of his subcommittee's first executive session on October

2 The Fort Monmouth Scandal

12, the Monday afternoon following his return from the British West Indies, Senator McCarthy called in the press to proclaim that he had unearthed a trail of *"extremely dangerous espionage"* at the Army's Fort Monmouth, New Jersey, research laboratories.

"If it develops," said the senator, "it will envelop the *whole Signal Corps*. . . . This espionage is *recent* and deals with our entire defense against atomic attack."

But in order to understand *exactly* what has been uncovered and accomplished so far by the Senate Permanent Investigations Subcommittee on the subject of disloyalty at the Fort Monmouth installation, it is necessary to go back a little to the security program created by President Truman in 1948.

These security procedures, designed to keep communist agents away from sensitive American military research, brought about an investigation of all federal employees. At Fort Monmouth it resulted within months in the suspension of thirty-five civilian scientists and other trained personnel, of whom all but two were eventually reinstated after intensive investigation of their backgrounds, activities, and attitudes.

Secretary of the Army Robert T. Stevens, an Eisenhower appointee, took office in February 1953. Conferring immediately on Army security with FBI chief J. Edgar Hoover, the Army Secretary asked the Bureau to reinitiate a thorough probe into the Fort Monmouth setup. In a matter of weeks, also, President Eisenhower issued an Executive Directive revising President Truman's loyalty program and making it more stringent. Under the new procedures, all federal personnel had to be rechecked.

It seems that Roy Cohn came into possession of a condensed version of the Stevens-requested FBI report outlining security conditions at the Army's research laboratories at Fort Monmouth. Cohn, chief counsel to the subcommittee, had been an Assistant U. S. Attorney under Myles Lane in New York some two years before. Having assisted in the prosecution of the Rosenberg treason trial, he was familiar with most of the names turned up in the course of that investigation. When he read the condensed version of the new FBI study of Fort Monmouth, Cohn spotted in the confidential report a name or two which he thought he remembered from the files of the Rosenberg case. The names rang a bell in his mind and started him on his own subcommittee inquiry into the New Jersey situation.

By September 1953 fifteen Fort Monmouth cases had reached Secretary Stevens under the revised procedures with recommendation for suspensions. The employees involved had already been fully investigated a number of times, some being suspended and, as we said, cleared later after hearing. But on the basis of the reinvestigations and in light of the stricter rules, the Army Secretary decided upon suspension again.

It was about this time that Roy Cohn met with Robert Stevens and advised him that he believed "a bad security situation" existed at Monmouth; although one can safely assume the Army Secretary knew the facts from his own sources. Cohn added that the McCarthy subcommittee was preparing an investigation of the military installation. Sensitive to public criticism, especially from a congressional committee, the Army Secretary instantly issued orders to General Kirke B. Lawton, commanding officer at Fort Monmouth, to co-operate wholeheartedly with the Senate Permanent Investigations Subcommittee.

Roy Cohn, Francis P. Carr, the subcommittee's staff director, and David Schine, subcommittee consultant, immediately began their inquiry of the Signal Corps at Fort Monmouth. It was then the first week in October 1953.

On October 6, at the very moment the subcommittee staff was moving in, the Army announced that several employees of its Fort Monmouth laboratories had been "suspended for security reasons." It refused to furnish the number released, their identities, or the precise nature of the charges against them. But two days later the New York *Times* named three men who admitted that they were at least part of the suspended group. Each vigorously denied any guilt.

That very day and the next, Roy Cohn and staff interviewed eighteen Fort Monmouth civilian specialists. Advising the newspapers that the probe had begun, he then stepped into an airplane headed for Spanish Cay, British West Indies, and left Francis Carr behind to report at a second press conference that "important ramifications have developed"

2 The Fort Monmouth Scandal

in the Fort Monmouth inquiry. So important, added David Schine, they necessitated the emergency return of Senator McCarthy from his wedding trip. On the following Monday—October 12—McCarthy arrived in New York.

For the next five weeks Senator McCarthy conducted "secret" hearings—they were called "executive" sessions—but he furnished the newspapers with enough information at the end of each day to make frightening headlines. And during the same period Secretary Stevens continued to make public the suspensions, one after another, of civilian personnel at the Fort. Here is what happened.

On October 12, Monday afternoon, after the first day's "executive" session, when McCarthy issued his first startling charge of "extremely dangerous espionage" at Monmouth, he informed reporters that the subcommittee had questioned five witnesses, all civilians. Four were currently working at Fort Monmouth, and the fifth, he said, had left the installation in 1948. Identifying none of the witnesses by name, the senator admitted that the four current employees were "co-operative." It was the fifth witness, he charged, whose testimony, or lack of it when he pleaded the Fifth Amendment, raised grave suspicions. The senator was careful to admit, but not to emphasize, that this particular witness had been permanently suspended from the Air Force *five years before* because he had refused to answer questions during a security check. Since then the witness, no longer employed by the government, had not even been permitted within sight of any sensitive scientific activity.

But the headline Monday night in the nation's press, based on Senator McCarthy's remarks to reporters, was: "Spying Is Charged at Fort Monmouth."

On the Saturday *before* this first "executive" session, an almost unnoticed news story appeared in the New York *Journal-American,* a Hearst newspaper. It was under the by-line of Howard Rushmore, who not too long before had been the subcommittee's research aide and who was still on intimate terms with the senator and most of his subcommittee's staff. Rushmore confided to his public in this exclusive

73

dispatch that a feud had flared between the McCarthy subcommittee and the Justice Department over the right to interview federal prisoners. Rushmore said that McCarthy's staff had been seeking permission from the Justice Department to question Harry Gold and David Greenglass, former Soviet couriers serving prison terms in the Lewisburg, Pennsylvania, penitentiary. Despite the subcommittee's contention that both prisoners could supply important evidence in the radar case, the Justice Department, Rushmore revealed, had so far refused McCarthy permission to question the two spies.

This brief inside story is worth noting because many days later Senator McCarthy and his staff mentioned that, on the basis of evidence which they had only *then* discovered, it had become necessary to question Gold and Greenglass. Somebody had forgotten that the staff weeks before had leaked their desire to cross-examine the two convicted spies. Certainly they must have hoped the public had forgotten—or hadn't noticed.

On Tuesday, October 13, at the end of the second day's "secret" hearing, Senator McCarthy reported that his investigation had taken a new turn—a turn well worth a headline, to be sure: now the angle was allegedly missing confidential documents. "A sizable amount of top secret papers" had disappeared from three Signal Corps installations, was the way the senator phrased it, and he added that if the documents "got into the hands of an enemy they could be extremely dangerous to this country." McCarthy did not assert that his own subcommittee had just discovered the alleged loss. He admitted to reporters that a search for the missing documents had been initiated two years before by the armed forces.

Robert T. Stevens, now a spectator at the "executive" sessions, told the press that the Army was giving the subcommittee the "fullest cooperation." From Washington Charles E. Wilson, Secretary of Defense, indicated that the Army's own investigation of Fort Monmouth was turning up implications of a spy plot. He declared: "It looks like it might be worse than just a security leak." In Chicago, Senator Everett M. Dirksen (R., Ill.), a member of the McCarthy subcommittee, an-

2 The Fort Monmouth Scandal

nounced that the "26 top secret documents missing from Fort Monmouth had been found in the Russian Zone of East Germany." "The real tragedy," said Dirksen, "is that the whole secret of our radar defense screen may have been peddled off. That would be a colossal treachery." And to reporters Dirksen added mysteriously: "More than that I do not dare talk about now."

An ex-Army officer testified that the "registry logs" of the "documents" were accounted for in "destruction orders." Nevertheless, Senator McCarthy, for the moment a precisionist, told newsmen that the subcommittee was most eager to question the two Signal Corps officers who had signed the "certificates of destruction" for the registry logs. Mr. Stevens added that he would produce the responsible officer. At this point Senator McCarthy declared that his investigation *"definitely involves espionage."*

The "missing" documents were not the reason for Tuesday's session —only the reason for the headline. The session had been occupied with nine witnesses, including four civilians currently employed at the Monmouth radar laboratories who had been subpoenaed by the subcommittee. Patently the examination of the current employees was not newsworthy; none refused to talk; none sought his constitutional privilege of silence; none was involved in espionage. So—"missing" documents. But it was clear from the news stories that the civilian employees who had been brought before the subcommittee had been directed to appear because each had known or had once had some association with the executed Julius Rosenberg.

On Wednesday, October 14, the big news from Senator McCarthy at the conclusion of his closed hearing was that the Army had suspended five more Fort Monmouth civilian employees for "communist activities." McCarthy did not expressly take credit for the Army's action.

What did that day's testimony at the subcommittee hearing produce? "A top scientist" on the stand admitted that, having taken forty-three "secret documents" from the Evans Laboratory of Fort Monmouth to his home "for study" back in October 1946, he had been punished with

75

a ten-day suspension. Ignoring other testimony that it was a general practice for Monmouth personnel who had secrecy clearance to remove vital information from the files for such purposes, Senator McCarthy dramatically expressed his shock that despite this frightening carelessness the scientist had later actually been promoted. Though the senator refused to identify the newest Army suspendees, reporters printed some of their names. They were the same names that had been published the week before:

Harold Ducore, a thirty-four-year-old electronics engineer of Long Branch, New Jersey, who had worked twelve years on radar projects at Fort Monmouth. "I certainly intend to fight these charges," said Ducore.

Aaron Coleman, a thirty-five-year-old engineer who had served as a Marine lieutenant in charge of a radar unit in the Pacific during World War II. Declaring his "complete innocence," Coleman said that despite his "positive contributions" to aviation and radar defenses the government had told him he was being suspended because of people he once knew in college or had met at Monmouth. "Unfortunately," added Coleman, "I was in the same graduating class with Sobell and some others. I had no social relations with him after that. But in my capacity as a government project engineer I met him several times at the Reeves Instrument Corporation plant in New York."

Coleman was referring to Morton Sobell, who had been convicted along with Julius and Ethel Rosenberg and sentenced to thirty years in prison, not the electric chair, because his conviction did not involve atom secrets.

The third suspendee to be identified was Hyman G. Yamins, of Newton, Massachusetts, who had been assigned by the Army to the Massachusetts Institute of Technology as a liaison officer. Yamins' attorney announced that he would immediately file an appeal on behalf of his client because "we are convinced there is no basis for the suspension."

At this writing, we cannot say what the truth is with regard to these three suspendees. However, a respect for constitutional safeguards requires that these men not be publicly labeled guilty until all the facts

2 The Fort Monmouth Scandal

are in and until each has had his day in court. Of course immediate suspension from such sensitive positions may be completely justified. The publicized suspension of these men from strategic positions in atomic research, however, seems to have been evidence enough for many frantic Americans that each suspendee was guilty and that the McCarthy subcommittee from the beginning knew precisely what it was doing.

The testimony of Friday, the sixteenth, again provoked awesome headlines. This time the story was that the Rosenberg spy ring "may still be in operation" at the Monmouth laboratories. The news was based on Senator McCarthy's statement that day to the press that Julius Rosenberg's name had "cropped up frequently in testimony in the last week" before the Senate subcommittee. That Rosenberg's name did not crop up accidentally can be seen from the subcommittee's reported examination of witnesses; the *questioners* introduced Rosenberg's name. What is more, McCarthy announced his own finding that the Rosenberg spy ring had "free access" to top secret material at the Fort Monmouth radar center.

Twelve additional witnesses from Fort Monmouth and elsewhere had appeared that day before the Senate Permanent Subcommittee in closed session at the United States Courthouse in Foley Square, New York. Their names were not disclosed. However, in light of the revelations concerning the Rosenberg ring, said Senator McCarthy, he was convinced that *"it is now absolutely necessary to interview David Greenglass."* He would "make the necessary arrangements" with the Justice Department.

By this time the hearings were going so well that Senator McCarthy and his staff pushed ahead with their daily "executive" sessions—and daily press releases. The result was a juicy headline in Saturday morning's papers: "Radar Witness Breaks Down: Will Tell All about Spy Ring."

Senator McCarthy was again the one to reveal this "most important development." In a tense voice he told the press that a "key" employee

I Cross-Currents in America

at the Army's Fort Monmouth laboratories had been placed in "protective custody" because he "is now afraid for his own personal safety." "I want to ask you a favor," McCarthy said to the press in the ensuing excitement, "if by chance you learn the identity of the witness, please don't use his name."

The Wisconsin senator explained that the witness, having been recalled after testifying "a day or so ago," had just given testimony regarding members of a suspected spy ring in government agencies, including the Signal Corps; the FBI would be supplied with a transcript.

The situation had been most dramatic. A few minutes after questioning by Roy Cohn, the witness had broken down and was led out of the hearing room by Frank Carr to a small anteroom across the courthouse corridor where, face ashen, he sank into a chair. Guards held back reporters and photographers while a doctor, trailed by a nurse carrying a tray with medical equipment, were admitted to the private chamber. It was reported that the witness, who was "shaking with fright," responded after a stimulant.

The press then filed back into the hearing room for *their* daily stimulant from Senator McCarthy. "I have just received word," intoned the senator, "that the witness admits he was lying the first time and now wants to tell the truth." Further, he had confessed to being a close friend of Julius Rosenberg. "They shared an apartment at one time," the senator added ominously.

Asked if the man had been a member of the Rosenberg spy ring, McCarthy cautiously replied, "I don't want to say how much he participated in it." However: "This much I can tell you. The witness has indicated a great fear of the spy ring which has been operating within government agencies, including the Signal Corps."

In the furor about the subcommittee revelations, little notice was taken of a brief AP dispatch filed that day in Washington quoting the U. S. Army in answer to the week-old charges by Senator McCarthy that certain documents and other material had disappeared from Fort Monmouth and turned up in East Berlin. The Army announced it still had "no evidence that any documents had been compromised or that

2 The Fort Monmouth Scandal

files had been tampered with," and noted that if any secret papers had reached unauthorized hands "they represent new and previously unknown evidence in the cases now being investigated." Of course nobody, least of all the McCarthy subcommittee, had charged that there were any documents missing other than the missing-ones-which-had-turned-up-not-missing.

This was no longer important; but the witness, Carl Greenblum, who had broken down and agreed to tell all *was*. Names make news. A week of secret investigations had ended in a blaze of glory for the subcommittee.

With Sunday, a day devoted to more leisurely and considered newspaper reading, came caution. His inquiry, Chairman McCarthy reported that weekend, was hampered by the delay "of five to ten years" in pursuing the espionage trail. Because of this, he said, the three-year statute of limitations might operate to bar full prosecutions for espionage. No longer was it *current* espionage; the alleged spy work had occurred years before!

Sufficient unto the day was the headline thereof. There was a new culprit. McCarthy would now seek a contempt citation, he said, against a former civilian employee who had not worked at Fort Monmouth since 1948. Two other witnesses, current employees, who had just been before the subcommittee were relatively minor, he admitted.

Before the weekend was over, Harold E. Rainville and Robert L. Jones, assistants respectively to subcommittee members Senator Dirksen and Senator Charles E. Potter (R., Mich.), announced to the press that they were ready to make their individual reports to their superiors. Rainville said:

"The growing number of former employees and executive personnel at Fort Monmouth who have now taken refuge under the Constitutional protection of the Fifth Amendment clearly indicates that there was widespread communism in one of the Government's most secret enterprises, and at the most critical period."

Read Mr. Rainville's statement quickly and you might have the impression that *current* executive personnel had pleaded the Fifth

Amendment. As a matter of fact, no current employee did, and Rainville did not say they did. The word "former" in Rainville's carefully prepared comment applied to "employees *and* executive personnel." It should be noted, too, that Rainville was now talking about alleged subversive activities that were long ago rooted out and punished.

Mr. Jones indicated that his particular report to Senator Potter would include the following: "The Rosenberg spy ring may still be an operating conspiracy . . . the major damage has already been done. Everything brought out by Senator McCarthy in the last week should have been brought out ten years ago."

It did not strike Mr. Jones, either, that his statement threw the lie into the teeth of all the previous headlines about *current* espionage.

In the meantime the U. S. Army announced more suspensions that day. And, ostensibly because its statement the previous day about the allegedly stolen documents might not have been seen by enough people, the Army repeated its denial:

"There is no evidence that any documents have been compromised or that files have been tampered with in the Signal Corps Intelligence Agency. The documents alleged to have been missing at that time were accounted for. Under lend-lease agreements during World War II, a free exchange of information with allied nations was authorized. Since the termination of lend-lease agreements after World War II, we have no evidence of microfilm copies of any classified documents having gone astray."

McCarthy and his men spent the following Monday in Washington. Tuesday morning they arrived at the Monmouth County airport to be taken, in the company of Secretary Stevens, on a two-hour inspection of the electronic and radar laboratories in the area. Though the press reported that Roy Cohn was in the party, gossip had it that he was barred from restricted buildings and made quite a fuss about it.

In the ensuing interview, McCarthy and Stevens, talking affably with the reporters, were fulsome in their praise of each other. Said the senator: "I have been very favorably impressed with the forceful and aggressive step taken by the Secretary and the Commanding General

2   The Fort Monmouth Scandal

of the area to clear up the situation. . . . An extremely bad and dangerous situation has existed here over the years. Some past and present —until recently present—employees have been very unfaithful. . . ."

The Secretary and the senator went on to talk about the high degree of morale at the Fort because conditions were being so effectively corrected. "They are just as happy as we are," said McCarthy, "to see these few bad apples—twelve of them—being thrown out by Mr. Stevens and General Lawton."

Not one of the twelve employees suspended by the Army Secretary has even received a copy of the charges against him as yet, or has had a first hearing. Surely McCarthy had no legal basis for concluding that the employees were guilty—"bad apples." And Stevens, ignoring the obvious oversight, adopted exactly the same position when he interrupted to say:

"I can put that up a little. That figure is too low. More than twelve have been suspended."

Could the Secretary tell the reporters the exact number? No, he could not do that, it would not be in order for him to do so. "But I can say that this is good evidence of the kind of teamwork between the Executive and Legislative Branches of the Government which will clean up any situation that needs cleaning up."

Could anyone be surprised that the public assumed the treason of these civilians? After all, the Secretary of the Army wasn't waiting to hear them; he knew the facts.

(Suppose the Army hearing boards and all the reviewing boards conclude, after the evidence is in, that there is no basis for the accusations, and therefore recommend the reinstatement of the twelve employees. Will the Secretary be able to approve such recommendations—or has he gone too far out on a limb?)

On Thursday the subcommittee held its hearings at Fort Monmouth, and Senator McCarthy used the opportunity to announce that the Army had suspended three additional civilian specialists as security risks. He identified none of them. He did reveal that he had questioned five more witnesses regarding possible espionage at the radar center,

| Cross-Currents in America

and, pressed by reporters, gave enough details for the careful observer again to note that no present employee had hidden behind constitutional privilege.

The big news of the day was the testimony of a German scientist that during World War II the Russians had access to secret radar information from the Evans Signal Laboratory of the Army at Belmar, New Jersey. The testimony was a tape recording of an interview James Juliana, a staff assistant, had conducted during a quick trip to Germany from which he had just returned.

But the newspaper reporters were beginning to catch on. They pressed McCarthy to say whether evidence had been uncovered indicating an espionage ring *still* in operation at Fort Monmouth. The senator refused to comment. (The Washington *Times Herald* didn't catch on. The following Saturday, crediting itself and the Chicago *Tribune* with discovering "the damning report" of the German scientist, it said editorially: "Call it disloyalty or call it stupidity, something is rotten when two newspapers and a congressional committee must act to break up a spy ring at the secret research center where electronic war devices are developed and the nation's radar defenses are planned by the signal corps.")

Friday night's story was more of the same. McCarthy announced that the number of suspensions of civilian specialists at the Fort had risen to twenty and might rise to many more; he had summoned twenty-three additional employees for interrogation the next week. Not only that, but he had testimony linking nine of the twenty-three with the executed spy, Julius Rosenberg. Again, no details. The testimony he did describe for reporters that day came from witnesses who were *not* Monmouth employees. But you had to read the day's dispatches carefully to make the distinction.

Of course the non-Monmouth witnesses included admitted ex-communists and some others who pleaded the Fifth Amendment. And though the hearings were still being conducted in secret, the senator nevertheless again revealed rather complete details and even some of

2 The Fort Monmouth Scandal

the witnesses' names. None of the admitted communists heard that day were Jews. The other witnesses were.

Monday night, October 26, McCarthy's staff members came up with a natural for the next morning's headlines—Alger Hiss. To be sure, there was only a peripheral connection with him, but for this variety show, Hiss was a sure headliner. With the senator back in Wisconsin for some undisclosed purpose, the staff, it was revealed, had questioned an "important civilian section head in the Evans Signal Laboratory" on his connections with a figure named as a member of the Alger Hiss spy ring. Details? As usual, they were less in evidence than even the "missing" documents. But David Schine added that civilian suspensions now totaled twenty-seven.

By then, it seemed the subcommittee staff had exploited all the Monmouth angles, for new channels of investigation were already being hinted at. Roy Cohn informed newspapermen that the subcommittee had become interested in interviewing Igor Gouzenko, former code clerk in the Soviet Embassy at Ottawa, Canada. And David Schine announced: "We will suggest to Senator McCarthy that we soon get to the matter of the loyalty boards which cleared Communists or individuals who were communist risks, particularly the screening board of the Department of the Army in Washington."

From that day on, Fort Monmouth was crowded into the background by attention-getting daily reports of tangential subcommittee activities: questioning William Perl in the Federal Penitentiary at Lewisburg, Pennsylvania; compiling lists of top Army screening board members "so that we can summon those who reinstated persons suspended for Communist activity" (the Army instantly denied subversion in its loyalty boards); interviewing Greenglass and proclaiming his disclosures of espionage in the radar field (Greenglass' lawyer subsequently denied his client had supplied the subcommittee with anything of substance); visiting Harry Gold in prison and announcing he had implicated a person dismissed from the United Nations staff. All of these scare stories and the subsequent denials made exciting and shocking newspaper headlines, and were covered by most of the major press in full dramatic detail. McCarthy, active on the West Coast, was telling reporters he was subpoenaing a suspended security official of a loyalty board. (The Army immediately denied it had suspended any loyalty board official.) And then the subcommittee started to concern itself with its next investigation—"communism" in defense plants. But . . .

Suddenly, last Friday, Secretary Stevens, pressed by newspaper reporters, particularly the Washington *Post's* Murrey Marder, openly denied that the investigations of the Fort Monmouth installations had uncovered evidence of current espionage. He also reported that thirty-three civilian employees at the laboratories had been removed; however, several had been reinstated. McCarthy yesterday struck back at Stevens by scheduling public "showdown" hearings.

Apparently the Army Secretary in the last few weeks realized that if the public believed there was still espionage at Monmouth it would conclude that he himself was to blame; he had been in charge ten months. He therefore issued this long-overdue refutation.

For the first time, Secretary Stevens is personally embroiled with Senator McCarthy over the Monmouth mess. He has publicly slapped Senator McCarthy, expert extraordinary in the art of the open brawl. Look for trouble.

Yesterday a press interview with Carl Greenblum, the Fort Monmouth witness who had been led away in hysterics after breaking down under Roy Cohn's "grueling cross-examination," resulted in a completely different picture from the one the subcommittee had furnished to the newspapers.

Greenblum identified himself as the mystery witness. He had reluctantly decided to make public his part in the hearings, he said, because his family was being persecuted by neighbors.

You will recall that when Senator McCarthy first released the Greenblum story he claimed the witness confessed he had lied and now "wanted to tell everything." Yesterday Greenblum denied he had falsified at any time, contended that he had always been a loyal American, and offered a different reason for his collapse. His mother had died forty-eight hours before the hearing, he said, and he had been in no state to undergo an intense, lengthy examination. He disclosed that

2 The Fort Monmouth Scandal

he had *never* been suspended from the Monmouth laboratories and insisted he had *never* been questioned either by the subcommittee or by the FBI about matters that concerned him personally.

At the United States Courthouse in Foley Square last night, Senator McCarthy was pressed by reporters about Greenblum's denial of any connections with the Communist Party. Said Senator McCarthy: *"I would not want to comment on that."*

More of the story will have to be learned before we can come to any final conclusions about the truth in the Greenblum matter.

The public, of course, is still anxious about "the great espionage ring" at Fort Monmouth, especially because every few days a brief dispatch appears in the press identifying various suspendees, who are now preparing to prove their loyalty and win back their jobs at Monmouth.

So the rumors of prejudice continue to increase.

Whether the large percentage—exactly what percentage we don't know—of Jews among the suspended Monmouth employees is the result of anti-Semitic malice obviously cannot be determined from the sources at hand. One searches in vain through the huge pile of newspaper clippings, magazine articles, and other published materials for the *facts* on which the Monmouth removals were ordered. The Army has revealed nothing except that it suspended these men; publicly it only insinuated their guilt. McCarthy has revealed nothing except to say, while also insinuating treason, that he has subpoenaed the suspendees and they have testified.

Our conclusion: the mere number of Jews involved in this situation raises a sufficient question to suggest the need for conferring with Army Secretary Stevens. Certainly he must have heard the same rumors which have come to us; perhaps he has some answers. It will be important to have his response since McCarthy is now planning to rerun his Monmouth hearings—this time for the benefit of the public.

NOVEMBER 17, 1953
Library to BRE

The only pertinent data in our files on a possible anti-Jewish slant to the Fort Monmouth case is as follows:

In the spring of 1952 we received a detailed memorandum from a suspended Fort Monmouth scientist relating alleged difficulties Jewish and Negro employees were being subjected to at the Watson Laboratories, the Air Force Signal Laboratory, the Evans Signal Laboratory, and the Army Signal Corps Laboratory—all located at Fort Monmouth. The scientist stated that there had been eighteen cases based on loyalty or security grounds, and that with one possible exception all the persons involved were Jews and Negroes. In addition he counted eleven employees who, he believed, were in "suspect status," that is, had been reduced to a restricted security clearance, involuntarily transferred, delayed in promotion, or otherwise repressively dealt with.

The scientist contended that Jews and Negroes *generally* were suspected of being pro-communist by the Fort's Security Section, and that anyone who expressed any sympathy with the problems of minority groups was also considered suspect. While the memorandum appeared to be persuasive, it lacked documentary evidence, grounded, as it was, primarily upon the arithmetic of the suspensions (predominance of Jews among disciplined employees) and upon hearsay and secondhand reports.

The scientist himself had been suspended in October 1950, after fourteen years of government employment, the last eight years as an engineer with the Fort Monmouth Signal Corps. A week or two prior to his removal he had received a promotion. The charges against him included, among other counts, an accusation that he had associated with Communist Party members, one man in particular; that he had been a member of a communist-dominated local civic association; that he had attended a meeting of Friends of Soviet Russia; that he had "followed the Communist Party line." These charges he categorically denied as false.

2   The Fort Monmouth Scandal

After carefully analyzing the memorandum we conferred with our local representatives familiar with the problem at Monmouth, and came away convinced that the charge of bigotry by the scientist could not be documented one way or the other. Within a few days, however, we received word that the scientist had been completely cleared and reinstated. We decided to sit tight and watch; it was June 1952.

In March 1953 we were advised by our Washington, D.C., office that the scientist, after his reinstatement with back pay, had resigned from his Fort Monmouth job and obtained employment in private industry working on Signal Corps contracts. However, he quickly lost that job and two others—because Army security officers refused him clearance even though he had won his case at Monmouth. In desperation, he sought the help of his congressman.

Like the scientist, the congressman got a run-around from the Army and Air Force, but eventually his official position, he informed our office, enabled him to get through and clear the scientist for sensitive employment. In the course of his inquiry the congressman was told by responsible sources that "the Fort Monmouth people were unfriendly to Jews."

On October 2, 1953, our New Jersey office received a telephone call from an attorney representing several Fort Monmouth suspendees. The lawyer was distressed over the fact that, of ten individuals at the military installation who had just recently been suspended as security risks or had their security clearances canceled, nine were Jewish and the tenth was married to a Jew.

The attorney stated further that over the preceding two-and-a-half-year period a number of employees at Fort Monmouth, Jews and Negroes in the majority, had been charged with being loyalty risks. In the last few days, he added, a group of engineers at Camp Evans received notice of cancellation of security clearance and, in some cases, suspension under loyalty and security procedures. Every engineer so notified had been a government employee for from ten to fifteen years through both World War II and Korea, and had been examined and cleared for classified and secret work many times. The attorney named fourteen individuals—all Jews except one whose wife was Jewish. Several of the suspendees were convinced, he added, that anti-Semitism was at the root of their difficulties. Each pointed to known anti-Semites at the installation: one a Jew-hater who loudly vaunted his bias, another who openly distributed anti-Semitic literature.

The lawyer supplied one other fact. General Lawton, he said, had been questioned about the presence of anti-Semitism and offered the countersuggestion that the reason for the removals was "maybe the college these boys went to."

This private information recorded in our files, plus what we have gleaned from the McCarthy subcommittee hearings and newspaper reports, is the sum of our knowledge on the subject. Thus far we have undertaken no independent investigation.

DECEMBER 11, 1953
BRE to AF

Next Monday two members of our Executive Committee and I will meet with Secretary Stevens to discuss our fear that anti-Semitism—our only concern—might be a factor in the Fort Monmouth situation.

DECEMBER 12, 1953
AF to BRE

In preparation for your visit with Secretary Stevens you wanted my summary of events brought up to date:

Senator McCarthy is in the middle of his public hearings on Monmouth, and nothing has developed that in any way clears the confusion of fact, fancy, and publicity.

To begin with, before the public hearings opened, Secretary Stevens narrowly averted a frontal clash with McCarthy on whether there was current espionage at Monmouth. Stevens withdrew his challenge by inviting the senator to lunch with him at the Merchants Club in New York City and then by calling in reporters to say that he had been misquoted.

2 The Fort Monmouth Scandal

"When I stated at a press conference that the Army has no proof of current espionage," Stevens explained, "I want to make it unmistakably clear that I was speaking of the Army investigation only, and not of the inquiry by the Senate Permanent Subcommittee on Investigations, of which Senator McCarthy is chairman."

The Secretary then added that spying in the Signal Corps laboratories at Monmouth had extended through the postwar years and possibly as late as 1951—thereby agreeing, as far as he went, with the Wisconsin senator.

Their truce will not last, I am certain. Only a day or so ago McCarthy taunted Stevens again with a charge that the Army loyalty boards are doing a "foul" job.

Meanwhile, others have stepped in to fight: Joseph Rauh, Washington attorney and vice-chairman of the Americans for Democratic Action, assailed the hearings as a "hoax on the public." "McCarthy charges espionage at press conferences twice a day," Rauh said. "I predict he will have nothing to support the charges once the public hearings start."

On November 24 the public hearings began, and at this writing Rauh's prediction seems to be standing up well.

The only current Fort Monmouth employee that the subcommittee has put on the witness stand so far is Aaron Coleman, whose testimony McCarthy was unable to shake. The suspended radar scientist, claiming no constitutional privilege against self-incrimination, flatly denied under oath that he was a communist, that he had ever stolen secrets from government research centers, that he had ever seen his classmate Julius Rosenberg in the sixteen years he had been out of City College in New York. Coleman admitted only that he might have been guilty of carelessness when, some years ago, he took some classified papers home with him for study.

McCarthy produced Army records to show that Rosenberg had been employed at Monmouth from 1940 to 1945—which was not exactly news. The senator put an assorted handful of ex-Monmouth employees, all out of the laboratories since before 1948, on the stand and listened to each refuse to say whether he had ever been a communist. McCarthy did introduce into evidence an affidavit his staff apparently succeeded in obtaining from David Greenglass, in which the convicted spy went through his relationship with Julius Rosenberg—a story Greenglass had told many times; the one, in fact, which helped to send Rosenberg to the electric chair. The single new statement in the Greenglass affidavit that, "as far as he knew, these operations never stopped and could very possibly be continuing to this very day," carries little weight. Greenglass has been in prison for three and a half years.

Not a single witness was brought forward who could or would testify about actual espionage at Fort Monmouth in the present period.

In other words, the public hearings are helping to prove exactly the opposite of what the senator promised they would show.

This is being recognized. Last week the New York *Herald Tribune* printed on its editorial page a feature article by Walter Millis, entitled "The Scandal at Fort Monmouth." In it Millis charged that "this really vital and sensitive military installation has been wrecked—more thoroughly than any Soviet saboteur could have dreamed of doing—by the kind of anti-Communism of which Senator McCarthy has made himself the leader and champion."

Millis reported that conservative Republicans are talking about demanding a congressional investigation "into the processes of witch-hunting, bigotry, cowardice, race prejudice and sheer incompetence which have turned one of our top-level military-scientific operations into a mare's nest of exasperation, fear and futility."

Millis makes a direct statement on the question we are taking to Secretary Stevens. He says: "The strong elements of racial and religious bigotry and prejudice in the case can only increase the damage it has done to the common defense. . . ."

If prejudice of this kind is present, it will be found somewhere in the Army proceedings. McCarthy seems only to have followed the leads of others. He may or may not have provoked some suspensions, but he did not select the men to be suspended. His is not the guilt of removing them from their jobs; his is the guilt, if they are innocent, of destroying their good reputations. The anti-Semites, if they are involved, remain to be found elsewhere.

2 The Fort Monmouth Scandal

DECEMBER 15, 1953
BRE to AF

We conferred with Secretary Stevens. He, too, is concerned about the rumors of anti-Semitism, but he cannot verify the truth of the reports, since he has been shown no evidence to substantiate the charge. While prompted to doubt that anti-Semitism has been a factor in the security proceedings, he would immediately remove anyone guilty of religious prejudice if facts coming to his attention warrant it.

The Secretary invited us to submit any data we have or can obtain on the subject. He would welcome help in this direction, he said, and we advised him that we would go ahead with an investigation.

DECEMBER 17, 1953
AF to BRE

The public sessions ended today, adjourned to an indefinite time by the chairman. Most of the newspapers reported that McCarthy was shown up in the "showdown" hearings; there was no proof of current espionage.

What remains now is to prove or disprove the presence of anti-Semitism as a factor in the suspensions. Our investigation has begun.

JANUARY 14, 1954
Press Department to BRE

The New York *Times,* expressing uneasiness about McCarthy's successful but "shameless scramble for publicity," also censured the Army's Security Screening Board for being "arbitrary, unreasonable and lacking in loyalty to its employees." Said the *Times,* too:

An atmosphere has been created in the United States that leads to this type of undemocratic persecution, and for that Senator McCarthy is partly to blame. Certainly, he has become the symbol and has provided the name—McCarthyism—for the sort of phony crusade that Fort Monmouth represents.

The Army had been investigating its Monmouth workers for months before Mr. McCarthy came along. Army investigators found no spies and neither has Senator McCarthy, yet the Senator was given sensational headlines last October on supposed espionage and communism at Monmouth. His charges have thus far proved false or exaggerated, but they were published at the time. It has taken weeks of reportorial effort to get at the true facts and publish them, but meanwhile Mr. McCarthy has had his publicity and Fort Monmouth has had its morale shaken badly, and it will doubtless lose valuable scientists who do not need to take suspicions and insults.

For the newpapers Fort Monmouth has been a lesson that will not quickly be forgotten, but the reading public should understand that it is difficult, if not impossible, to ignore charges by Senator McCarthy just because they are usually proved exaggerated or false. The remedy lies with the reader. If the Senator should hit upon something genuine there will be corroboration, but until there is the intelligent reader should refuse to accept a McCarthy charge as valid. Perhaps the Fort Monmouth case will prove valuable in the end as a typical example of McCarthyism that could be exposed.

FEBRUARY 4, 1954
AF to BRE

We have completed our inquiry into the Fort Monmouth problem. We found the following:

There are approximately six hundred civilian professional men and women retained in sensitive employment at all the laboratories encompassed by the Fort Monmouth installation. It is estimated that about twenty-five per cent of the personnel are Jewish, and it is generally believed that so large a number of Jews work in these government laboratories because private industry in this field practices religious discrimination.

All employees at the laboratories were subjected to an intensive security check and cleared by one or more federal investigative agencies prior to their employment. This is routine. Whatever doubts were

2 The Fort Monmouth Scandal

later cast on their loyalty by the lifting of their clearances or by actual suspension were precipitated in the Office of Civilian Security through the initiation of a security-risk proceeding.

The local chief of Civilian Security at the military post is the one who in most instances starts such proceedings by a written statement based either on facts which have come to his attention or upon accusations made by others against the employee.

We have experienced some difficulty in establishing exactly the number of civilian Monmouth employees who have been suspended from their jobs or who have been declassified and removed to so-called non-sensitive responsibilities. On November 14 the Army announced that thirty-three civilian employees had been suspended as security risks. But Secretary Stevens said at the same time that several of the employees who had been suspended were now reinstated.

Simultaneously several newspapers looking into the situation came up with varying figures. Mitchel Levitas, whose series of articles on Monmouth was published in the New York *Post,* reported that of forty suspensions or declassifications thirty-five were Jews and one a Negro. He further pointed out that about fifty per cent of the accused men had attended the College of the City of New York, from which atom spies Julius Rosenberg and Morton Sobell were graduated.

In Walter Millis' feature article on the suspensions, published in the New York *Herald Tribune,* it was said that within a month—in the period of October surrounding the McCarthy Subcommittee hearings—at least thirty scientists, many whose services with the Signal Corps had gone back ten to fifteen years, had summarily been suspended from the Army without pay. Millis indicated that eleven additional scientists had had their security clearances withdrawn, "thus putting them into a leper colony where they can be little more useful than twiddle their thumbs."

Shortly after the Millis story a series of articles appeared in the Newark *Evening News* reporting the results of an investigation made into the Fort Monmouth situation by John O. Davies, Jr., staff correspondent. These articles, which appeared from December 20 to 22, stated, among other things, that the Army security regulations were

| Cross-Currents in America

sharply revised last October 10, and from that time on, rules affecting security were rigidly changed. Davies reported an interview with Harry Green, of Little Silver, New Jersey, an attorney representing many of the suspendees, wherein Green alleged that at least forty men were involved in the aftermath of the revised security regulations. Green confirmed Levitas' observation that most of the suspended or declassified employees are graduates of the College of the City of New York where they studied engineering with Julius Rosenberg and Morton Sobell or in classes just before or after them.

Davies further reported that a study of the original statements of charges in attorney Green's possession shows that employees have been suspended because of alleged subversive activities of parents, sisters, brothers, and in-laws. He then went on to cite a number of cases supporting these allegations.

According to the publication Special Regulations, No. 620-220-1, Civilian Personnel—Security Investigations and Adjudications (issued by the Department of the Army, December 18, 1953), nineteen criteria are set forth for determining the effect that employment of the individual concerned might have on national security. Do the regulations point out that the activities and associations listed in the criteria are of varying degrees of seriousness? Yes. And do the regulations point out that, therefore, the ultimate determination of whether retention in employment is clearly consistent with the interests of national security must be an over-all common-sense one based on all available information? They do.

Our first inquiry was into the criteria used by the Department of the Army in its determination of security risks.

Here follow the criteria as set forth in SR 620-220-1:

1. Commission of any act of sabotage, espionage, treason, or sedition, or attempts thereat or preparation therefor, or conspiring with, or aiding or abetting, another to commit or attempt to commit any act of sabotage, espionage, treason, or sedition.

2. Establishing or continuing a sympathetic association with a saboteur, spy, traitor, seditionist, anarchist, or revolutionist, or with an

espionage or other secret agent or representative of a foreign nation, or any representative of a foreign nation whose interests may be inimical to the interests of the United States, or with any person who advocates the use of force or violence to overthrow the Government of the United States or the alteration of the form of government of the United States by unconstitutional means.

3. Advocacy of use of force or violence to overthrow the Government of the United States, or of the alteration of the form of government of the United States by unconstitutional means.

4. Membership in, or affiliation or sympathetic association with, any foreign or domestic organization, association, movement, group or combination of persons which is totalitarian, Fascist, Communist, or subversive, or which has adopted, or shows a policy of advocating or approving the commission of acts of force or violence to deny other persons their rights under the Constitution of the United States, or which seeks to alter the form of government of the United States by unconstitutional means.

5. Intentional, unauthorized disclosure to any person of security information, or of other information disclosure of which is prohibited by law.

6. Performing or attempting to perform his duties, or otherwise acting, so as to serve the interests of another government in preference to the interests of the United States.

7. Participation in the activities of an organization established as a front for an organization referred to in (4) above when his personal views were sympathetic to the subversive purposes of such organization.

8. Participation in the activities of an organization with knowledge that it had been infiltrated by members of subversive groups under circumstances indicating that the individual was a part of or sympathetic to the infiltrating element or sympathetic to its purposes.

9. Sympathetic interest in totalitarian, Fascist, Communist, or similar subversive movements.

10. Any behavior, activities, or associations which tend to show that the individual is not reliable or trustworthy.

11. Any facts which furnish reason to believe that the individual may be subjected to coercion, influence, or pressure which may cause him to act contrary to the best interests of the national security.

12. Participation in the activities of an organization referred to in (4) above, in a capacity where he should reasonably have had knowledge of the subversive aims or purposes of the organization.

13. Sympathetic association with a member or members of an organization referred to in (4) above. (Ordinarily this will not include chance or occasional meetings, nor contacts limited to normal business or official relations.)

14. Currently maintaining a close continuing association with a person who has engaged in activities or associations of the type referred to in (1) through (9) above. A close continuing association may be deemed to exist if the individual lives at the same premises as, frequently visits, or frequently communicates with such person.

15. Close continuing association of the type described in (14) above, even though later separated by distance, if the circumstances indicate that renewal of the association is probable.

16. The presence of a spouse, parent, brother, sister, or offspring in a nation whose interests may be inimical to the interests of the United States, or in satellites or occupied areas of such a nation, under circumstances permitting coercion or pressure to be brought on the individual through such relatives.

17. Willful violation or disregard of security regulations.

18. Acts of reckless, irresponsible, or wanton nature which indicate such poor judgment and instability as to suggest that the individual might disclose security information to unauthorized persons or otherwise assist such persons, whether deliberately or inadvertently, in activities inimical to the security of the United States.

19. Refusal by the individual, upon the grounds of constitutional privilege against self-incrimination, to testify before a Congressional Committee regarding charges of his alleged disloyalty or other misconduct (Executive Order 10491, 14 October 1953).

Our next inquiry was into the security and investigation *procedures* which led to suspension, loss of security clearances, and declassifications at Fort Monmouth.

On the basis of many interviews, including sources within the Army, we learned the following, which we believe to be accurate. However, in the absence of official information, this description cannot be considered authoritative.

Fort Monmouth, like other Army installations which have civilian employees, has a Civilian Security Officer—hereinafter called the "C.S.O." At Fort Monmouth the C.S.O.'s operation is variously referred to as "Civilian Security" and "Civilian G-2." He is under the supervision of the Post Military G-2 head who, in turn, is responsible to the commanding general.

Generally it is the responsibility of the C.S.O. to maintain "civilian security" at Fort Monmouth. He and his staff are responsible for seeing to it, for example, that safes are properly locked; to insure that confidential material is properly guarded; to prevent gambling, disorderly conduct, etc.

In addition—and probably a primary function—it is the C.S.O.'s job to file and collate all information forwarded to his office concerning the loyalty of the civilian employees or any other information pertinent to civilian employee security. He receives this kind of information from his own staff of security officers and through an informer system; with respect to the latter, there had been *developed a group of informants both among employees at the post and within the communities around Fort Monmouth who systematically furnish him with information about alleged subversive or suspicious activities, or affiliations on the part of civilian personnel. Who these complainants are, what motivated them, whether they were prompted by religious or racial prejudice, cannot be discovered—because their identities are kept secret.*

When the C.S.O. accumulates enough information of a derogatory nature which in his judgment makes any individual employee a security risk, he submits the file to his superior, the Military G-2 officer of the post.

It is believed that in forwarding such a file the C.S.O. also makes a recommendation for removal of security clearance.

The Military G-2 head in turn presumably ratifies the C.S.O.'s recommendation and passes the file up to the commanding general (now Major General Lawton).

If the commanding general concurs in the recommendation, he may immediately suspend the employee or remove his security clearance.

The commanding general then forwards a report to G-2 First Army (Governors Island). If this echelon ratifies the action, it is then passed up to G-2 Department of the Army, Washington, D.C. Ratification of the action by this echelon then brings the file to the Screening Board of the Department of the Army. If this body, in turn, approves a suspension, it sends the suspended employee a statement of charges.

Must a suspended employee receive a statement of charges within thirty days of the suspension? Yes, otherwise he is automatically reinstated. This rule may account for a number of situations where employees have been suspended, reinstated, and resuspended.

The foregoing is a description of the C.S.O.'s routine operation over the period of years during which he has been head of Civilian G-2 at Fort Monmouth.

In April 1953, President Eisenhower issued an executive order directing a reinvestigation of security risks within executive departments. As interpreted by the Department of the Army, this order required not only more intensive investigation of new employees but a security review of anyone employed on or before May 27, 1953, including those who had been previously charged and cleared. The responsibility for conducting these reviews was assigned to individual military installations. Thus, presumably, under the direction of Major General Lawton, it became the responsibility of the C.S.O.'s office to determine which employees at Fort Monmouth had to be subjected to reinvestigation.

Another *possible* impetus for a derogatory evaluation of employees by the Monmouth Civilian Security Section came from reports prepared by the FBI and other government branches. As an example, we are told that a comprehensive investigation conducted by the FBI into the associations of Julius Rosenberg produced unfavorable information regarding certain employees at Fort Monmouth. This information about specific employees went through channels of the Department of the Army in Washington, through G-2 First Army, and ultimately to the Civilian Security Section at Fort Monmouth. This kind of information, though perhaps insufficient in itself to warrant a full-scale investigation of the individual employee by the FBI or any other governmental agency, would be added to the already existing dossier in the C.S.O.'s office. If, in its judgment, the total

2 The Fort Monmouth Scandal

picture showed a security risk situation, it would then proceed to process the file—as described above, through the Military G-2 officer of the post and up through each succeeding echelon to Washington, D.C.

In not every case is a complaint or an unfavorable report necessarily the only provocation for investigation leading to suspension or declassification, etc. We have learned that when an employee is promoted or has his assignment changed to a higher security rating a review by the Civilian Security Section automatically follows. Such review presumably can lead to information which may result in loss of security clearance or worse.

We then proceeded to examine the charges made against some of the suspended Fort Monmouth employees. This information was made available to us in the cases of ten employees. Fairly typical of this entire group are the charges made against four employees, which will be set forth at this point:

Charges against Mr. B.

a. It has been reported that you were an active member and officer of at least one committee of the Monmouth County Chapter of the American Veterans Committee in 1947.

b. It has been reported that you failed to take a positive stand on the issue of admitting Communists to the Monmouth County Chapter of the American Veterans Committee.

c. It has been reported that you made it possible for M.U., a coworker and employee of the U.S. Air Force, to have access to classified reports which M.U.'s work did not require. M.U. has been reported to be a Communist Party member. The Communist Party has been cited by the Attorney General as a "subversive" organization which seeks "to alter the form of government of the United States by unconstitutional means."

d. It has been reported that your father registered as an affiliate of the American Labor Party from 1937 to 1941.

The Monmouth County Chapter of American Veterans Committee and the American Labor Party are referred to in these charges because of reports that they have been infiltrated or dominated or controlled by Communists and Communist sympathizers.

| Cross-Currents in America

Charges against Mr. C.

1. It has been reported that you were a member of, and active in, the United Public Workers of America—CIO.

2. It has been reported that you expressed approval of Communist views and stated that you thought that the Russian government had the best method of handling its people and that the United States Government was too liberal.

3. It has been reported that you associated with reportedly suspected Communists or Communist sympathizers, including, among others, A.S. The Communist Party has been cited by the Attorney General as a "subversive" organization which seeks "to alter the form of government of the United States by unconstitutional means."

4. That you married and have continuously resided with your wife who:

a. In 1944 was reported to be an active member of Monmouth County Local 236, United Federal Workers of America—CIO; in 1946 and 1947 continued activities in the successor organization, Monmouth County Local 236, United Public Workers of America—CIO, and served as secretary of the Local in 1947.

b. Is reported to have been associated with L.K. over a period of years, reportedly a known Communist sympathizer.

c. Is reported to have expressed pro-Communist statements.

d. Is reported to have distributed United Public Workers of America literature at the Army Electronics Standards Agency in July 1946 with L.K.

The United Federal Workers of America—CIO and the United Public Workers of America—CIO are referred to in these charges because of reports that they have been infiltrated or dominated or controlled by Communists and Communist sympathizers.

Charges against Mr. D.

1. While attending Brooklyn College from 1947 to 1949, you were an officer of the American Veterans Committee at the College. The leadership of that organization is reported to have been influenced by Communists and to have followed the Communist line in its activities and publications. It is also reported that the faculty advisor of that organization in 1947 had refused to testify before the Rapp-Coudert Committee which was an official New York State legislative committee investigating Communism in New York schools.

2. While attending Brooklyn College you were a member of the

2 The Fort Monmouth Scandal

Physics Club in 1949, of which Professor M.P. was the faculty advisor. It is reported that Professor P. had been dropped from her position at Brooklyn College because of her failure to testify before a Congressional committee concerning membership in the Communist Party.

3. You registered to vote as an affiliate of the American Labor Party in the years 1947 to 1949.

4. You have maintained a close association with your brother S.B. who is reported:

   a. To have been an active member of the International Workers Order, Lodge No. 817, in Brooklyn since 1946. The International Workers Order has been cited by the Attorney General as a Communist and subversive organization.

   b. To have been a delegate of the Wholesale and Warehouse Workers Union, Local No. 65, Brooklyn to the American Youth Congress in 1941. The American Youth Congress has been cited by the Attorney General as a Communist and subversive organization.

   c. To have declared the Communist Party an ineffectual party that should be permitted to operate legally and not be suppressed.

   d. To have registered to vote as an affiliate of the American Labor Party from 1946 to 1950.

5. You have maintained a close association with your mother, R. who registered to vote as an affiliate of the American Labor Party in 1946 and 1949, and with your father, J. who registered to vote as an affiliate of the American Labor Party from 1945 to 1947 and in 1949. The American Labor Party is cited in the above charges because of the reports that the Party in Brooklyn was dominated and controlled by Communists as early as 1944 and by 1948 it was generally known that the Communists had assumed control of the American Labor Party in New York.

Charges against Mr. E.

1. Your brother-in-law, T.S. was reported to be a Communist Party member in 1947, Treasurer of the New York County Communist Party in 1949 and an employee of the New York Communist Party through July 1950. Since 1941, T.S. has resided at the home of your mother with whom you have continued to be closely associated.

2. You attended and assisted in preparing for a rally sponsored by the New Jersey Independent Citizens League which was held on the property of Mrs. E.S.G., a reported Communist Party member.

3. You have been an associate of several reported Communist Party

members and sympathizers, among whom were H.G.Y., R.W., and B.D.

4. Your wife was reported to be a member of the United Federal Workers of America in 1944. It is reported that this union was Communist dominated.

5. Your sister, Mrs. T.S. signed Communist Party nominating petitions for Amter-Holmes and Isidore Begun in 1941 and 1943, respectively.

On December 17, 1953, we interviewed Oliver Pilat and Mitchel Levitas of the New York *Post* regarding the Fort Monmouth situation.

Pilat's only involvement in this problem had been with respect to a report which he had received charging that in an address to employees of Fort Monmouth General Lawton had made a statement favorable to Gerald L. K. Smith. Pilat doubted that the report was true and expressed a "feeling" that the story had been invented. (Subsequently Pilat interviewed General Lawton and other individuals and was satisfied that there was no truth to the report.)

Levitas feels, on the basis of his investigation, that it is going to be impossible to *prove* that there was an anti-Semitic motivation in the suspensions and declassification of the Fort Monmouth workers. One knows nothing about the character of the accusers. However, he pointed out that, in the current disciplinary proceedings of forty-two employees suspended or declassified, thirty-seven were Jewish. He regards this high ratio of Jews as extremely suspicious—particularly since the charges against many are fundamentally frivolous. Also, none of these employees has invoked the Fifth Amendment in his appearances before the McCarthy Committee or loyalty boards. Levitas recognized, however, that anti-Semitic motivations could be established only if it were discovered that non-Jews (against whom the evidence of possible disloyalty was as strong as or stronger than that against the suspended Jewish employees) were *not* suspended or declassified.

Levitas concluded that, since such an investigative task is out of the question for any agency except the Army itself, it would be well to concentrate inquiries upon the Security Section at Fort Monmouth which was responsible for initiating the disciplinary proceedings.

2 The Fort Monmouth Scandal

Levitas furnished us with the name of one man who he felt might be helpful. This man is Mr. F., interviewed by us on December 22.

F. impressed us as being astute and sincere; he said he had been troubled for several months about the Fort Monmouth situation because, on the basis of his experiences at the Fort, it was his feeling that anti-Semitism provoked the recent happenings there.

F. told us that for some years he was employed in a civilian capacity at the Fort—security and administrative officer in an important position in the laboratories. One of his duties, he explained, was to execute any orders relating to security which resulted from investigations by G-2, then headed by the present C.S.O., and he had frequent contacts with this C.S.O. respecting cases that involved security clearances. *F. expressed as his definite judgment that, in all these contacts with the C.S.O., the latter had followed a consistent pattern of delays in clearing Jewish employees, but was expeditious when it came to non-Jewish employees.* While F. "sensed" this pattern from firsthand observation, he could offer no documentation.

Had F. ever heard the C.S.O. make any statement with respect to Jews? He had not. On the other hand, he said, *one Jewish Fort Monmouth employee (a scientist who is still at the installation) told F. that he had heard the C.S.O. refer to F. as "a dirty Jew."* F. said that he had tried to persuade this Jewish employee to make a statement to this effect, but that the man is deathly afraid and refuses to do so. F. refused to identify the man.

F. said that he had taken it upon himself to go back to the Fort Monmouth area and make inquiries regarding the situation. He was going there that day "in order to see people" who could, if they were willing, give him information regarding any anti-Semitism at Fort Monmouth.

F. told us that he himself had been under a "cloud of suspicion" for about a month, after which time *his own commanding officer told him that the complaints against him were unfounded, and that he, F., had been the victim of anti-Semitism.*

In F.'s judgment, the task of proving anti-Semitism was "next to impossible." People are afraid to talk; those who may be willing to talk can offer only hearsay and other inconclusive evidence. He pointed out what we already know: if the Army wants to do an honest investigation of the charges of anti-Semitism, it can do so simply by sending in investigators to determine who the accusers were, what precipitated the charges against Jewish employees, how the investigations were carried on, whether non-Jewish employees were subject to similar investigations, etc.

F. promised us that he would let us know within a few days if he obtained any information which he felt free to share with us.

On December 29, F. advised us that he had been out to Fort Monmouth and had spoken with four or five Jews who had worked with him when he was at the Fort and who are still employed there.

Without exception, these people—who refused to let their names be used—told F. that there is no community anti-Semitism; that Jews and Gentiles get along very well together as neighbors; and that they have seen no evidence of anti-Semitism in terms of their work. They pointed out that many Jews had been promoted in jobs at the Fort, and their feeling is that General Lawton bears Jews no animus.

What did they think of the arithmetic of the suspensions? Well, it looks suspicious, they admitted. And if anti-Semitism were at the root of the Jewish suspensions, they suggested the place to look for it would be in the Civilian Security Section of G-2 which conducted the investigations and recommended the disciplinary proceedings.

We checked the background of the Civilian Security Officer and his chief asssistant, with a number of different sources. It comes out this way: The C.S.O. began as a policeman in the village of Eatontown, New Jersey, an armed guard in the Signal Corps Laboratory there. With this training, he was placed in charge of Civilian G-2 at Fort Monmouth. The C.S.O.'s assistant is described as a "professional veteran," who regards all non-veterans with suspicion and is hostile to veterans who do not join the American Legion or the Veterans of Foreign Wars. However, these sources have never seen any indications that point to anti-Semitism on his part.

On December 24 we interviewed Walter Millis, editorial writer and columnist of the New York *Herald Tribune*. We explained that we

2 The Fort Monmouth Scandal

were interested in determining whether there had been any anti-Semitic motivation behind the suspensions at Fort Monmouth, and that we had come to him because he had expressed the feeling in his report that religious and racial bigotry was responsible.

Mr. Millis has the same "sense" of anti-Semitic discrimination at Fort Monmouth many others have had, without being able to establish it by evidence. Throughout our discussion it became evident that he regarded Fort Monmouth as just one aspect of a much more serious problem—"mccarthyism." He pointed out several times that "mccarthyism" produces the Fort Monmouth situations that breed anti-Semitism.

Murrey Marder, the Washington *Post* reporter, was also interviewed. Marder stated that he had seen no evidence that the suspensions were motivated by anti-Semitic bias. He indicated, however, that he was disturbed over the possibility that there might have been such motivation. He was told that there was some feeling in New Jersey that there had been anti-Semitic activities in the Fort Monmouth area. Did his investigation disclose the reason for this feeling? He said he was told that it was based upon the fact that a number of years ago the area had been the scene of KKK activities; that there had been some "book-burning" incidents; that the Minute Women had been active; and that there had been some distribution of anti-Semitic literature.

On January 13, 1953, we interviewed a reporter who had written a series of articles in a major newspaper on the Fort Monmouth situation. We explained our interest and asked point-blank whether or not he had found any evidence of anti-Semitism. The reporter replied he had discovered no tangible proof, but did indicate a feeling that some anti-Semitism was prevalent. He told us that, in his opinion, we would never be able to prove an anti-Semitic motivation for the suspensions—unless we could get inside the minds of the accusers and the others responsible for the removals. He felt that the best way for us to determine the presence of anti-Semitism would be to ascertain whether there were any significant number of non-Jewish employees who should have been investigated as security subjects but were not.

1 Cross-Currents in America

The reporter told us that, as far as he knew, none of the defendants could offer any direct proof of anti-Semitism. He stressed, however, that the question of anti-Semitism had been tangential to his main line of inquiry.

We met with the managing editor and the city editor of a local newspaper in the area to learn what they knew about the situation.

The managing editor indicated that they, too, on the paper, had been disturbed by rumors of anti-Semitism. Had they looked into it? Yes, he said, but despite intensive checking they had found nothing but further rumor and hearsay. The city editor added that he had now assigned a reporter to study the charges themselves. Both men felt that the basis for the rumors could be traced to the belief that the C.S.O. is prejudiced. "It was the general opinion in the community."

(In a subsequent interview the two editors advised us that they had made a diligent attempt to run down the allegations of anti-Semitism against the C.S.O. The managing editor stated that he talked with a colonel of the Jewish faith who had been stationed at Fort Monmouth for many years, and who is intimately acquainted with all the people involved in this matter. Both men had complete confidence in the colonel; he had never given them a "bum steer." And according to this colonel, the C.S.O. is not an anti-Semite.)

It was the managing editor's belief that, in a setup like that of the scientific laboratories, fertile grounds for informants and stool pigeons existed. With one quarter of the civilian scientists and engineers in the Monmouth laboratories Jewish, and consequently Jews competing against non-Jews, the editor said there was resentment on the part of some non-Jewish personnel. This might, in his opinion, impel them to turn in bits of gossip to the security officers about the Jewish employees. To support his argument, he pointed out that it was "common knowledge" that few really top-notch Christian engineers were working at Fort Monmouth, since the very superior ones were able to get employment in private industry; and that conversely, since Jewish scientists and engineers of very great ability could not readily get outside employment, they had to take jobs such as those at Monmouth.

2   The Fort Monmouth Scandal

The managing editor further informed us that the difficulties involving suspected loyalty stemmed back to 1946; since that time there had been constant dismissal, suspension, and loss of security clearance involving the Jewish employees. He stated that those who fought the charges ultimately were returned to their jobs.

We asked the managing editor what the reputation of General Lawton was in the community, and whether or not there was any evidence linking him to anti-Semitism. There was "no indication whatsoever," he replied.

On the same day we interviewed a local rabbi, whose pulpit and residence are in this area of New Jersey. The rabbi stated that, while not an Army chaplain, he has fulfilled many such functions at Fort Monmouth since 1934. In his work with the Army he had never found, he said, one iota of anti-Semitism at Fort Monmouth. On the contrary, "they" lean backward to avoid it. The rabbi informed us that he is a personal and dear friend of General Lawton and that the general would not tolerate it for a moment. He also denied hearing any rumors that anti-Semitism was involved in the cases of Jewish engineers denied security clearance or labeled as security risks. We then asked him whether he was familiar with an article in a New York City newspaper indicating that *he* had gone to General Lawton complaining about anti-Semitism at the post. He vigorously and categorically denied ever having gone to Lawton for this purpose and again proceeded to extoll the virtues of Lawton and the complete absence of anti-Semitism at the Fort.

We asked the rabbi whether he was familiar with the arithmetic of the situation, and he replied that he was not.

On December 17, a New Jersey attorney prepared a statement regarding a Fort Monmouth employee, Mr. G., non-Jewish.

G. was declassified in the fall of 1953. His clearance was restored, revoked again, and once more restored some months later.

G., in an interview with the attorney, stated that his immediate superior was one X; that the section chief supervisor of both G. and

I Cross-Currents in America

X was a now suspended Jewish employee; that after the supervisor was suspended in October he asked X whether this was a witch hunt. The attorney says that, according to G., X thereupon said: "There will be more Jews suspended. They are the ones likely to be spies and espionage agents because they are a Godless bunch. The ones least likely to be spies are Catholics."

G. told the attorney further that similar sentiments were expressed by a former high Army officer, employed in the same section as G., who was in G-2. G. also identified two others with anti-Semitic attitudes at Fort Monmouth.

The attorney's statement does not indicate that G. offered any evidence against the latter two men; nor did he give any more specific information on the Army officer.

Mr. H., another former Fort Monmouth employee, was interviewed on January 14. In the course of the interview H. indicated his suspicion of the Army officer in question. H. felt that the officer was an informant and had been responsible for turning in many people. In H.'s opinion the Army officer is anti-Semitic.

H. could not prove this, but pointed out that the Army officer had a manner of using Jewish names in a way calculated to emphasize Jewish involvement in Fort Monmouth activity. H. said that the officer had made the statement: "My father was a member of the Ku Klux Klan." Pointing out that the KKK is a subversive organization, H. said he felt that, had a Jew or a Negro made a similar statement linking a parent with a subversive agency, security action would have been instituted.

H. said: "There is a gradual departure from Fort Monmouth of Jews, even those not under duress." He explained that "the competent Jews who can get jobs in any field anywhere are leaving because of the atmosphere at the Fort. The less proficient Jews are 'shaky.'

"You will have a difficult time proving that anti-Semitism exists at the Fort. There are Jews at Fort Monmouth who have been cleared for top secret work by the Army and I know Jews at Fort Monmouth who have 'Q' clearance." "Q" clearance, he explained, is even more im-

2 The Fort Monmouth Scandal

portant than top secret because it is the highest form of clearance, and is given for work with the Atomic Energy Commission.

Another point which H. emphasized time and again was that Jews currently employed at Fort Monmouth will not talk. "The atmosphere is very bad at the Fort and everyone is scared. No one trusts the man next to him."

H. indicated that our only hope of getting facts would be from former employees like himself who either were suspended or never again want to be involved with Civil Service or Fort Monmouth. One of the reasons for the prevalent reticence, he felt, was the operation of "at least three thousand people who are informants for the Civilian Security Officer."

H. added that he knew that he himself had been watched by people under the C.S.O.'s jurisdiction during his last days at Fort Monmouth. One enlisted man under him had kept a diary of his activities and was the principal source of information on him.

"This soldier," he said, "went so far as to pick up a newspaper which I laid down after reading it, just to establish what I was reading. The soldier was always looking over my shoulder to see what I was reading or doing. No matter to whom I spoke, the moment I completed my conversation and left the room, the soldier would run up to the person I had been talking to and would demand to know what the conversation was all about.

"It is this type of activity by a mass of informants," H. concluded, "that has discouraged many."

H. did say that there was a pattern of anti-Semitism in existence at the Fort and explained: *"If, say, one Willum Kuningam* (example), *white, Protestant, is reported through the informer system on five counts, he may escape without punishment of any sort. But let Abraham Garfinkel* (example), *be reported on the same five counts, he would be immediately picked up and would receive a letter of interrogation asking him to answer the charges made against him."* H. arrived at this conclusion on the basis of his years of employment and constant observation at Monmouth.

H. was hired at Monmouth in 1941, along with other Negroes and

Jews, "on the basis of no discrimination," strictly on engineering ability. Jews and Negroes had been driven into the Civil Service field, he said, because of discrimination in private industry.

H. first experienced a certain tension in the Fort when war began and local people, for the most part, got the minor jobs, while the scientific and engineering groups, which rose to as high as 15,000, had a large concentration of Jews. This tension, he felt, was sharpened by bigotry in the community.

H. rose to section leader; and as a leader he knew that a "spy system" had been set up which involved fellow employees as informants. He told of the incident of one Y. who worked under his supervision and was later suspended along with him. He said that Y. had been approached to become an informant and had refused. At the time he felt that those who had approached Y. had done so as a test; and when Y. was suspended, one of the charges made against him was his refusal to assist the informer system. H. did not know what finally happened to Y., although he knew that he had lived at one time in Long Branch, New Jersey.

In the fall of 1949, H.'s clearance was lifted. He continued to work until January 1951 while a background investigation was conducted to determine whether he was a security risk. (During the course of investigation, it is the policy at Fort Monmouth to "neutralize" the suspect by removing him from classified work. The employee loses his white badge and is given a green badge. In this period of neutralization, highly qualified engineers can be taken off secret work without the loss of rank or pay and put to work "counting nuts and bolts." The suspect is naturally not eligible for promotion.)

Finally charges were drawn against H.; he was suspended and given thirty days' notice, during which time he turned in his badge and equipment, his salary was suspended, and he was not allowed on the premises. (This is the procedure followed at Monmouth for all those suspended.)

There were three separate charges against H.:

1. He had allowed the *Daily Worker* to be brought in and read by members of this group.

2. He had been an officer of the United Public Workers of America, which had been expelled by the CIO because of alleged Communist domination, and

3. He did not reprimand a fellow employee for a pro-Soviet remark.

H. came before a Security Hearing Board which receives evidence from two kinds of witnesses—confidential witnesses who are usually government sources, and non-confidential witnesses who are usually fellow employees who have denounced the suspended individual. Neither type usually appears at the hearing. "In many instances," said H., "the board apparently does not know who the confidential witnesses are." The suspended individual may invite his own witnesses, he added, but has no power to subpoena sources who may have accused him. The local board's report goes to the Secretary of the Army, who has the power to overrule its decision.

H. was fired. There followed a year during which H., unemployed, fought back, appealing to each higher authority until his case reached Washington, D.C.

In this final appeal one must request permission to submit new evidence, but one cannot produce new witnesses. "The rules of evidence do not apply." H. said, "One must actually sell oneself to the board and make them believe you."

By hard work, H. said, he secured the affidavits of twenty-one of the twenty-three individuals working under him in which they stated that they had not made the charges against him. This left two unaccounted for—one a woman, and one a nondescript mechanic. These then were the informants, H. said, and he set about proving that the woman had a record of insanity, hated Negroes, and hated the idea of working for a Negro.

"I proved the same about the mechanic," H. concluded, explaining that this mechanic had refused to shake hands with H.'s identical twin, because of his race.

H. won reinstatement and was given a certificate clearing him for secret work by the Army. Did he go back to Fort Monmouth? Yes, he said, and he worked a short while until he had been given complete clearance. Then he left to take his current position in private industry.

He has had no difficulty in his new job, a "sensitive" one, and has been cleared by the Air Force for top secret work.

H. revealed that last year he was called by the McCarthy Committee and went to New York where he was interrogated by Francis Carr. Before going he went to his employers, one of the world's leading scientific laboratories, and told them that he understood that he was to be subpoenaed and that he would like to go on his own volition. What was the laboratory's reaction? we wanted to know. The authorities indicated they were pleased with his concern for their institution, he said. But they wanted him to know that they were not frightened by Senator McCarthy.

To use H.'s own words, "This experience has left me shaken, I admit. I will not join anything. I will not sign anything. I have had my T.B. and I don't want to take any chances of contracting it again."

Concerning the forty suspended, thirty-six of whom are reported to be Jewish, H. said he believed the figure must be even higher than forty. Besides those suspended, he indicated that there are many who get letters of interrogation asking them to reply to certain charges; of these, many resign and leave the Fort.

In the case of Y., one of the charges brought against him when he was removed was that, while chairman of the AVC, during a discussion of whether communists should be in the post, he, Y., took a neutral position and did not take a vigilant stand against communism. H. simply pointed out to us that Y., as chairman, was *supposed* to be neutral during a discussion.

Finally H. stated that proving a general pattern of anti-Semitism would be difficult because there are still Jews in the most secret projects at Monmouth, and many Jews there have been selected for the highly classified Bikini atomic energy project.

Mr. J., an attorney, advised us that he had provided an affidavit concerning the C.S.O.'s attitudes. He had given this affidavit to an attorney for a suspended employee. In his affidavit, of which we have a copy, Mr. J. stated:

1. I am an attorney at law of New Jersey, and in the years 1947–1948 I was a corporal, later sergeant, assigned to Headquarters, Fort Mon-

2 The Fort Monmouth Scandal

mouth, where I worked in the Security and Intelligence Division; the present C.S.O. was then to the best of my information and belief the Chief of said Division. I was a subordinate of his; I worked in the same building and came into contact with him from time to time.

2. *I know of my own personal knowledge that this C.S.O. was accustomed to refer sarcastically to Jewish people as "tribesmen" and he did so in conversation with me.*

3. *On one occasion, the date of which I cannot specify, he related in my hearing a joke of such an extremely anti-Semitic nature that I was constrained to object.*

4. *On another occasion, in January 1948, he gave me directions that whenever I came across any job applications of "your tribesmen from CCNY," I should bring them to his personal attention rather than process them along with other job applications in a routine manner.*

J. offered the name of an Army officer, now on active duty, as a witness to the C.S.O.'s behavior. According to J., he and the attorney for a suspended employee spoke with the officer on the telephone and the officer verified J.'s affidavit.

The officer further agreed to execute an affidavit. However, when such an affidavit was sent to him, he returned it with a notation that he had been advised not to get involved.

We passed this information on to one of our field directors, who on January 14 spoke on the telephone with the officer who again declined to make an affidavit on the grounds that this might jeopardize his Army career. The officer who is now stationed at Camp ——, advised our representative that he had been the C.S.O.'s subordinate in the latter's office at Fort Monmouth in the late '40s. The officer declared that his opinion of the C.S.O. was based upon the latter's habit of referring to Jews as "tribesmen" and to a statement by the C.S.O. on at least one occasion that he "would not have any Jews working for him."

We interviewed Mr. —— in his law office in ——, New Jersey. In this man's estimate, there definitely is an underlying anti-Semitism to the suspension and declassification of so many Jewish employees. He could offer no evidence for this other than unverifiable information which he and another lawyer had been collecting, and which corre-

Cross-Currents in America

sponds to the hearsay and gossip which have been described in the foregoing pages. Indeed, the only concrete evidence he knows about is Mr. J.'s affidavit. He is not familiar with what additional concrete evidence we have cited.

The attorney stated that even today those who were either declassified or suspended find that when they return to active status, upon being cleared, their old jobs have been taken. Without offering any proof he also stated that in every case the returning Jewish employee finds himself in a rank lower than that which he had occupied previously, his former position taken by a non-Jew.

We interviewed still another New Jersey attorney who is now associated in the defense of a number of the suspended employees and obviously has been directing the defense strategy. This lawyer is convinced that anti-Semitism was rife at the Fort Monmouth establishment, and that it extended from the top down.

We tried to get a specific idea from the attorney as to the total number of employees suspended; proportion of Jews, etc. Here is what he told us:

Since September thirty-three individuals were suspended and nine were declassified, making a total of forty-two individuals disciplined as security risks. Of these forty-two, thirty-eight were Jews. Of the thirty-three suspended, up to this time, twenty-two have been served with charges. Of the twenty-two served with charges, five have had their cases heard by the Hearing Board at Governors Island.

It is obvious that even these two lawyers are unable to describe precisely who has been suspended and when, who has been reinstated, who has been declassified and then suspended, etc. One of the reasons for this confusion lies in the fact that under the law reinstatement in thirty days is automatic when written charges are not presented.

The attorney told us that he has been advised by a friend he trusts, who is also a friend of the C.S.O., that the latter disclaims any responsibility for what has taken place. According to this mutual friend, the C.S.O. insists that he is a scapegoat in the charges that the recent suspensions, declassifications, and loss of security clearance stem from

2 The Fort Monmouth Scandal

his operation. His explanation is that "higher-ups" saw fit to order these purges and that he turned in the information that came to him without any evaluation on his part. We obtained no documentation for this.

We interviewed the executive editor of another local New Jersey newspaper in the Monmouth vicinity at great length. His paper had conducted an inquiry into the Monmouth scandal and has taken what is generally an anti-Senator McCarthy and anti-General Lawton position. However, the paper has not charged anti-Semitic motivation in the suspensions; and when we asked the editor directly whether, in his opinion, there was any evidence of this motivation, he stated that in his opinion there was not.

As a long-time resident of the area, he was able to point out that, although loyalty investigations had been continually undertaken, the pace had been accelerated recently. This placed an added burden on an administration which he contended was inadequate, and compounded the current confusion, mismanagement, and uncertainty at the Fort. General Lawton he described as a narrowly religious martinet, who had given strict orders on the post that all personnel should attend religious services; and who undoubtedly is of the opinion that anyone who does not go to such services is untrustworthy.

What did he think motivated the present investigations? we asked. Senator McCarthy, he replied, through pressure on the Pentagon, has been getting copies of all loyalty investigation reports emanating from military establishments, particularly in sensitive areas such as Monmouth. This, together with the scope of the President's loyalty review order of April 1953, had been a factor.

Was he aware of the Gerald L. K. Smith statement attributed to General Lawton? He replied that he was; that he had assigned some of his crack reporters to the story, but they had been unable to get verification.

Was he familiar with the C.S.O. and his assistant and, if so, what was their general reputation? Yes, he said, he had known the assistant for twenty-five years, and on the whole had found him to be an uninformed, narrow-minded individual and a "professional veteran." And he had come in contact with the C.S.O. on several occasions and been unimpressed with him as an individual.

We asked whether either the C.S.O. or his assistant was in any way responsible for the current investigations. In his opinion, they were not. In fact, he stated, recently the assistant had complained bitterly to him that ninety-five per cent of the cases which the G-2 establishment on the post had referred to Washington were turned down by higher authority.

This editor impressed us as being very conscientious and well informed. He pointed out that, to understand what has happened at Fort Monmouth, one must understand the total community situation. This is how he sees it:

The major portion of the non-scientific civilian personnel at the Fort is composed of relatively untrained people from the surrounding New Jersey communities, who have been unable to make satisfactory adjustments in private industry. Men such as the security officer, typical of this group, are fundamentally suspicious of outlanders, particularly New Yorkers, and are hostile to intellectuals, readers of books and liberal publications, etc. Given this narrow outlook, it is plain that the New York men who have come to work at Fort Monmouth over the last ten or twelve years, largely Jewish, would be the kind of people naturally, almost instinctively, distrusted by men like the C.S.O. These New Yorkers, too, are competent scientists who have achieved on their merit promotions and salaries beyond the capabilities of local residents. This fact, the editor, who is not a Jew, concluded, has created jealousies, antagonisms, and rivalries, all of which provide grist for the mill of informants set up by the Fort Monmouth Security Section.

During our talk with one of the lawyers, he introduced us to two suspended employees, both Jewish, who had already had their hearings before the Review Board at Governors Island. They were Mr. B. and Mr. C. Mr. B. acted as spokesman for both; he seemed highly intelligent and objective.

2 The Fort Monmouth Scandal

B. was of the opinion that the C.S.O. is not an anti-Semite, nor did he think the current suspensions were motivated by anti-Semitism. B. judged, however, that were the C.S.O. and his security associates in no way anti-Semitic, but merely everything else they are—suspicious of New Yorkers, intellectuals, liberals, etc.—and that were the suspended employees not Jewish but merely everything else *they* are—liberals, intellectuals, members of the AVC, former members of the United Public Workers of America—the results would have been the same. "In my opinion," he said, "everything that has happened is almost a natural consequence of the intensified loyalty program ordered by Washington."

Did he know any non-Jewish employees against whom security charges could have been made but were not? The question made him uncomfortable because, as he pointed out, this would put him in the position of being an informant. We promised him we would keep any names he gave us in confidence. He told us of a non-Jewish Fort Monmouth employee who had been a member of a car pool with a former Fort Monmouth employee identified as a communist, whose wives had played cards together. B. said that, as far as he knew, no charges had ever been preferred against the man—although similarly insignificant facts were sufficient in the cases of Jews to cause removal.

B. also recalled the case of a non-Jewish lieutenant colonel who was assigned to transport a piece of top secret equipment to Europe and lost it en route. So far as B. knew, no action was ever taken against the officer, although the removal of similarly secret documents for home study had been the basis for suspension of Jewish scientists at the installation.

Just one final word: We believe deeply in the need for a government employee security program. To be as effective as possible such a program must be as flawless as the human mind can render it. If the written charges filed against the Monmouth suspendees were based in fact, additional investigation of these men is certainly warranted; some of the alleged associations raise serious security questions. If, however, the charges were rooted in falsehood, the security program procedures must have omitted essential safeguards.

Cross-Currents in America

Conclusion

I. In the foregoing, there is evidence sufficient to conclude that the C.S.O., in the capacity of his office, was one of the prime factors in initiating suspensions and losses of security clearances at the Fort Monmouth installation.

II. There is evidence and hearsay which would justify a reasonable man in concluding that the C.S.O. at Monmouth is bigoted.

III. On the basis of I and II, we nevertheless *cannot* conclude (in the absence of further evidence) that the C.S.O.'s bigotry was necessarily a motivating factor for the suspensions he initiated.

IV. The presence of one other circumstance in this situation would eliminate doubt and lead to the clear conclusion that bigotry *was* a motivating factor. The presence or absence of this circumstance should be established. *Did the C.S.O. treat the cases of non-Jews differently from the cases of Jews? Did the C.S.O. fail to process for action cases involving non-Jewish personnel where the adverse information respecting such non-Jewish personnel was virtually similar to the adverse information he accumulated with respect to Jewish personnel?* This can be established only by a careful examination of the files of each of the approximately six hundred civilian scientists and engineers at the Fort Monmouth installation.

Obviously such an examination can be made only by direction of the highest Army authorities. It is recommended that the Secretary of the Army be requested to initiate such a confidential examination.

V. In view of the widespread belief and more widespread rumor that anti-Semitism was a precipitating factor in the investigations and suspensions at the Fort Monmouth installation, fairness to all concerned requires that the above recommended examination of the personnel files be made.

VI. Whether anti-Semitism was or was not a factor in the Monmouth situation, it seems quite clear that the established criteria for security evaluation are so devoid of safeguards that malicious rumor and the most careless hearsay can be the bases for suspensions and losses of security clearances. If situations such as these are to be avoided in the future, either the criteria have to be tightened or highly trained experts with sophisticated evaluation abilities must supervise investigations.

The unfortunate public impression that communism was rampant among the suspended civilian personnel at Fort Monmouth, and that it was rooted almost without exception in Jews, came largely from the

2 The Fort Monmouth Scandal

collateral activity of the Senate Permanent Subcommittee on Investigations. This committee, headed by Senator Joseph McCarthy, conducted public hearings of present and former civilian personnel of the Fort Monmouth installation. As far as is known, none of the present Fort Monmouth employees who appeared before the Senate Subcommittee pleaded the Fifth Amendment or refused to answer questions. Some of the ex-employees who appeared did plead the Fifth Amendment. By intermingling former and present employees in the course of the subcommittee hearings, the impression was created across the country that personnel currently employed at Fort Monmouth had "refused to talk" and were therefore guilty.

The foregoing report should now be submitted to Secretary Stevens.

JULY 16, 1954
BRE to ADL Commission

This memorandum reviews what has happened since February 8, the date on which we submitted to Secretary of the Army Stevens a full report of our intensive six-week investigation.

On February 26, John G. Adams, department counselor of the Army, acknowledging receipt in behalf of Mr. Stevens, indicated that our study would be "used to assist the Department of the Army in the study of the situation." Mr. Adams graciously rejected our offer to discuss personally our findings and proposals for follow-up investigation.

On March 3 we wrote to Mr. Adams, again urging an opportunity to meet with the Army Secretary. Two and one half months later, with still no sign that Mr. Stevens or his representatives were willing to meet with us, we wrote again to the Secretary. It was May 19, and the Army Secretary was completely engaged in a public controversy with Senator McCarthy. In our letter we urged that, while we understood his current affairs required his fullest attention, fairness to everybody concerned also required that the truth about Monmouth be placed on the public record.

| Cross-Currents in America

More than a month later, on June 24, a response came from Lewis E. Berry, Jr., deputy to Mr. Adams.

After stating that the "appropriate staff agencies" within the Army Department had completed a review of our report, Berry revealed that the Army had also conducted its own "independent investigation." But since he did not indicate the nature of that investigation, we have no way of knowing whether it followed our suggestion that an analysis be made of the six hundred personnel files.

In any event, wrote Berry, the Army was "unable to establish that religious bias had a bearing upon the activities of the security officer or other personnel responsible for the initiating or processing of security cases."

Mr. Berry omits any reference to original accusers; and apparently no inquiry was made into their characters or motives. Of course, Mr. Berry assured us, "were facts available which clearly demonstrated improper motivation on the part of any individual responsible for security actions, appropriate corrective steps would be taken." Racial and religious prejudice, he added, have no place in the operation of the Department of the Army; and in order to make certain that such influence cannot gain a foothold, the Chief Signal Officer at Fort Monmouth has been directed to take the necessary steps. But the basis for the Army's conclusions remained obscure to us, so we wrote Berry still another plea to meet with either the Secretary or his designee.

On July 7, with assurances that our "very excellent, exhaustive and candid study" has received considerable attention, Mr. Berry regretfully replied that because the cases in question are "still being adjudicated," discussions with us are necessarily foreclosed. This was not reassuring, all former assurances considered.

Perhaps someday in the future we may meet with the appropriate Army officials regarding this problem. Until we do, and until the Army embarks upon and completes the proposed investigation of the six hundred personnel files at the Fort, the problem will also involve a riddle; and the answers we have will remain conjectures no matter how strongly we believe them to be accurate in the main. And we do believe them just that.

2 The Fort Monmouth Scandal

Up to August 1953, when Secretary Stevens' administration first began to remove scientists, thirty-five Monmouth employees had already been suspended under the old Truman Security Regulations; thirty-three of them already were reinstated. Put this first group aside and consider only the second batch—the suspensions begun by Secretary Stevens immediately prior to the McCarthy Subcommittee executive sessions and ended along with the public hearings.

Thirty-six men in all were suspended from their originally assigned responsibilities. Eleven were automatically reinstated after the failure of the Army security authorities to file formal charges; three of these men then resigned. Seventeen were reinstated after hearing or appeal. Eight were permanently dismissed after hearings.

The McCarthy Subcommittee had subpoenaed twenty-five of these men to its closed sessions; to its public hearings, one.

This means that twenty-eight of the thirty-six, insisting upon fighting back, eventually returned to their jobs. But all, in simply righting themselves, suffered great losses—frequently their entire savings, and more often than not their good reputations.

Despite subcommittee headlines and the innuendoes of Army spokesmen, not one of the suspendees, including those finally dismissed, was charged with committing or attempting to commit espionage, of being a communist, otherwise subversive, or disloyal. The sum of all the accusations only touched the question of the risk in continuing them at their assignments. The question was one of predictable reliability, not treason or subversion.

The one happy fact, and its uniqueness makes it outstanding, is that the Army loyalty boards themselves were careful to permit no sign of religious prejudice in their hearings; our examination of all the hearing transcripts was completely reassuring. The damage suffered by all American Jews, because of the irresponsible hints during the investigation that made "Jew" just about synonymous with "communist spy," cannot, however, be so quickly reassured away.

The heartache and near tragedy in the lives of twenty-eight men has been told in the preceding pages without bringing the human element to the fore. Let us take the case of a single individual confronted by precisely the same circumstances to see its effect in purely personal terms.

Abraham Chasanow was a civilian Navy clerk . . .

Three   The Chasanow Story

APRIL 16, 1954
Press Department to AF

As requested by you, we are forwarding all available clips dealing with the Navy's dismissal of Abraham Chasanow. Included are the stories carried this morning by the New York *Times* and New York *Herald Tribune*.

APRIL 16, 1954
AF to BRE

I have phoned our Washington office to get the full texts of the statement and other documents which Chasanow's attorney, Joseph A. Fanelli, issued to the press yesterday. This morning's papers carried only a general story on his public appeal to top Defense Department officials to reinstate Chasanow in his job at the Navy's Hydrographic Office. The full text of Fanelli's statement may amplify what he said about the element of anti-Semitism tied up with Chasanow's dismissal.
   It certainly is odd, as suggested by Fanelli, that the five Jews, includ-

ing Chasanow, who lived in Greenbelt and worked at the Hydrographic Office have all had security difficulties; while not one of the eight non-Jews who resided in the same town and are employed in the same office has been disturbed or even investigated.

What must be added to this circumstance is that the accusations against Chasanow stem from Greenbelt. Chasanow himself feels that anti-Semitism had something to do with the charges, to the extent, at least, that in the past there has been anti-Semitism in Greenbelt. Equally noteworthy is that one of the more serious accusations against Chasanow is that he has been an active leader of a radical group in Greenbelt. Every time we tried to pin down the allegations of anti-Semitism in the Fort Monmouth cases, we seemed to be poking into a cloud. But here, in the accusations against Chasanow, we may very well find that bigotry is a concrete factor. Here, at least, we have some solid leads to go forward on.

APRIL 19, 1954

Washington, D.C., Office to BRE

We have informed Robert B. Anderson, Secretary of the Navy, of our grave concern over the Chasanow case. Our office has received numerous calls from people associated with Mr. Chasanow in B'nai B'rith who were disturbed, as we are, by the fear that anti-Semitism is present in the case, especially since the Navy gave no reason for what appears to be an arbitrary reversal of the first board's decision that Chasanow is innocent. This we pointed out to the Secretary in asking him to institute a review of the case.

As quickly as we have a response, we will let you know what it is.

APRIL 20, 1954

Washington, D.C., Office to AF

We have spoken to Fanelli and have obtained the full text of his statement released to the press on the fifteenth, as well as a copy of the

3 The Chasanow Story

charges filed against Chasanow, Chasanow's reply, the ruling of the first Security Hearing Board, and the Chasanow petition to the Secretary of the Navy to reconsider the Assistant Secretary's decision which overruled the board. These are being sent under separate cover.

Fanelli tells us that it is difficult to pinpoint exactly where, if at all, anti-Semitism may have been involved in the dismissal of Chasanow. But what leads him to believe that the proceedings may have been tainted with anti-Semitism somewhere along the line, and call for some explanation by the Navy Department, is the fact that the five Jewish residents were all involved in security proceedings whereas not one of the eight non-Jews has been involved.

Of the five Jews, three resigned while under investigation. At least one, according to Fanelli, did not know he was under investigation when he resigned. The fourth was recently given a hearing and is now awaiting the board's decision. He, like Chasanow, who is the fifth case, is also represented by Fanelli.

If anti-Semitism has in any way tainted these proceedings, the foregoing facts would appear to indicate that it may have entered at either of the following levels: (1) the source of the accusations against Chasanow: Chasanow states that the accusations against him were motivated in part by an anti-Jewish animus on the part of four former residents of Greenbelt; (2) those conducting the investigations may have been so motivated.

Since the Assistant Secretary of the Navy assigned no reasons for the decision reversing the Hearing Board, Fanelli speculates that: (1) perhaps the Navy officers were so thin-skinned that they have penalized Chasanow for an article on his case which appeared in the *Reporter* magazine; or (2) perhaps the Office of Naval Intelligence investigators sold the appeals board a bill of goods which they were unable to sell to the Hearing Board, which was composed not of Navy officers but of Defense Department officials—two civilians and an Army colonel.

I Cross-Currents in America

APRIL 22, 1954
AF to BRE

Fanelli's press release is an eloquent statement and a precise summary of the case. It is worth reading in full. Here it is:

I have this day filed a petition for reconsideration of the decision by the Assistant Secretary of the Navy in security proceedings against Abraham Chasanow, my client.

Mr. Chasanow, who is 43 and lives at 11-T Ridge Road, Greenbelt, Md., has been a civilian employee of the Navy Hydrographic Office for 23 years. On July 29, 1953, he was charged as an alleged security risk and suspended from duty without pay.

On October 9, 1953, a three-member security hearing board found unanimously after three days of hearing that Mr. Chasanow's employment was "clearly consistent with the interests of national security."

On April 7, 1954, the Assistant Secretary of the Navy for Air, James H. Smith, Jr., overruled the decision of the Security Hearing Board, and terminated Mr. Chasanow's employment. No reasons were given for this decision.

Our petition today is directed to the Assistant Secretary of the Navy for Air, the Secretary of the Navy and the Secretary of Defense. It asks that the decision to dismiss Mr. Chasanow be reconsidered and reversed, or that at the very least the reasons for that decision be stated.

We have also decided to take the unusual step of making the Chasanow case public. We do so with some reluctance because of possible further injury to Mr. Chasanow and his family, but we find hope in the statement by President Eisenhower last week:

"In the long run you may be certain of this—America believes in and practices fair play and decency and justice. In this country public opinion is the most powerful of all forces, and it will straighten this matter out wherever and whenever there is real violence done to our people."

It is difficult to ask time and attention from the public for Mr. Chasanow when bigger subjects and more important names are in the headlines. But we feel the Chasanow case is of great significance, in part because it involves an unimportant man, and a man who by the loosest conceivable standard cannot be considered a risk to security. If

3 The Chasanow Story

Mr. Chasanow can be dismissed, then no American is safe. In support of that statement we make the following points:

1. The very charges against Mr. Chasanow amount to nothing. There is no charge that he was ever affiliated with the Communist Party or any organization on the Attorney General's list. There is no such charge against his wife or family.

There is no charge that in more than 20 years of handling security material Mr. Chasanow ever failed fully to protect the security of the United States.

There is no charge that he is the kind of person who consciously or unconsciously would disclose classified information to an unauthorized person.

The main charge against Mr. Chasanow is that he belongs to a "radical group" in Greenbelt. At the hearing witnesses called by the Navy as well as those called by Mr. Chasanow agreed that he had nothing to do with any supposed radicals. The hearing board found that he was in fact "a moderating, constructive and conservative influence."

2. Undisputed evidence shows that Mr. Chasanow has been exceptionally security-conscious in his job and anti-Communistic and ultra-patriotic in his life.

During World War II, Mr. Chasanow recommended moves to keep Navy charts from enemy hands and the Chief of Naval Operations accepted the recommendations.

During World War II he took steps to keep classified material from the scrutiny of visiting Russian officers.

In 1950, he acted to prevent useful nautical charts from getting into the hands of shipmasters from Iron Curtain countries. . . .

The *Reporter* magazine, March 2, 1954, had an article on this case at an earlier stage and without identification of anyone connected with it, other than myself. Today we withhold nothing. . . .

Some 97 affidavits were presented in Mr. Chasanow's behalf. Despite legitimate fear of reprisal, 24 present or former Navy associates of Mr. Chasanow came forward on his behalf, including two former Hydrographers—a retired Rear Admiral and Captain—and other Naval officers. Affidavits from present or former Greenbelt residents included one from the Mayor, the City Manager, the City Clerk, the Protestant minister, the former Jewish rabbi, a former American Legion post commander and Americanism officer, and the Director of Public Safety, who is a graduate of the University of New Hampshire and the F.B.I. school.

| Cross-Currents in America

Most of these affidavits are more than routine expressions of regard for Mr. Chasanow. They assert deeply felt belief in his patriotism and integrity; they should be read in full.

The question of course arises: Why has this long punitive action been taken against Mr. Chasanow in total absence of any scrap of evidence indicating he might be a bad security risk?

One thing must be understood:

The Security Hearing Board which found unanimously in favor of Mr. Chasanow had before it all the material in the case, including confidential reports. Under law and Navy regulations the final decision to separate Mr. Chasanow was made on exactly the same facts which the hearing board had. If any new evidence or reports came in, the Navy was required to reopen the hearing. Assistant Secretary Smith has confirmed that he made his decision on recommendation of a Navy Department Security Appeals Board which studied only the same material that had been before the hearing board.

We can only guess at the reasons that a hearing board composed of non-Naval employees of the Defense Department—an Air Force Colonel and two defense establishment officials—found entirely in Mr. Chasanow's favor, while Naval officials found against him on the same evidence.

Many sources, including both Navy and defense witnesses at the hearing, spoke of loose charges such as "radical" or "long-hair" that are freely tossed around by disgruntled persons at Greenbelt. These include accusations by those who don't like cooperatives against those who do (Mr. Chasanow was active in cooperative enterprise); by anti-Semites against Jews (Mr. Chasanow is Jewish), and by former subsidized tenants in Federal Housing against those who wished to buy their homes from the Government (as Mr. Chasanow did). The Security Hearing Board put it this way: "Such terms as crackpots, long-hairs, radicals, pinkos and communists have been bandied about loosely by disgruntled individuals."

It is our belief that disgruntled individuals at Greenbelt have made false charges against Mr. Chasanow and others, and that the Navy—or at least its police arm, the Office of Naval Intelligence—has committed itself to believing these charges.

Some confirmation for this theory is offered by several residents of Greenbelt. They have their own statements bearing on the kind of investigation carried on in Greenbelt by Navy intelligence agents.

Mr. Chasanow's case has significance beyond his own life and reputation because it is the first that has gone through the entire new

3   The Chasanow Story

security procedure of the Navy. Presumably standards set by this case—under which virtually every citizen of the United States could be described as a bad security risk—will continue unless the decision is reversed.

The case is also significant for Greenbelt. Several other Greenbelt residents who are Navy employees have been charged as security risks, and in those connections the Navy has by implication accused some 20 others of being "radicals." Many of these persons hold highly confidential jobs with the Army, Air Force and other Government agencies, and none to my knowledge currently faces security proceedings. So far as is known no agency but the Navy has paid any serious attention to unsubstantiated backbiting at Greenbelt.

APRIL 22, 1954
BRE to AF

The Fanelli documents are most impressive. It is difficult to grasp what Chasanow has endured—to be thrown out like that after a lifetime in a job. It there a personal side to the story?

APRIL 29, 1954
AF to BRE

The ordeal of Abraham Chasanow began one hot summer afternoon in 1953. What happened to him on that day is a story of our times, and his agony was the agony of too many other federal employees caught in a hazardous situation—working for the government. It was a day Chasanow was never to forget. It still disturbs his sleep.

The day—July 29—started out conventionally enough, and seemed no different from so many others in Chasanow's twenty-three years of government service.

He settled comfortably into the morning's routine at the Navy Department's Hydrographic Office. He knew his job; his work interested him. A long record of accomplishment lay behind him. On the strength of his competence and energetic devotion to his job, he had risen from the bottom to his present post as chief of a large section handling marine charts. His superiors both liked and respected him. His ratings over the years were excellent. He had helped to tighten the Navy's security system and won the commendation of the Chief of Naval Operations during World War II for this. He had always held the confidence of Navy officials, who once sent him on a secret mission around the world. He had won two Meritorious Civilian Service Awards, besides a cash prize for recommendations which saved the Navy many thousands of dollars.

And Chasanow had no cause to be personally concerned over the distemper which has been destroying government employees in the name of national security.

His own life was above reproach. He was devoted to the country's interests; there was nothing in his background to prove otherwise. Twenty-three years of unwavering loyalty to the federal service left an impressive record. Others might be suspect as security risks, not he.

The morning went rapidly. After lunch, shortly before the day's end, Chasanow's phone rang and he was asked to come to the personnel office. He believed the summons involved some routine office matter.

But shortly, in a matter of minutes, what had taken him twenty-three years of routine to build was to cave in. The personnel officer handed Chasanow a sheaf of official papers. Chasanow was befuddled ... he could not believe what he read ... he tried to steady himself.

He was glad to escape to his own office, where he hoped to be able to wrestle with the meaning of what had happened. He placed the papers on his desk and read and reread the hard type. The words "security" ... "communists" kept leaping up at him. It was unmistakable ... he stood condemned as a security risk. This was formal notice that he was suspended from his job, without pay, as of that day.

Eight charges were listed against him. These Chasanow scanned rapidly, but they trailed off in a blur, his mind too fuzzy to follow all the angles of the document's language. But what was clear was that he was accused of associating with a number of named individuals specified as known communists; and there was another group of individuals described as having "communistic tendencies." He was also

3 The Chasanow Story

charged with being a leader of a radical group in his home town of Greenbelt, Maryland. These seemed the more serious of the charges.

Chasanow felt he was slipping into a phantom world. Who was after him? Why? His suspicions struck out in all directions.

But before taking leave of his old, familiar surroundings, Chasanow had some minor details to attend to, like surrendering his badge and his office pass. These were the last traces of his former identity as a human being who had—over a period of twenty-three years—faithfully served his government.

This done, he quickly left the building, somehow to get home. Outside, with the homeward, hurrying traffic all about him, he had a sense of chill isolation. Then, for the first time, he began to think of his wife, Helen, and their four children; and his numbness was no proof against the sharp twinges of anxiety.

He finally reached home. The house and town had a look of bleak hostility in the hard, lingering light. He walked blindly in. One look at his face, and his wife said, "Abe, what happened?" And he gave her the papers.

Blank days, dull, sluggish days, followed. But now, at least, Chasanow had someone to share his isolation, someone to help him get through the processes of living. The Chasanows pulled down the blinds and shut themselves in. Already news of Chasanow's suspension had begun to get around; there was even a rumor that he had been picked up for espionage.

The difficult days went on; and he dreaded the long nights. The struggle to sleep was exhausting; it left him lightheaded, hardly able to control his thoughts. His thoughts took over. They dragged him across the same ground over and over again. Long-forgotten events, hardly remembered people, scraps of conversations. Had any of these led to his present state? Over and over again.

He was drawing closer to the breaking point. He needed help and sought out his rabbi, but his rabbi was ill. Late one night he telephoned the minister of the Community Church, the Rev. Eric Braund, who came by and found Chasanow in a dazed state, his voice strange. The two talked for hours, into the early morning. Braund advised that the charges had to be fought, and left in great distress at Chasanow's condition.

Chasanow had already decided to fight the charges, and after some inquiries among attorneys met a lawyer with some experience in handling loyalty cases. His name was Joseph A. Fanelli, a former special assistant in the Department of Justice.

This was the beginning of many days, days of long hours, spent in preparing Chasanow's case, and the painstaking effort of obtaining close to a hundred affidavits in his behalf.

At last, in late September 1953, Chasanow was summoned to appear before a Navy hearing board.

The hearing was held in a large Navy conference room, where his judges, three high-ranking Defense Department officials, sat around a long table. They were joined by a legal officer who conducted the interrogation.

When Chasanow entered the room he felt strained; an air of suspicion seemed to hang over the room. He saw himself as a common criminal, come to hear his sentence. But after the first day this feeling wore off and he loosened up.

Where were his mysterious accusers? They were nowhere to be seen. They were not here to meet the test of corroboration and veracity. An impossible challenge was being thrown at Chasanow. His was to be a defensive role and nothing more, and under interrogation it was to be his burden to establish clearly that he was innocent of the charges.

The session lasted three days. On the first, several witnesses testifying in Chasanow's behalf were cross-examined. On the second and third days Chasanow took the oath and was examined. The questions put to him dealt primarily with his home town of Greenbelt and some of its residents, who now appeared to be the source of the accusations against him.

Toward the close of the hearing, the only witnesses for the government were produced. Their interrogation took a surprising turn when they testified favorably for Chasanow, not against him. Both swore that they never gave any information against Chasanow, that any derogatory statements attributed to them were misrepresentations.

3 The Chasanow Story

The legal officer was puzzled. She questioned the two witnesses closely.

"Didn't an investigator visit you and talk to you about Chasanow?" she asked each witness.

Each said yes.

"And didn't you say he had associated with suspicious persons?"

Both denied it.

"Are you sure?"

Both were sure.

One of the two witnesses added this:

"The investigator who saw me was a young man who took no notes at all the whole time we were talking. He seemed to be trying to get me to say that Mr. Chasanow was associated with some of these people you listed."

The members of the Hearing Board looked surprised on hearing this testimony.

On October 9 the Hearing Board unanimously rendered its verdict that Chasanow was not a security risk.

The board's decision was that Chasanow did not associate with known communists or persons with communistic tendencies. In regard to some of the other charges brought against Chasanow, the board stated:

The evidence establishes that Mr. Chasanow was present at a social party sometime during the year 1941. This function was attended by many residents of Greenbelt, some of whom were reputed to have "radical" and "left-wing" tendencies and others whose reputation in the community was unquestioned. It was established that money was raised at this affair for the support of some Spanish relief organization, the exact nature of which is not clear. The United Spanish Aid Committee, which allegedly was the recipient, was not placed on the Attorney General's list of subversive organizations until eight years after the party.

The evidence established that Mr. Chasanow did subscribe to a publication known as In Fact some twelve years ago. There is evidence to indicate that he never renewed his subscription. The evidence does not show that the publishers of this periodical appear on the Attorney General's list.

| Cross-Currents in America

The evidence establishes that in 1939 Mr. Chasanow became a member of the National Lawyers Guild for one (1) year. At that time lawyers of national prominence were members and contributed articles to the quarterly published by the organization. There is no evidence that the National Lawyers Guild was considered a subversive organization when Mr. Chasanow was a member.

Mr. Chasanow, as well as his wife, were connected in some minor capacity with the Greenbelt Gazette. His connection, like others, was on a voluntary basis. Copies of this newspaper which were received in evidence and perused by the Board failed to reveal "radical" or "left-wing" tendencies. Rather, these issues reflected an account of the activities of a small town. No competent evidence was produced to establish that the Gazette was ever a member of the "Washington Bookshop Association." . . .

There is a lack of credible evidence to establish that Mr. Chasanow was a leader of or active in radical groups in Greenbelt. In fact, the weight of the evidence points to the non-existence in Greenbelt of "radical" or "left-wing" groups, as the words are loosely used.

The evidence reveals an enlightening and interesting insight into the operations of a cooperative city such as Greenbelt. Since its inception, Greenbelt has been a subject of controversy.

From without, it has been eyed suspiciously as a "queer" experiment. Many believed the Government had no business starting it. The extent of the cooperative undertaking was viewed by many as something apart from conventional private enterprise. The result has been that rumor and gossip have given Greenbelt a "radical" or "leftist" reputation.

Within, management has been characterized by frequent disagreements. The testimony shows heated disputes that often developed into personal animosities. As a result such terms as "crackpots," "radicals," "pinkos" and "Communists" have been bandied about loosely by disgruntled individuals.

In this environment a civic-minded individual—whether conservative or otherwise—is bound to be exposed to criticism. In the case of Mr. Chasanow, who took part in many activities, the testimony showed that he was, if anything, a moderating, constructive and conservative influence.

Based on all the evidence heard by the Board and the reports of investigation furnished by the Government, the Board could reach no other conclusion but that Mr. Chasanow's employment is clearly consistent with the interest of national security.

3 The Chasanow Story

Such were the findings of the Hearing Board. The complete vindication it gave Chasanow, however, was only a momentary sense of triumph and relief. For his case was the first under the government's new security regulations, which now required an additional step before final clearance—a review by a security appeal board. Chasanow looked upon this with no great concern; his clearance would now be a matter of routine. And he settled back to wait with grim but hopeful patience for the call to return to his job.

Month after month passed with no word. He greeted the arrival of each new day with fresh hope. This was it . . . the day of good tidings. . . .

A new year—1954—arrived; still no word. The silence was overbearing; what had been a certain hope became a nervous suspense. The excitement of the sight of the mailman became the deadening expectancy of disappointment.

His resources had run dry; he had cashed in his bonds and was now living on borrowed money. He decided to open a law and real estate office in Greenbelt to carry on. So his friends and neighbors rallied around in encouragement and support, and it gave him the needed strength to keep going.

Spring was approaching when a young and enterprising reporter for the Washington *Daily News* wrote a series of articles on the government's security program and the Chasanow case. The reporter, Anthony Lewis, later described the Chasanow case, without identifying the principals, in the *Reporter* magazine. It helped enlist the interest of the public in the case.

The following month, April 4, 1954, Chasanow got word to appear at the Hydrographic Office. He drew a deep breath. At last, it was all over. He hurried to his office, where a letter awaited him. It was from James H. Smith, Jr., Navy Assistant Secretary for Air. Chasanow ripped open the envelope. . . . The letter said that the Hearing Board's decision was overruled and "your employment is hereby terminated." There was no further explanation. . . .

Cross-Currents in America

APRIL 30, 1954
Washington, D.C., Office to BRE

We have received a reply from the Secretary of the Navy to our letter of the nineteenth.

Secretary Anderson's response, dated April 27, assures us "that the Department of the Navy adheres firmly, conscientiously, and wholeheartedly to the American principle that there shall be no discrimination against any person by reason of race, color or religion." Further, he informs us that Chasanow's counsel has already been advised "that he may submit any additional pertinent facts and information" on the case, to be considered on May 3.

The reopening of the case is heartening, and we shall, as observers, so write to the Secretary.

MAY 3, 1954
Washington, D.C., Office to BRE

Fanelli and Chasanow have been requested to appear before Assistant Secretary Smith for oral arguments. Things are beginning to stir.

MAY 4, 1954
Washington, D.C., Office to BRE

Smith announced that the Chasanow case will be given a full hearing.

JUNE 21, 1954
Washington, D.C., Office to BRE

Chasanow's rehearing starts today.

3 The Chasanow Story

AUGUST 15, 1954
BRE to Washington, D.C., Office

It is now almost two months since the rehearing on Chasanow's case was completed. It is already more than a year since Chasanow was removed. How much more can they drag this out? Any straws in the wind?

AUGUST 31, 1954
Washington, D.C., Office to BRE

Smith has phoned Chasanow and informed him that he has been reinstated. It will be publicly announced tomorrow.

SEPTEMBER 1, 1954
Washington, D.C., Office to BRE

Assistant Secretary Smith today publicly apologized to Chasanow for his thirteen-month ordeal. Mrs. Chasanow was present to witness her husband's exoneration. Smith told a press conference that a special hearing board found Chasanow an "above average, loyal American citizen."

The Assistant Secretary denounced the unidentified informants, Chasanow's accusers, who had on re-examination "either failed to corroborate their original testimony or were unable to produce specifics of earlier allegations."

Smith said these informants did a "disservice to the security procedures of the nation," and he confessed that the Navy had been "probably a little naïve" in not checking their credibility. The security procedures of the department were being revamped, he said, expressing the hope that a way would be found to throw out the testimony of

Cross-Currents in America

irresponsible persons who were unwilling to "come in and back it up when the chips are down."

Smith further stated that the special board found "that any contact with individuals or organizations alleged to be subversive, which Mr. Chasanow may have had, were at a time when such individuals or organizations were not generally considered to be subversive, and that such contacts were isolated, short or casual and were brought about by Mr. Chasanow's normal civic activities and for no other purpose."

Now that the Navy has corrected its error, Smith said, it wished to return Mr. Chasanow to his job and restore his reputation in the eyes of the public. He ordered Chasanow reinstated as of July 1953, the month of his suspension from duty. The long nightmare is over.

Chasanow, too deeply moved for words, nevertheless managed this simple statement:

"All I can say is that it seems like I woke up from a bad dream and the sun was shining."

An editorial in the Chicago Daily Tribune *of September 4, 1954, commenting on Chasanow's reinstatement, remarks that if it is true that anti-Semitism was involved in the case, "the Anti-Defamation League may choose to interest itself."*

The main point of the editorial, however, is in its conclusion. Says the Tribune: *"No 'McCarthyism' is involved, and this must be a severe blow to those who prefer to talk about McCarthyism rather than Mc-Brownellism or McFlanderism."*

Would that "mccarthyism" had not been involved. The Tribune *misses the point. What "mccarthyism" (as distinguished from Senator McCarthy) has come to mean is the irresponsible exploitation of political and public media for the furthering of personal or political ambitions; defamation of personal or political opponents; the mixture of fact and gossip. It means the cultivation of prejudice and fear; it means the increased reliance upon "secret" informers; unproduced evidence in the processes of justice. It means that a person is guilty until he proves himself innocent.*

3 The Chasanow Story

Chasanow's reinstatement is cause for rejoicing. But let's not forget about the others. The New York Times, *on September 3, reported that "The Navy was asked today if it was reopening the cases of Mr. Chasanow's four colleagues to determine whether the same discredited informants were responsible for the accusations against them."*

The Navy answered that it would release no data "for security reasons"; if they wished to, the individuals involved could make statements. And the Times *then noted that "The four often rode to and from work with Mr. Chasanow. The charges against them were markedly similar to those against him."*

Over and above all the facts and conclusions elicited in the Chasanow case and in our intensive inquiry into the motivations behind the large percentage of suspension of Jews at Fort Monmouth, a number of glaring weaknesses in the security program became patent; weaknesses which in an ascending period of hysteria result, as we have seen, in the wrongful destruction of men's reputations and of their right to work undisturbed in their chosen professions.

Let us examine the operation of a federal security program that permitted such injustice. The most striking finding developed by our Fort Monmouth inquiry is that nearly eighty per cent of the suspendees won their cases. In other words, in eight cases out of every ten the formal charges brought by the government against its employees proved to be groundless. This arithmetic reveals some of the unnecessary hardship and heartache of the security program. The policy and practice is that the employee against whom charges are filed must first be suspended or declassified, yet in the overwhelming majority of cases, if past experience is a guide, he will ultimately be reinstated with back pay.

But reinstatement with back pay cannot completely undo the damage wrought by the practice of suspending first and hearing afterward. At Fort Monmouth reinstatement took an average of nine months; the duration of the security proceedings ranged from one to eighteen months. Meanwhile, the employee was severed from his job, a wall of suspicion was erected between him, his neighbor, and his fellow employees. Demoralization set in.

I Cross-Currents in America

It seems clear, too, that the security officers who formalized the complaints that precipitated the suspensions at Fort Monmouth and of Abraham Chasanow in Maryland were guilty, at least, of passing the buck. Failing to stop a thin or hollow case at its very inception, they preferred to let the issue go to a hearing board for determination. We expect a district attorney to have the decency and sense of duty to refuse to take a case to court if it is too thin. We expect a judge to toss out a case without letting it go to a jury if the evidence has raised no real issue of fact. We should expect no less of security officers.

A clearly indicated reform, then, would be to hold security officers responsible for sending along batches of untenable charges that conscientious preliminary examination or a face-to-face meeting with the employee would have exploded.

The only excuse a security officer can have for initiating such suspensions is that he has incorporated in his complaint only what is proper under the criteria established for him. In such case, the security regulations themselves are the culprits and they must be refined and corrected.

A key question has never been answered in the Monmouth cases; it was never even probed. In the Chasanow case, it seems to have been answered. That question is: Were any of the accusers in any of the Monmouth suspensions or in the Chasanow suspension motivated by religious bigotry? In the Chasanow situation, enough was learned about some of the accusers to make an educated guess that prejudice was present. But with respect to Monmouth, not even the barest hint was ever given as to the character or attitude of any of the accusers; not a single one was identified.

The concept of secret accusation is repulsive to democratic tradition. It is basic in American jurisprudence that the accused confront his accuser and be permitted to question his good faith openly and intensely. Were this a requirement in the loyalty program, anti-Semitism could never have been a factor.

In several instances other than Monmouth and Chasanow, when the accuser was cross-examined, superficially serious charges quickly evaporated. Improper motivation, impossible to determine while an accuser

3 The Chasanow Story

remains anonymous, was easily ascertained when the accuser was compelled to face the man he accused. An obvious reform, then, in the loyalty program would be a provision that an accused employee should have the right to come face to face with his accuser.

Finally, there is a need to revise the security program so that it will no longer be mandatory to suspend an employee against whom formal charges are filed before adjudication. Suspension before hearing could be reserved as a discretionary power in those cases where the evidence against the employee is especially grave and where he holds an especially sensitive position.

The virtues of a properly drawn employee security program are many. Such a program would not prejudice the legitimate, vital interest of national security, yet it would strengthen the traditional American guarantees of fair play. It would promote national security by strengthening morale and enhancing confidence in the fairness and humaneness of government. Finally, it would prevent the political opportunist and the gutter bigot from doing the damage which our recorded memoranda demonstrate they have perpetrated.

Clearly, the genuine threat of communist subversion requires a foolproof security program.

Four   The Reactionaries

Three overlapping forces seem to be coalescing as we begin the presidential election year 1956—the hate groups, welded to one another by the anti-Semitism they all exploit; latter-day know-nothings who in their fear of communism oppose civil liberties as a weakness in our ramparts; extreme political reactionaries who are unable or unwilling to recognize the bigots among those joining their movement.

The three forces are unified on many issues, including opposition to the present programs and leadership of the Republican and Democratic parties, to the United Nations and its UNESCO, to modern education as we know it in the United States, and to the socio-economic changes that have come on the domestic scene over the last two decades.

In the previous pages we have examined the men in the field of professional bigotry, the mechanics of their operations, and the ugly substance of their propaganda. We have seen the panic created by the know-nothings and how they have hurt people. To complete the picture, we should direct our attention to the activities of the reactionary movement, probing for a moment its motivations, the character of its contribution to current events, and its impact upon our nation.

| Cross-Currents in America

Typical of this last group is Merwin K. Hart's National Economic Council in New York City, the first propaganda agency to sound a call to action immediately the 1954 congressional elections were over.

On November 5, 1954, Hart sent word across the nation by means of his Economic Council Letter *that the Republican Administration had been "repudiated" by the American people—a Republican Administration run "not . . . by a President" but "by a junta—that powerful, usually ruthless kind of a group that has so often ruled despotically in . . . other countries."*

"It need not have happened," said Hart. "But it did—through communist infiltration among those who have surrounded the President and kept him virtually a prisoner. . . . For an Administration of a major Party, which takes its very name from the Republic itself, to have perpetrated this assault upon the fundamental character of the United States is reason enough for the voters to disavow that party."

The solution, said Hart, is obvious: "A coalition should be established between conservative Republicans and Democrats of both North and South."

Five months later, in April 1955, Hart set out for the West Coast to attend a little-noticed meeting held in San Francisco under the auspices of an organization known as the Congress of Freedom. What happened there will be told in full in later pages.

The Congress of Freedom is today most representative of the reactionary movement we are considering.

Created in the fall of 1952 with an impressive list of sponsors, the Congress of Freedom has established a record which strongly suggests the need for continued observation of its affairs. Although no evidence of anti-Semitism was apparent, and its purposes were well within legitimate political and economic bounds, the persistent attempts of notorious patrioteers to join its ranks could only excite suspicion.

Arnold Kruckman, a seventy-three-year-old Washington, D.C., public relations specialist, founded the Congress of Freedom as a sounding board for conservatives strongly opposed to the United Nations. But a number of the men and women who gradually joined the National

4 The Reactionaries

Advisory Committee of the newly established agency spelled trouble. Included were:

P. A. Del Valle—*who was ignominiously defeated in 1954 in a bid for the Republican gubernatorial nomination in Maryland, is a retired U. S. Marine Corps lieutenant general, closely associated with Merwin Hart, and an admirer of Robert Williams. He has publicly endorsed Williams'* anti-Semitic pamphlet, Know Your Enemy, *and recommended the Californian's monthly newsletter as must-reading to delegates attending the 1952 Republican National Convention in Chicago.*

W. L. Foster—*a Tulsa, Oklahoma, geologist who has been a financial contributor to the anti-Semitic Christian Nationalist Crusade headed by Gerald Smith.*

John Bross Lloyd—*who is a long-time supporter of Joseph P. Kamp, identifies himself as a Greenwich, Connecticut, philanthropist. In 1941, Lloyd distributed through the mails, unsolicited, copies of booklets by William Dudley Pelley, one of the most notorious pre-World War II seditionists in the United States.*

Lucille Cardin Crain—*a self-described educational editor of New York City who has collaborated with Merwin Hart and Joseph P. Kamp. Mrs. Crain, editing the now defunct* Educational Reviewer, *made it a guiding force in extremist attacks upon the modern educational system.*

Verne P. Kaub—*the president of the American Council of Christian Laymen, Madison, Wisconsin, who has engaged in anti-Semitic activities. Kaub has worked closely with Allen Zoll, the propagandist heading at least one organization which has been cited by the U. S. Attorney General as "subversive."*

Kalenik Lissiuk—*who has spoken under the auspices of Conde McGinley.*

Trouble in the Congress of Freedom came sooner than anticipated, and in the spring of 1954, Kruckman disassociated himself from the organization, leaving one Robert LeFevre to take control as the executive director. Perhaps the reason for Kruckman's resignation can be found in the following two reports written in the winter of 1953.

I Cross-Currents in America

NOVEMBER 5, 1953
Research to BRE

You will recall that in the summer of 1952 an organization calling itself Operation America, Inc., stage-managed a "third party" conference in Chicago in opposition to the presidential conventions of the two major parties. The result was the formation of a Constitution Party which, after it fell into the hands of rabble-rousers, rapidly dwindled to little significance.

Under the presidency of Arnold Kruckman, Operation America, Inc., renewed its search for politically-minded people of substance, and last summer realized that it had the answer in his original idea—the Congress of Freedom.

Operation America, Inc., then took a motherly interest in the Congress and became the sponsor of its annual national get-together to be held in October 1953, at Omaha, Nebraska, saluting it as a gathering of "patriotic organizations and groups seeking to revive original Constitutional Government administrative practices."

Omaha was chosen as the site because "it is in the heart of what is probably the greatest area of native-born in the United States"; and Kruckman was to be the guiding spirit of the Congress sessions. Even though he had expressed the notion that anti-Semitism was unconstitutional and anti-American, he also believed that Merwin Hart, Gerald Smith, and Father Coughlin were "much-maligned" souls. Obviously he was acceptable.

The task of crystallizing the objectives of the Congress of Freedom, however, was assigned to one Aldrich Blake, of Los Angeles, whose America Plus led the drive for the "Freedom of Choice" amendment to the California Constitution in 1952. A pamphlet he wrote entitled *The Second Bill of Rights* was included with Operation America's original call; it stressed the need for a "virile conservative—rightist mass movement . . . to win back from the Marxists the individual freedoms and private property rights which they have stolen from us."

Blake's pamphlet suggested the adoption of a series of amendments which would: "Safeguard the press, radio, television and the cinema against bureaucratic dictation . . . Guarantee to businessmen, property owners and employers the right to choose their own guests, patrons, tenants, neighbors and employees. Extirpate indoctrination of collectivism from the nation's schools . . ."

Blake also urged an amendment to assure the selection of "Presidential Electors in such manner as to prevent the election of our Chief Magistrate by the minorities in a few large cities."

Operation America, Inc., released a list of sponsors of the Omaha Congress. The committee included such names as Dr. E. G. "Parson Jack" Johnston, anti-Semitic publisher of the Columbus, Georgia, *Tribune;* Austin F. Hancock, anti-Semitic leader of the American Heritage Protective Committee of San Antonio, Texas; Verne P. Kaub; and Thomas Creigh, a former vice-president of Merwin K. Hart's Economic Council.

Among the ladies, the sponsors included Dr. Ella Lonn, Minute Women leader of Baltimore, Maryland; Mrs. Lucille Cardin Crain; Helen P. Lasell, anti-Semitic president of the New York Chapter of the U. S. Flag Committee; Florence Braunsdorf, of Operation America, Inc., who has attended Gerald Smith meetings; Mrs. Katherine R. Peugnet, president of the Dames of the Loyal Legion of the U.S.A., and a former officer in Allen Zoll's organization, the National Council for American Education.

In September 1953, before the Omaha Convention, Operation America, Inc., mailed a series of bulletins about the forthcoming Congress; and by the middle of the month Kruckman had lined up a number of "distinguished Americans" to address the convention. They included Colonel Archibald B. Roosevelt, who had agreed to serve as the Congress' general chairman; Frank E. Holman, inveterate foe of the United Nations; Frank Chodorov, associate editor of *Human Events,* an extremely rightist Washington newsletter; former Congressman John T. Wood[1] from Idaho; and Representative Ralph W. Gwinn of New York, who for many years has been closely associated with Merwin K. Hart.

---

[1] John T. Wood died on November 2, 1954.

| Cross-Currents in America

In addition to these keynote speakers, Operation America, Inc., announced that a series of panel discussions would be held "to crystallize the thought and the conclusions of the Congress" on such topics as foreign affairs, taxation, states' rights, and freedom of choice.

More significant than the agenda was the list of organizations and individuals who had "filed returns" for the Congress of Freedom. Operation America's call had been answered not only by a number of Minute Women groups, but also by Joseph Beauharnais' anti-Negro White Circle League, Mrs. Jessie W. Jenkins' anti-Semitic and racist National Patrick Henrys, Myron C. Fagan's Cinema Educational Guild, and Keith Thompson's American Committee for the Advancement of Western Culture.

From the Midwest, former Christian Nationalist Andrew B. McAllister's Pro-American Information Bureau responded, as did John W. Hamilton's racist National Citizens' Protective Association, anti-Semitic Stephen Nenoff's Paul Revere Club and Verne Kaub's American Council of Christian Laymen. The Ohio anti-Semites, the Rev. Millard J. Flenner and Peter Xavier, were also on the roster, along with Florida Klansman Bill Hendrix; Christian Nationalist Stephen Goodyear; and W. Henry MacFarland, Jr., whose American Flag Committee led the vicious attacks against UNESCO.

Operation America, Inc., subsequently explained that a listing of individuals and organizations "was not a registration." The final "processing" would be up to its Credentials Committee, among whose members were Aldrich Blake, Mrs. Helen Lasell, and Verne Kaub.

The fact that Operation America, Inc., did not repudiate the suspect organizations which had answered its call was apparently of concern to some of the "distinguished Americans" slated to address the gathering. In one of the Congress' bulletins, John T. Wood noted that he and Frank Holman had both "heard some similar reports on subversion on the part of some of the backers of the movement." But, said Wood, "Mr. Holman had the whole thing completely investigated by the FBI" and it had been given a clean bill of health.

This might have been less of a comfort to Mr. Wood had he reflected that it was highly improbable that the FBI would undertake any investigation for the purpose of furnishing information to private citizens. Still, he seems to have been temporarily reassured.

Meanwhile, Kruckman continued to issue glowing reports about "the most important meeting of its kind to be held since the days when our forefathers met to decide that the path of the Colonies was outside the orbit of England." He predicted that one thousand or more accredited delegates and observers would be on hand for the proceedings.

The Congress was held the first three days of October. Attached is a copy of the report we received yesterday about it from Omaha, Nebraska.

NOVEMBER 4, 1953
Omaha Office to Research

Approximately five hundred delegates and observers—half the number originally predicted by Kruckman—attended the three-day session of conferences and panel discussions which got under way on schedule at Omaha's Hotel Paxton.

The principal speakers delivered their expected arguments against the evils of socialism and the threat of internationalism. Frank Holman once again urged the passage of the Bricker Amendment and charged that the "treaty law" now before the UN was a threat "to individual rights and rights of self-government." Representative Ralph W. Gwinn warned the delegates that "we are already so sunk in socialism that it is too late to call a halt in Washington." Lucille Cardin Crain urged American education to rid itself of "alien ideas." Frank Chodorov charged that the income tax was "the open sesame to all our Socialistic experiments," and demanded the repeal of the Sixteenth Amendment.

Considerable local interest was aroused by the appearance of Mrs. Crain. The Omaha Education Association, an organization representing twelve hundred Omaha public-school teachers, had been invited to attend the Congress, but announced that it would boycott the sessions because Mrs. Crain and other "enemies of public education" were listed among the speakers.

| Cross-Currents in America

Mrs. Crain denied that she was against public education, and at the conclusion of her speech announced that her *Educational Reviewer* would be forced to suspend publication after the October 1953 issue because of lack of funds. The implication was clear, and Archibald Roosevelt, who chaired the meeting, announced that he would contribute a substantial amount toward a fund to keep her publication going.

Subsequently Mrs. Crain conducted the Congress' Seminar on Education and Communication, which was attended, among others, by Myron C. Fagan. Fagan, who once boasted that "we cleaned UNESCO out of Los Angeles," and whose play, *Red Rainbow,* was recently withdrawn after twelve performances in New York, charged that the "communists" have "absolute control" over Broadway and dominate radio and television.

At the end of the three-day session the delegates met to sign a "declaration of purpose" in which they unanimously agreed that "freedom in America is not being adequately protected." They also passed a series of resolutions which showed them both anti-Republican Administration and anti-Democratic Party. A familiar slant in certain quarters.

The Congress of Freedom delegates heartily endorsed the discriminatory McCarran-Walter Immigration Act; called for an end to foreign aid; charged that the United Nations "in its present form [was] deplorable and unforgivably shameful"; and recorded their opposition to federal aid to education, progressive education, and "socialized" medicine.

While there was no evidence of bigotry at any of the Congress' formal sessions it was reported that during a panel discussion one of the participants commented that B'nai B'rith was dissatisfied with the "slow process of mongrelization in America." It was further noted that an anti-UN pamphlet published by Gerald Smith's Christian Nationalist Crusade was included in the literature made available to the convention delegates.

A list of those who had attended the Congress was not released to the public during the Congress, but observers reported that Florida's

4 The Reactionaries

Bill Hendrix, for one, was very much in evidence. So was Charles B. Hudson, who formerly published the hate sheet *America in Danger,* and Harry James Johnson, of Phoenix, Arizona, a public admirer of Gerald Smith and Robert H. Williams.

The presence of the anti-Semitic Hendrix, wearing a convention badge that identified him as an "observer" from Tallahassee, Florida, was apparently of no concern to the Congress' Credentials Committee. Several delegates, however, felt that his presence would result in unfavorable publicity for the Congress and demanded that Kruckman remove his name from the official roster. A newspaperman who subsequently checked the story with Kruckman was told that Hendrix had "left town one day before the end of the convention" and that his name was being removed from the roster.

The nation's press generally ignored the Omaha proceedings, with the exception of the Chicago *Tribune,* which sent one of its top reporters, Frank Hughes, to cover the sessions. Hughes, who was enthusiastically received by Kruckman and his associates, pointed out to Chicago *Tribune* readers that "Many Congress of Freedom delegates have taken part in third party movements . . . designed to capture anti-New Deal sentiment of southern Democrats and conservative sentiment of Northern Republicans."

The Chicago *Tribune* praised the "third party" theme in an editorial of October 4 entitled "The People Speak." Said the *Tribune:*

More than five hundred Americans have been meeting in Omaha . . . to discuss viewpoints on national policy which at present are given expression by neither political party. . . .
They hope that time will see a political realignment which once more will bring to the fore the dominant American motives of nationalism, individual liberty and constitutional government. . . .

The *Tribune* added:

It is significant that the people are becoming restive . . . and it would be well if the Republican Party paid them heed. If it does not, it will awaken some day to discover that its former supporters have left it behind.

At the end of the convention, Operation America, Inc., announced

| Cross-Currents in America

that it had organized regional groups to carry on its work. Another convention is scheduled for next year.

NOVEMBER 6, 1953
BRE to AF

There is certainly room in America for genuine movements which are critical of the United Nations or unhappy with the major political parties or dissatisfied with the methods of public education. Such movements, however, take on a different meaning when they become permeated with elements representing racial and religious prejudice.

It occurs to me that possibly the extreme reactionaries in the Congress of Freedom who are intensely politically-minded will also permit these questionable elements to infiltrate if and when they organize along political lines. Please keep me informed.

JUNE 8, 1954
AF to BRE

A new movement has cropped up. There are many personalities in it who have not been participants in the Congress of Freedom, who are extremely conservative, and have never shown signs of religious prejudice. However, others in the new organization are either themselves anti-Semitic or are intimately associated with known anti-Semites.

The new organization is called For America.

For America seems to be a refurbished and rededicated ghost of the America First Committee which led the prewar isolationist movement. Its general orientation shows that it finds many of the old isolationist theories still politically attractive. Should the new organization attain any degree of national prominence, it would unquestionably draw a large body of the old America First faithful. And a bigoted lot that would be. It bears watching. Let me give you a rundown of its history to date.

4   The Reactionaries

Following several months of preliminary and unpublicized activity, For America was formally announced May 7 in Chicago. A charter of incorporation was obtained in the state of Illinois, and central headquarters were set up in Chicago.

Colonel Robert McCormick, publisher of the Chicago *Tribune,* was host to a luncheon gathering which formally announced For America and its primary purposes: (1) to combat "super-internationalism and interventionism" and (2) to campaign in the fall election for candidates supporting their aims.

Clarence E. Manion, former dean of law at Notre Dame University, who quit the Eisenhower Administration (as chairman of the Presidential Commission on Inter-Governmental Relations) to support the Bricker Amendment, and General Robert E. Wood, former head of Sears, Roebuck & Co. and onetime chairman of the America First Committee, are co-chairmen of the new group.

The organizing committee of For America is made up of prominent isolationists: Burton K. Wheeler, former Democratic senator from Montana; Hamilton Fish, former Republican congressman from New York; Howard Buffett, former Republican congressman from Nebraska; John T. Flynn, of New York, writer and radio commentator; and Dr. Manion.

Fish, spokesman for the luncheon group, emphasized that For America is "no third party," but that it plans to work for a new political alignment in both major parties. He said it intends to go beyond the America First Committee's single objective of keeping out of war, and proposes to take a position on every important issue—such as the Bricker Amendment and communists in government.

Though Fish himself said the new organization would not try to be the nucleus of a new political party, I cannot seriously believe he would be content if this remained true. Ever since he was read out of the Republican Party by Governor Thomas E. Dewey, the ex-congressman has had one primary aim in life—the formation of a third political party.

"People have nowhere to go," Fish said. "There should be an organization to take care of people who want realignment. There is no organization representing states' rights except what are represented here. It is evident that even the Republican Party has gone over to internationalism and interventionism."

The declaration of principles announced by For America implies a panic about the state of the nation. "Save America," its first stated aim, suggests that we are about to lose our country. "Restore and uphold our Constitution," the second aim, suggests that we have already lost our national charter. The other essential planks, for "states' rights" and against "super-internationalism," "giving away our money," and "one-worldism," are familiar reactionary scare words that, in this context, serve to direct the panic against the present Administration.

Positions on the new organization's executive board were accepted by some prominent, extremely conservative business leaders, and by others known primarily for their preoccupation with dubious causes. On the executive committee, and also active in the Congress of Freedom, are Richard Lloyd Jones, of Tulsa, Oklahoma, and Robert Donner, of Colorado Springs—more on these two later.

The emergence of For America provoked extensive coverage in the nation's news columns and editorial pages. For example, two major dailies in the deep South, the Atlanta *Journal* and the New Orleans *Times-Picayune,* viewed with retentive memories the reappearance of the America First leaders. The Atlanta *Journal* declared (May 11):

> It is sad to see the discredited take up the torch of isolation once again. If ever a movement wound up in disrepute, it was that one called America First.
> It started with big names, men who lent their wealth and prestige. . . . The dates have changed but the times are not altogether different. . . . What will it take to disband this group? Another Pearl Harbor? World War III? . . .

> Maybe [says the New Orleans *Times-Picayune* (May 24)] world communism can be combatted without super-internationalism and one-worldism—(we think it can)—but to combat it without a touch of interventionism, on behalf of allies; without internationalism, though alliances; without "free-worldism," would offer the same grim prospect that the "America First Committee" was holding out when Nazism was rampant . . .

4   The Reactionaries

A newspaper from another section of the country, the Boston *Traveler,* says (May 12): "This new group . . . looks like the same old hat with a touch of new trimming."

But the executive committee of For America includes a number of figures whose backgrounds are not so well known as those of Fish, Wheeler, Colonel McCormick, or General Wood.

Robert Donner, for example, a retired steel tycoon, first emerged as a self-appointed guardian of the American educational system when, in 1941, he conducted a campaign to get the Rugg textbooks eliminated from the public schools of Colorado Springs. Early in 1948, Donner also demanded that Colorado College abolish its social science department because it was "wittingly or unwittingly fostering subversive thinking."

Donner called for the removal from the college's library of "such leftist-side propaganda" as the *Nation,* the *New Republic, Survey Graphic, Christian Unitarian Register,* the *Bulletin of Atomic Scientists,* the *United Nations Bulletin,* and the Catholic publication *Commonweal.* Also books by John Dewey, George Counts, and others.

Donner has also been for years a strong supporter of such talents as Joseph P. Kamp, Allen Zoll, Merwin K. Hart, and Robert H. Williams.

Another member of For America's executive committee is Robert M. Harriss, a onetime financial adviser to Father Charles E. Coughlin. During the thirties Harriss was in and out of all manner of political ventures. In connection with these activities he often supported known anti-Semites, though on occasion he also publicly professed a belief in religious and racial tolerance. And he made financial contributions to Merwin K. Hart's National Economic Council.

A frequent attendant at the policy meetings of Hart's National Economic Council was Howard Buffett, the former congressman from Nebraska, now a member of For America's organizing and executive committees.

Still another member of the executive group is Richard Lloyd Jones, editor of the Tulsa *Tribune.* "Would to God," wrote Gerald L. K. Smith (*The Cross and the Flag,* March 1953), "we had more daily papers like the Tulsa *Daily Tribune.*" The same issue of Smith's publication ran one of Jones's editorials on the United Nations, "Get Out of the Hate House." It is not known whether Smith had authorization for the reprint. Says Jones:

"We must withdraw our country from the United Nations organization and tell the U.N. delegates to pack their bags and scram . . . we never should have brought these rats to our shores."

Other Jones editorials have been widely distributed and reprinted by the anti-Semitic press, particularly one, "The American Flag for All of Us" (February 27, 1943). Whether this was authorized is also not known. Jones writes:

The habit of the Jew, wherever he goes, is always to remain Jew. He stays racial. He is inclusive, therefore exclusive. . . . The Jew maintains no missions. He sends no missionaries, as do Christians, both Catholic and Protestant, to make converts. . . . The very thought of a Gentile, seeking membership in a synagogue, would astonish even a liberal Jew. . . .

The For America group may pour money into the fall elections, strengthening candidates who espouse its program; but it will meet its real challenge after the November balloting—and as we draw close to the 1956 national election campaign. Can it continue to build on its present base or will it follow its predecessor, the America First Committee, into spectral oblivion?

In the meantime, we must regard this new organization as a part of the reactionary movement—a stronger, more effective part, because of its large number of respectable, respected, and affluent elements.

FEBRUARY 7, 1955
AF to BRE

Enough has happened since the announcement of the formation on November 14 of Ten Million Americans Mobilizing for Justice to evaluate the role it plays in the reactionary movement.

Although it is not necessarily pertinent, we should stress that we found no evidence of religious prejudice among the leading personali-

4 The Reactionaries

ties who lent their names and efforts to this recent fruitless move to whip up public opinion against the proposed Senate resolution censuring Senator McCarthy. Behind the scenes, however, there is abundant evidence that the signature-soliciting organization itself has been a magnet for a large number of America First, Congress of Freedom, and For America fans. It is also clear that some of the Ten Million Americans leadership rushed to it in the hope that it might be an effectively dramatic rallying point for a third party.

For one thing, Lieutenant General George E. Stratemeyer, national chairman of Ten Million Americans, is one of the national directors of For America. That TMA was hardly a spontaneous reaction to the plight of the ill-fated senator from Wisconsin was revealed by reliable information that this movement was originated, among other reasons, as a means of creating a national mailing list for future political purposes.

If a list of selected followers was the real motive of the anti-censure hoopla, it cannot be said to have failed. While TMA now seems to be fading rapidly since the passage of the censure resolution, somebody has walked away with the names and addresses of 2,287,143 Americans; that at least is the certified count to date with more petitions allegedly still untallied.

But the list has a great weakness. Those who accumulated it made the hasty error of believing it composes a mass of Americans oriented in one political direction. It does not. Which is why the anxious efforts of Rear Admiral John G. Crommelin and Major John Racey Jordan to turn TMA's mass following into a permanent national body are failing.

The big Madison Square Garden rally, held by TMA on November 29, was an obvious fizzle. Despite a promised overflow meeting, only 13,000 men, women, and children filed into the 22,000-capacity arena. Even Senator McCarthy himself, using an old arm injury as an excuse, did not attend the gathering held in his behalf.

Men of the three major religious faiths were on the platform to testify to the absence of religious prejudice on the part of the rally's promoters. Their very caution, however, exposed a degree of advance uneasiness; and the character of scores who filled the Garden seats belied the well-meaning gesture of tolerance. Gerald L. K. Smith, Joseph P. Kamp, and a generous representation of other "pros" were sprinkled around the vast auditorium.

Gerald Smith, in his enthusiasm unable to remain away, nonetheless recognized the harm to the movement in his attendance. At the very outset of the rally a local newspaper reporter spotted him concealed under a ten-gallon hat and approached for an interview. Insisting that he was "Walter Philips, of California," the man arose, turned, and rushed out of the meeting. But two weeks later, in his regular newsletter, Smith acknowledged that the reporter was not in error.

There was little disorder at the rally, and no heckling, with the exception of two minor but revealing incidents. Lisa Larsen of *Time* magazine, assigned to get candid shots of attendees in the reserved section of the Garden, received some rough treatment. As she conscientiously snapped away, hoping to make identifications later, several men in the audience began to fidget, and finally rushed at her. Amid shouts of "Dirty Jew" and "Hang the communist bitch," Miss Larsen was jostled and shoved until police, coming to her assistance, led her out unharmed. A second near riot was avoided when a young college student who had refused to stand and applaud with the others fled from the arena in time to escape two men in the row ahead who had begun to berate him in loud and menacing tones.

After the program had started, an unidentified enthusiast walked across the main floor carrying a poster bearing the legend, "JOE MCCARTHY FOR PRESIDENT FOR 1956 OF OUR GREAT CHRISTIAN NATION. KEEP IT CHRISTIAN."

The one speech that had undertones of direct concern to us was delivered by Rear Admiral Crommelin. Crommelin, who retired in 1950 after his suspension for divulging confidential military information, warned: "There is some Hidden Force or some Hidden Power or Something that is influencing our people. . . . They don't act like Americans." This Hidden Force, Crommelin went on, had agreed upon the elimination of Senator McCarthy, the one man who, alone, has been able to arouse the people of the United States to the menace of the Hidden Force in their government.

4 The Reactionaries

While the retired admiral's choice of phrase may have been entirely innocent, no well-versed reader of the professional anti-Semitic press present that night, and there were many, could have failed to note his use of their own euphemism for "international Jewish conspiracy."

On the other hand the admiral's choice of phrase may not have been an unfortunate accident. In the hectic days before the rally Crommelin had worked long and hard, much of the time on long-distance phones to all parts of the nation—from the New York City office of Joseph P. Kamp.

In the audience for the occasion, or active behind the doors of TMA's headquarters, or working from their own office desks, were these very familiar figures:

Pedro A. Del Valle.

Mrs. David D. Good—a national committeewoman of TMA. This Philadelphia lady is also a member of the board of governors and a vice-president of Allen Zoll's National Council for American Education. In 1939, at a meeting of the National Defense League, she introduced with high praise retired General George Van Horn Moseley, the so-called "man on the white horse" of the pre-World War II native fascist movement.

Fred H. Goodwin—TMA leader from New York City who was an early associate of Joseph P. Kamp, a frequent attendee at Merwin K. Hart affairs, and a participant at a dinner Hart arranged for Upton Close.

John B. Trevor—national treasurer of TMA. As the onetime president of the American Coalition of Patriotic Societies, an organization of 115 member agencies, many of them quite legitimate, Trevor welcomed into its ranks a significant number of super-nationalist outfits well known for their Coughlinite, pro-Fascist, or anti-Semitic character.

Mrs. Grace L. H. Brosseau—one of the founders of TMA. In 1939, Mrs. Brosseau was a member of the Americanism Award Committee of Joseph Kamp's Constitutional Educational League. As program chairman in 1953 of a women's patriotic conference, she invited Major Robert Williams to be a featured speaker. Also a vice-president in Zoll's "educational" organization.

| Cross-Currents in America

Loren Berry—an officer to TMA whose record includes soliciting funds for Merwin Hart's National Economic Council.
Louis D. Carroll—TMA committeeman who was active in the Constitution Party in 1952, and a member of the National Assembly of the Congress of Freedom.
Marque O. Nelson—national TMA committeeman from Tulsa, Oklahoma, who has been a financial contributor to Gerald Smith's Christian Nationalist Crusade.
Edward Fleckenstein—self-announced New Jersey state chairman of TMA, with a long record of neo-Nazi activity.

The full list of active TMA supporters contains many other Hart, Kamp, and Zoll stalwarts. A number of the workers in TMA's New York headquarters were rank-and-file volunteers in the New York offices of the old America First Committee. Finally, the following persons active in TMA should be recorded as members also of such agencies as For America or Congress of Freedom: Hamilton Fish and Robert M. Harriss, of New York; A. M. Owsley, of Texas; and Spruille Braden, of New York.

Reason would suggest that TMA is another facet, at least potentially, of the pressure for a third party now being exerted by extreme right-wingers unhappy with Eisenhower. Yet observe the denials: For America, openly raising campaign funds, insists that it is not and never will be a third party; Senator McCarthy, encouraging everybody, recently said that, for the present, he has no interest in or intention of joining any third party; Admiral Crommelin, maintaining that he is riding a political "grass-roots movement," protests that he is not sure it would be proper procedure to attempt the formation of a third party.

Why the denials? And what is that mailing list for?

APRIL 30, 1955
San Francisco Office to Research

The Congress of Freedom, describing itself as a "coalition of right-wing forces," convened in this city April 25 for a five-day, anti-United Na-

4 The Reactionaries

tions convention that brought forth a predictable spate of anti-UN oratory and a series of resolutions calling for American withdrawal from the world body.

The repetitious denunciations managed to include not only the inevitable UN but Presidents Eisenhower, Truman, Roosevelt, Chief Justice Earl Warren, the federal income tax, and fluoridation of the nation's drinking water. "Mass medication," declared one speaker, "is the first step by the communists."

The solemn deliberations were climaxed by a banquet at which Merwin K. Hart warned the guests that the tenth anniversary of the United Nations would be celebrated in June "to further the ideas of the United Nations and world government." Hart also declared that "we're speeding toward world government under which all American traditions and ideas would be lost. . . . The biggest hold-over of the Roosevelt and Truman administrations is the man in the White House."

Another featured speaker of the convention was columnist Westbrook Pegler, who called for an "American resistance movement." He said he favored United States withdrawal from the UN, but added, "I'd settle for the Bricker Amendment."

On the final day Robert LeFevre, the executive director, looked back upon the week's proceedings, pronounced them "good," and offered his personal verdict that the Congress of Freedom had solidified its position in San Francisco because of wiser leadership than in past years. He then returned home full of plans for another convention next year.

The convention's sharpest disagreement arose when Dr. V. Orval Watts, author of *The UN—Road to War,* unsuccessfully attempted to change the language of two resolutions which had some bearing on religion, so as not to offend non-Christians. He and a few supporters appealed to the Congress not to go on record as "just one segment of the religious movement in America"; and he pointed out that freedom of religion was one of the foundations of the nation.

But there were cries of "No!" and efforts to cut him off as he tried to explain that his long experience in fighting socialism and communism had taught him the necessity of getting support from "many who are not Christians, but Jews, for example." Further, he noted that he had been asked if he were a "foreigner," despite having lived in the United States for forty years, and he added that "that spirit is what worries me about this Congress."

His remarks, at first interrupted, later went unheeded or contradicted.

An Indiana physician, Dr. A. G. Blazey, declared that the "American" movement consisted "chiefly of Christians." And Mrs. Frank Cunningham, of Santa Monica, urged "this Christian gathering" not to deny Christ by supporting Watts but to join together in the "fight against the anti-Christ."

LeFevre, director of the Congress of Freedom, told the convention it had been deliberately set for April to interfere with the San Francisco observance of the tenth anniversary of the founding of the United Nations. The UN commemorative session had had to be delayed until June "because we already had the booking," he claimed. "We didn't stop it, but we sure dislocated it."

LeFevre listed this as one of the three great victories scored by anti-UN forces during the year. The other two, he said, were the revisions forced in the handbook of the Girl Scouts, removing "internationalist" references, and the success of the United States Day committee. All who had helped finance these efforts to "knock this incredible monster (the UN) in the head," were thanked.

The keynote speaker, George S. Montgomery, Jr., a New York attorney and board member of the National Economic Council, set the tone.

"We do not have an ally in the White House," he declared. The White House, apparently multihanded as well as underhanded, was, according to him, responsible for the "ambushing, waylaying, handcuffing and stabbing in the back" of Senator McCarthy; for "scuttling the Bricker Amendment"; and for refusing to listen to the advice of Clarence Manion on that and other subjects. Eisenhower, he said, "is not fighting on our side for national sovereignty."

Portions of the American press were also found wanting, particularly the New York *Times,* which, he charged, "printed more favorable pictures of Chou En-lai, the Red Chinese premier, in recent weeks than they have of Senator McCarthy during his whole career."

Reviewing the history of the last thirty-five years, Montgomery bitterly condemned Presidents Roosevelt, Truman, and Eisenhower, Justices of the Supreme Court Oliver Wendell Holmes and Felix Frankfurter, and the late British socialist, Harold Laski, whom he called "a draft-dodging little Englishman."

At this session telegrams were read from Admiral William Standley, former ambassador to Moscow, Brigadier General Bonner Fellers, Clarence Manion, and Colonel Archibald Roosevelt, who urged the convention to adopt the slogan, "Let's Take the U.S. out of the UN and Toss the UN out of the U.S." Messages were also received from Lucille Cardin Crain and Dan Smoot of Facts Forum.

After welcoming ceremonies, the convention broke up into various symposiums to hear, according to the advance billing, "America's greatest patriots in panel discussions aimed at preserving the American way of life."

These "foremost authorities" and "greatest patriots" included the following:

Myron Fagan, self-styled anti-communist, and author of *The Eisenhower Myth.*—"It is beyond question," he declared, "that the man in the White House should be impeached." President Eisenhower was, in Fagan's opinion, "guilty of destroying sovereignty" by subscribing to the UN. Moreover, Eisenhower "came out for world government, yet he took an oath he would defend the sovereignty of the United States. He lied." Fagan also suggested that Chief Justice Earl Warren should be "impeached" for his part in the Supreme Court's ruling against segregation in the nation's schools. Several references were made to the activities of "President Rosenfeld" by Fagan, who also democratically observed: "We do not need a strong majority, but rather a strong minority. Two million would be sufficient."

Corinne Griffith, former movie star, president of the Organization to Repeal Federal Income Taxes, Inc.—"The root of all our evils is the federal income tax," which she defined as "legalized thievery," "a method of national suicide," and communist-inspired as well. Miss Griffith said she referred only to personal, not corporate, income taxes—"and believe me, if it weren't for this money we wouldn't have the United Nations." Also, without disclosing her exact source, she said she had read in newspaper columns how an "invisible group" was running the country and planning for its domination and downfall. Neither did she disclose the group. She attacked Harry Dexter White, Dean Acheson, the Morgenthau Plan for Germany, the Ford and Rockefeller Foundations, the Standard Oil Company of New Jersey, and Paul Hoffman.

Mrs. Suzanne Silvercruys Stevenson, founder of the Minute Women of the U.S.A., Inc., an extreme right-wing group.—Described the UN as a plan for world federation, which would come to fruition at charter-revision time. Further, she outlined some alleged "failures" of the United Nations, perpetrated with American complicity; among them that "we failed our real friends, the Arabs." As remedies, she recommended passing the Bricker Amendment and moving the UN to Switzerland.

George Todt, public relations executive, ex-TV commentator, president of the Pasadena chapter of the Sons of the American Revolution. —Terming the UN an instrument of "international Marxism," organized along the lines of the Russian constitution, he proposed that the United States take over any movement to achieve a world order. . . . "We ought to make the UN join the U.S. . . . if other nations expressed the willingness to be like us, then they should be permitted to join when the time is right. . . . Britain or France might apply to be the 49th state in the Union." He charged that television, radio, and press are controlled by "the propaganda ministry of the United States." Proof? He had had a program for fifty-seven weeks on the NBC outlet in Los Angeles until one day he attacked the United Nations. The next day, said Todt without furnishing evidence, he was fired at the personal direction of General David Sarnoff; and with great indignation he added, "When a thirteenth-generation American can be fired by an immigrant without recourse—then it makes me think that McCarran was right. We should cut off immigration."

4 The Reactionaries

The Rev. Claude Bunzel, executive secretary of the American Council of Christian Churches of California.—The subject of his speech was "Creeping Totalitarianism," based on the thirteenth chapter of Revelations, which depicts a serpent covering the world. Internationalism, in his interpretation, is this serpent "engulfing Christian virtues." In a less allegorical vein, he said that Stalin once told Elliott Roosevelt that Russia was for world police; and he attacked Bishop G. Bromley Oxnam as one of the group advancing the concept that, since nations are interdependent, a world police is needed. The whole impetus for world government Bunzel found in the UN Charter. And international law, as in UN, he said, can bring about further infringements on religion, because the UN Declaration of Human Rights is really a declaration of human control. Bunzel did not explain, when he proposed the Gospel of Christ as the only solution, just how this Gospel, even as he saw it, excluded our neighbor nations and the world family of races from enjoying human rights according to our American precepts. And how would *any* government survive abandoning "human control"?

Miss Leora Baxter, legislative chairman of the California Chapter of Pro America, a group of extreme right-wing women.—She outlined the purposes of Pro America and its opposition to world government, attacking the whole development of internationalism from President Wilson on, including President Roosevelt's Four Freedoms. After identifying former Secretary of State Dean Acheson as an architect of the United Nations, despite historical evidence to the contrary, she emphasized the alleged creative role played by Alger Hiss and Harry Dexter White in building the world organization. Miss Baxter saw any strengthening of the UN as increasing the infringement of personal freedom; and cited Korea and Palestine as proof that the UN is completely ineffectual in foreign relations. The Baruch plan for control of atomic weapons she also criticized, and posed the question: How influential is Bernard Baruch in the State Department?

Mrs. Alice Widener, publisher of the magazine *U.S.A.* and author of the forthcoming book, *Behind the UN Front.*—Offering no proof, she claimed that she was dismissed after six months as a free-lance contributor to the Voice of America because she attacked communism too strongly. In line with this, she charged that the American delegation to the UN was mainly communist, and that all higher departments of the UN are "heavily infiltrated by Communists and Communist sympathizers" who are American citizens. But the UN, she added, also contains "a strong freedom underground" fighting communism.

Mrs. Jessica Payne, lecturer and writer.—Saluting her audience as "fellow country savers," she said the UN was "unconstitutional, un-American, and un-Christian." "There is too much treason in the United States." Why, it was easy for the communists to "fool the very elect" in the churches, she declared; and cited the Presbyterian, Lutheran, and Baptist denominations as getting their material from subversive sources. "They're such wonderful people to be confused," the lady confusingly added. Modern education to her is a plot for inculcating world-mindedness at the cost of the three R's; among the plotters—the National Education Association, the late John Dewey and, of course, the archvillains, the UN in general, and UNESCO in particular. Mrs. Payne made repeated references to "this Christian nation"; and once, at a pitch of exasperation, she asked, "Is this a Christian nation or isn't it?" Someone in the audience shouted, "It *was!*"

Florence Fowler Lyons, of Los Angeles, who has been a leader in the fight to ban use of UNESCO material from the California schools.—Ingeniously defining UNESCO, the "United Nations Espionage, Sabotage and Corruptive Organization" and "devil loose in the world," she grimly asserted that many of the nation's best-known leaders were participating in a "national brainwash" to prepare for U.S. entry "into this permanent international snakepit."

C. O. Garshwiler.—He alleged that the use of UNESCO-influenced textbooks were having terrible effects in California schools. The introduction of one such text had increased the unmarried pregnancy rate in Chico, California, he claimed. (Even the most discerning observers were unable to understand the connection.)

Mrs. Mary D. Cain, of Summit, Mississippi, publisher of the Summit *Sun,* and founder of Individuals for Liberty.—Urged that the U.S. get out of the UN, repeal the Sixteenth Amendment, elect Governor J. Bracken Lee, of Utah, President, and "get back to sane government and decent presidents."

4   The Reactionaries

Freda Utley, author, lecturer.—"The UN was conceived in sin." The basis was Yalta. In Korea, we were not allowed to win, she charged, by the UN Command. UN's only function is to deliver the weak to the strong. The very people who supported intervention in 1942, she declared, now support the UN and withdrawal from the responsibility to fight communism. We should show our strength rather than just talk peace, she said, adding that through the UN we are losing our honor as well as our security.[2]

Joseph Zack Kornfeder, former member of the International Secretariat of the Communist Party.—He maintained that the UN, a child of the New Deal and communism, was organized as a communist political weapon, and that the non-governmental agencies included all the old communist fronts, now designed as "an ideal setup for creating internal warfare." On the home front, he contended, the U. S. National Labor Relations Board had been led by secret communists.

Thomas H. Werdel, former U.S. congressman from California.—He deplored the lack of a free press, stating that the CIO Newspaper Guild controlled the editorial and reportorial staffs of eighty-five per cent of newspapers. The Rockefeller Foundation, which he said helped promote Fabian socialism, and the Supreme Court, for its decision on segregation, were among Mr. Werdel's targets for attack. The decision, he suggested, is "not evolution but revolution." The real America, he said, can be found in the archives of the thirteen colonies. "Ninety-eight per cent of the Founding Fathers were Christians." He also attacked President Eisenhower.

These, then, were the symposium reports submitted on the resolutions which were proposed for adoption.

Almost all of the ten resolutions, voted on, and unanimously approved urged in one way or another that the United States should withdraw from the UN and from all participation in the financing of its agencies, and should order the UN headquarters moved from this country.

[2] Miss Utley later visited the Washington, D.C., offices of the Anti-Defamation League to state that she had been appalled by the anti-Semitic nonsense which she detected all around her during her stay at the sessions.

| Cross-Currents in America

One resolution proposed that Memorial Day be renamed "The Day of Shame," and rebuked President Eisenhower for not bringing more pressure to release the American fliers held prisoner in Communist China. The resolution urged that Americans wear signs of mourning, display their flags at half staff, and send postcards to the White House with the word "shame" on them.

Another resolution, denouncing UNESCO, called for an end to "Dean Achesonizing our children" in the public schools; it termed UNESCO "the main transmission belt" for the "communist one-world movement."

The Congress re-elected Robert LeFevre as executive director and Willis Carto, of San Francisco, secretary.

Carto declared on a local radio station that he was privileged to name as the Congress' sponsors Lieutenant General Albert C. Wedemeyer, Lieutenant General George Stratemeyer, Major General Sumter L. Lowry, Richard Lloyd Jones, and Colonel Alvin Owsley. (General Wedemeyer is a member of the national policy committee of the isolationist group, For America. General Stratemeyer is chairman of the pro-McCarthy group, Ten Million Americans Mobilizing for Justice. General Lowry has been a leader in a movement to have Congress dissolve UNESCO. General Stratemeyer and Colonel Owsley have both plugged John Beaty's anti-Semitic book, *The Iron Curtain over America*.)

The Congress, prior to the current convention, expanded its directorship and obtained for its National Advisory Committee such anti-Semites as Robert Donner, of Colorado Springs, Colorado, and Merwin K. Hart. Richard Lloyd Jones, publisher of the Tulsa (Oklahoma) *Tribune,* was also added to the committee.

The foyer of the Veterans Memorial Auditorium, where most of the convention sessions were held, was lined with literature set on tables, some free, some for sale. They included:

Joseph Kamp's *Headlines,* April 5, 1955, issue, a 28-page attack on the American Jewish Committee, the Anti-Defamation League of B'nai B'rith, and other Jewish organizations. This sold well.

Frank B. Ohlquist's tract, *The United Nations Is Treason,* which in

4 The Reactionaries

its opening sentences characterizes the UN as "the most diabolical scheme ever hatched by the International Rothschild bankers."
Merwin K. Hart's *Economic Council Letter*.
Literature of Myron Fagan.
Literature of the Californians for the Bricker Amendment.
Periodicals of the Minute Women of the U.S.A., Inc.
The right-wing magazine, *The Freeman*.
On the whole, the Congress' week-long deliberations got small coverage in the national and local press, and the convention's impact, for the present at least, amounts to something less than a tremor, even in San Francisco. It is evident, however, that the men and women who participated in these meetings do not mean to be quiet, with or without the Congress of Freedom, or to withdraw their influence, whatever it may be, during the 1956 elections.

Many of the irresponsible accusations against American public education stem from the very sources which traditionally agitate against the Democratic Party, the United Nations, the Eisenhower Administration, civil rights, civil liberties, and social progress in general.

Opposition to broad social change is the essential motivation of these groups; and in the area of public education they merely translate their philosophy into specific arguments against the changing methods of teaching.

The issue is a simple one. Education in America is grounded in democratic doctrine; and these critics would frustrate, if possible, every effort to develop techniques and experiences in the educational system which might give meaning to the principles of democracy.

Bigoted assaults on the nation's educational practices came first as part of the same hysteria that engendered mccarthyism. For example: in October 1950, in Englewood, New Jersey, the local branch of the American Association for the United Nations was celebrating UN Week with an open meeting at the Roosevelt School. As the principal speaker was being introduced, a man in the audience interrupted. He said his name was Frederick G. Cartwright and he demanded to be

1 Cross-Currents in America

heard. He had something to say about a speaker originally scheduled for the meeting—not, mind you, about the man being introduced. The original speaker, Cartwright said, was a "suspected Russian agent."

Cartwright had a claque with him; he read a prepared speech, cheered on by his followers. Police intervened and Cartwright was charged with disorderly conduct. As he was being led away a firecracker exploded, a girl became hysterical—and UN Week in Englewood was off to a bad start.

Before his trial Cartwright—a $200 contributor to Allen Zoll's National Council for American Education—demanded an investigation "into the activities and possible Communistic ties of some of the teachers in the Englewood public schools." The judge found Cartwright "not guilty," but deplored his behavior.

By that time Cartwright had an Englewood Anti-Communist League in operation; tension began to build up in the community. Cartwright and two of his associates went before the Board of Education and told of cases in which teachers were alleged to have communist sympathies. A long inquiry was opened by School Superintendent Harry L. Stearns, and Cartwright appeared as a material witness. He was not an impressive one. Rambling on disjointedly, he attacked textbooks which he admitted he had never read. The board, finding his charges were based on insubstantial hearsay, exonerated the teachers of "any implication of subversive activity."

Many equally unnecessary situations were fabricated in communities across the nation by similarly unenlightened men and women: in Oregon—Eugene and Portland; in Colorado—Colorado Springs and Denver; in California—Santa Monica, Antelope Valley, and Pasadena; also in Detroit, Minneapolis, Scarsdale, New York, Columbus, Ohio, and other places. After meticulous searching, the verdict—"no implications of subversive activity"—was always the same, although the outcome was not. In Pasadena, Dr. Willard Goslin, characterized by Time magazine as "one of the nation's ablest educators," was sacrificed to avoid further annoyance from the agitators.

The purpose of their sniping—to judge by results—is to emasculate good education, not to correct the bad. It bears no reasonable relation-

4 The Reactionaries

ship to the critical questioning of knowledgeable educators or informed observers. Never seriously analytic about the complexities of modern education, the snipers offer only elementary arguments: schools do not teach properly; schools cost too much money; schools overflow with "frills and fads."

Daily reports which have reached us from many authoritative sources lead us to these conclusions about the troublemakers' contentions: to "teach properly" means to teach only according to the narrow, nationalistic, anti-democratic standards of those who are attacking. The argument that "schools cost too much money," in the face of the scandalous, nationwide shortages of school buildings, equipment, and personnel, is merely bait for the taxpayer. "Frills and fads" is a slick euphemism for all educational projects designed to improve intercultural relations, interfaith understanding, and the students' appreciation of democracy.

Ignorant of teaching facts, the narrow-minded refuse to hear the truth. This makes it easier to charge that the schools attach too little importance to the teaching of American history, that the need for teaching moral and spiritual values is ignored, that children are permitted to "run wild" in classrooms, and that teachers are seizing responsibilities ordinarily reserved for the parents and home.

The organizations through which the reactionaries operate against American public education are different from those we have previously described. But the faces are the same even if the agencies have new titles. Not too well camouflaged by National Council for American Education is smooth-talking Allen Zoll, for example, whose only experience in the field consists of soliciting contributions for his work from men and women who once participated in the learning process when they undertook their formal if not effective education.

To get an idea how these agencies interlock with the isolationist and other propaganda movements, run down the list of some leaders in Allen Zoll's Council. Zoll, of course, is active in nearly every group in the field. Grace L. H. Brosseau, vice-president of his Council, holds the same position in Ten Million Americans. Jessica Paine, another Zoll vice-president, was a speaker at the San Francisco convention of the Congress of Freedom. Mrs. David D. Good, a member of the Council's

| Cross-Currents in America

Board of Governors, was actively associated with Ten Million Americans. J. H. Gipson, Verne Kaub, and Charles A. Macauley, all on Zoll's advisory committee, are also board members of the Congress of Freedom; in addition, Macauley is a member of TMA. Robert Donner, who agreed to be a member of Zoll's board so long as his name did not appear on the letterhead, is an executive committee member of the Congress of Freedom and, like Zoll himself, active in most of the other groups. And so on down the line.

Another imposing (in length of name) organization which has bedeviled American education calls itself the Committee on Education of the Conference of American Small Business Organizations. This group purports to evaluate textbooks and supplementary teaching materials in the public schools, "especially those dealing with American history and social sciences." But a perusal of its official publication, the Educational Reviewer, reveals that its guiding genius is none other than Lucille Cardin Crain.

In the vanguard, too, are such agencies as the National Laymen's Church League of America which operates from Chicago. Under the leadership of George Washington Robnett, an advertising executive with a convincing record of anti-minority-group activity, the League has upset one educational leader after another. When not occupied with the problems of public education, Robnett has spent his time plugging the books of the notorious Elizabeth Dilling; corresponding with Joseph P. Kamp; addressing the Citizens USA Committee; dubbing the Anti-Defamation League a destructive "gestapo"; or writing such pamphlets as Can We Preserve Our American System in the Post-war World? which Gerald Smith offered as a premium to prospective members of his own organization.

Also to be included are such agencies as the American Education Association, headed by retired Brooklyn, New York, high school principal Milo F. McDonald, and Friends of the Public Schools of America, led by Major General (Ret.) Amos Fries, of Washington, D.C. McDonald's point of view is suggested by the invitations he has extended to Upton Close and Allen Zoll to be featured speakers on the platform of his organization. Fries's magazine, Friends of the Public Schools,

4 The Reactionaries

somehow concentrates its fire on Catholics for alleged violation of the principle of church-state separation.

Of a piece with these agencies and the nation-wide war they are waging are myriad smaller groups which carry the campaign on the local level. Local Pro America chapters appointing themselves judges of the "subversive" content of textbooks, are typical. And Zoll's agency, which has emerged as the leading group in the field, also acts as the main connecting link to the professional bigots in the non-educational world.

The opponents of modern education were given a tremendous congressional lift in 1954 when Representative B. Carroll Reece (Tenn.) succeeded in re-creating a committee to investigate tax-exempt philanthropic and educational organizations. On the pretext that he would determine whether the large American foundations were using their huge resources for subversive or un-American activities, he issued a "preliminary report" even before his committee began its deliberations, charging that millions of dollars were being spent in the furtherance of an alien educational philosophy.

Congressman Reece never gave an aggrieved foundation or educational agency a chance to appear before his committee to defend itself; but he did welcome foundation critics. Because of the chairman's fantastic prejudgments and the thoroughly arbitrary manner of his one-sided inquiry, the Reece Committee discredited itself in any informed section of public opinion. Not, however, before the Tennessee legislator had welcomed to his congressional forum a selection of his own adherents, adherents with whom we are not unfamiliar.

Aaron Sargent was one of the witnesses; and his testimony is typical of the grade of thought Reece wanted to authenticate with the seal of the United States Congress. Sargent, a West Coast attorney and local leader in the Sons of the American Revolution, is a man with strange ideas. He blandly testified before the committee that teachings based on the philosophy of John Dewey, and supported by tax-exempt foundations, were subversive. These teachings, he declared, "as early as

| Cross-Currents in America

1892" sought to establish *"the federal income tax in order to pave the way for national federal socialism."*

This and similarly wild statements (*"The history of this [foundation] movement is a record of the greatest betrayal that ever occurred in American history"*) were perhaps more appropriate for back-alley rallies than for a congressional hearing. But Sargent had an appreciative audience. Present when he testified were Mrs. P. de Shishmareff of the Christian Patriotic Rally, Nancy Applewhite of the Militant Christian Patriots, Nagene Campbell Bethune of the Guardians of Our American Heritage, and Robert Donner, long a bright light among bigots.

During the proceedings Chairman Reece had words of great praise for the lady patriots. Quid pro quo, he received a petition protesting the "insolence" of Congressman Wayne Hays, of Ohio, his co-committeeman, who, objecting to Reece's tactics and views, was also unprepared to accept Sargent's contentions as gospel. The petition was submitted jointly by the Christian Patriotic Rally, Christian Parents for Better Education, the California League of Christian Parents, and United Christian Action.

The antics of B. Carroll Reece and the frenzied warriors against public education create but another skirmish in the continuing struggle between the mainstream of American thought and a secondary trend which periodically throughout our history has challenged and sought to halt the progress of that mainstream as it courses toward the fulfillment of the promise of American democracy. The secondary stream harbors the elements of reaction. It, too, was born with the Republic and has ever since tried to replace the dominant tradition. Such reaction has been mirrored in the Alien and Sedition Acts of the John Adams Administration, the Know-Nothing movements of the mid-nineteenth century, the hate movements of the latter part of that century, and, in our own time, the efforts to limit the development of civil rights and the spread of economic benefits to all of the people as the country grows and prospers.

Each upsurge of democratic growth brings with it efforts to turn progress into regression.

CROSS-CURRENTS
IN GERMANY

II

One   The Nazi Diehards

The cataclysms of its recent history, its geographical position straddling two worlds, make Germany an arena where all that is performed takes on an immediate international significance. We say "performed" advisedly; their position has made the Germans as conscious of their present role as a power in the world game as they once were of their Germanizing mission.

On December 3, 1954, the West German Supreme Court dismissed all charges against a Dr. Werner Naumann and seven associates. They were accused of plotting a Nazi comeback. The case was dropped for "lack of evidence."

Anyone reading the news reports of this dismissal must have been struck by the Court's fairly unique definition of "lack of evidence." Although, it was declared, there was "sufficient suspicion" that the prisoners, and Dr. Naumann in particular, had advocated "National Socialist and unconstitutional ideas," the Court was unable to "find beyond reasonable doubt that these efforts have been successful." Which is almost like saying: had the prisoners succeeded in restoring a Nazi regime, they would be guilty (though then, of course, not liable to prosecution); since they were not successful, they are found not guilty (though temporarily liable to prosecution).

II   Cross-Currents in Germany

When the reader of the news item goes on to discover that Dr. Naumann was former State Secretary in Goebbels' Propaganda Ministry, and that he intends to appeal the denazification sentence barring him from all political activity, he is quite likely to find himself asking some vexing questions.

The position of the Court is that the leaders of a small, neo-Nazi party, the German Reichs Party, are too inconsequential an influence to be punished for attempting to exercise that influence. Naumann's acquittal, therefore, taken at face value, amounts to a legal judgment that Naumann was ineffective. That he should interpret it as an opening to demand legal restitution of political rights, enabling him to broaden the influence he has just been acquitted for not having, shows a confidence in his personal prestige far beyond mere play acting.

What is the basis of Naumann's self-confidence? What are the extent and nature of his contacts mentioned in the press, and do they in any way explain this self-confidence? *The same news report also speaks of plans to penetrate the government coalition parties. Is there any evidence that this penetration has to any extent been accomplished? These are all questions an interested reader might ask after pondering the given facts.*

A widely publicized incident had taken place in Berlin two weeks earlier. The incident, marked by the grubby hysteria reminiscent of Nazi days, probably cannot be considered an answer to the question, but it certainly makes the asking of it extremely pertinent. This is what happened:

The Berlin section of the German Party, a member of the Adenauer coalition, called a large meeting to be held in the Sportpalast, which was, coincidentally, the scene of many Third Reich victory celebrations. Many German students came to observe, and the press, naturally, was there too. "Deutschland über alles" was sung. The official West German anthem begins with the third stanza, thus avoiding the line in the first, "Germany, Germany, over all in the world," which is too obviously tinged with Third Reich plans and sentiments to make it palatable to even the mildest anti-Nazis.

But the rally sang the anthem from its beginning; and two foreign newspapermen and a number of students did not join in. Their silence, a relatively passive demonstration at most, was soon noticed by the

1 The Nazi Diehards

omnipresent uniformed guards, who rushed down the aisles screaming insults at them, and quickly and none too gently threw them out.

A degree of excited feeling is always cultivated at large rallies. Sensitive nationalistic feeling, even to the point of violence, is almost predictable in a defeated country; predictable if not condonable. That these reporters and students were ejected to shouts of "You seem to have escaped the gas chambers," and "It's time you were sent back to the concentration camps," is another matter.

If such hatreds have survived the collapse of the Third Reich, it argues a survival so effective and widespread as to make the very existence of an official neo-Nazi party almost unnecessary. Unnecessary and possibly compromising to the long-term plans the neo-Nazi politicians harbor. Clearly, even a fully documented answer to the last question must raise others more difficult.

Anti-Semitism can hardly be an important political weapon now because of the sad fact that there simply are not enough Jews left in Germany to make attacking them worth while. Not for the moment and perhaps not ultimately. Incidents like the above bring quick reactions, if only for the reason that the German government is very alive to foreign opinion; and Die Deutsche Warte, *official organ of the German Party, was quickly banned by the American occupation authorities after the rally.* But the German societies for Christian-Jewish friendship also warned that extreme nationalism was on the rise in West Germany, that anti-Semites were reorganizing, that anti-Jewish publications were increasing, and that the courts were becoming too lenient in sentencing the initiators of anti-Semitic drives. Which brings us back to Dr. Werner Naumann.

For the time being, the German Reichs Party and most of the other neo-Nazi splinter groups are avoiding SS anti-Semitic hooliganism. It could, for one thing, bring them the sort of attention that the authorities would be forced to act upon; it might well, for another, uncomfortably remind too many Germans of what they would probably like to avoid thinking clearly about, a gap in their midst—the absence of Jews who left Germany, dead Jews. How long Naumann's discretion will continue depends, obviously, on whether such reserve is part of his program or merely a temporary political expedient. Anti-Semitism may not be an important political weapon, but its value as a con-

II Cross-Currents in Germany

veniently gaudy signpost to guide the dispersed fascist elements to each other must not be underestimated.

Let us take our interested reader's first questions and amplify them in the light of the subsequent discussion. Do the nature and extent of Naumann's contacts in Germany and abroad throw any light on how much he intends to revive of extreme nationalist theories and practices? *And* Is the nationalist extremism that seems to taint even the respectable German parties evidence of neo-Nazi penetration, or does it have its roots in the common recruiting ground of all the parties, the German people? *Lastly, and the first question we shall deal with:* How large a factor does anti-Semitism remain in German political and social life?

Let us turn to our files.

DECEMBER 20, 1954
AF to BRE

The attached folder contains a series of memoranda in chronological order, the first one dated June 12, 1953. They are selected to give as complete a picture as we can of the background to Naumann's acquittal.

I think that any questions you have asked about that acquittal are dealt with in the enclosed material. If any aspects of the story do not seem sufficiently detailed to you, we will try to supplement it with additional memoranda from our files.

JUNE 12, 1953
AF to BRE

Here is an extract from a memorandum of one of our German correspondents: Several winters ago, twenty years after they had fled Germany, their native country, Nina Straub's parents returned. Nina, an attractive girl of nineteen who returned with them, was herself a native Israeli, but spoke German without trace of accent.

1 The Nazi Diehards

The family had had some difficulty adjusting itself to Israel. In spite of the circumstances under which he had left, Germany remained home to Mr. Straub. He had been a successful furniture manufacturer in Berlin, and had hopes of regaining his property and rebuilding his life. He died soon after returning. Nina remained; she now has temporary employment and attends the University of Berlin.

She recounted her story to me with almost ironic equanimity and with a great show of detachment. Here it is:

"I came to Berlin more than willing to make it my home. You see, I had always been impressed with German family life—the solidarity, the neatness, the discipline. Perhaps what I was seeing was merely an idealized and multiplied image of my parents; I don't know. Yet even as a little girl the tidiness of individual Germans fascinated me.

"The first few months in Berlin were bleak, but my loneliness vanished when I met Johann. He was young and charming, and he made me laugh. Johann had spent two years in the States, but his character had been essentially fixed by a rigid family discipline. To me I suppose he was in many ways the typical German I had so long imagined and admired. Friendship became love; we were engaged.

"One evening Johann introduced me to his parents at dinner, and later we went to some public hall to become acquainted with a number of his young relatives. Johann's father, who had been a minor, unpolitical Nazi, and had amassed a fortune in wholesale groceries, boomingly informed me that he had done business with Jews over many years and that he was free of prejudice. However, he added that he objected to our marriage because it would arouse hostility among their relatives. He also expressed extreme concern over any children we might have, saying that they would be unnatural.

"That was the exact word—unnatural. I remember being both shocked and even slightly amused at this. But Johann was neither; and his father was quite serious. His mother had been hostile to me almost from the start; she spat her words out at me rather than spoke them. Eventually his father himself reached the point where he threatened to disown him if he married me, a Jewish girl.

"Poor Johann, with almost painful humility, pleaded with me to

II Cross-Currents in Germany

understand, to understand that his father would remove him from a well-paying job and take his automobile away. A docile boy, Johann. Domesticated. And so many pressures. The relatives had been brusque, cold, insulting; his sister-in-law had refused to speak to me. After twenty years, after a world war, it was plain that a Jew was a stranger here.

"One of the university professors of engineering was friendly. A scholarly man with a broad range of learning, he seemed stunned when I told him I intended to marry a German. Always polite, it was with the utmost courtesy that he expressed his opposition to such a union. It was bound to be unhappy, he explained, and would produce emotionally disturbed children. His tone was courteous; his meaning was clear. It burned.

"It may seem strange to you. It seems strange to me now; but I was in love and I would have married Johann even then if he had insisted. He didn't. He was afraid, afraid of losing family privileges and comforts; so it ended. Johann and I are still friends; we see each other occasionally. Friends . . .

"To augment my negligible income, I began studying bookkeeping at a school. The students there seemed friendly for a time. Then, during the Berlin Conference, there was a three-minute pause for silent prayer. The teacher said, 'This, of course, doesn't include you, Miss Straub.' That began it; from that time on, there was no letup. The students refused to collaborate on bookkeeping projects with me; when I asked a question in German, they pretended not to understand. How long can you stand being detested? I dropped the course after several weeks.

"I used to enjoy going to dances, and whenever I mentioned there that I was an Israeli people were curious. Then hostile.

"I shall never forget the time my landlady had a dispute with one of her tenants. Although she now depends on Jewish patronage for her livelihood, she nevertheless blurted out, 'Those damn Jews!' Her daughter was openly anti-Semitic. She took pride in her hatred, and once boasted that she would not even discuss the weather with a Jew.

"I'd say I've found a moderate amount of interest here in Israel, and

1 The Nazi Diehards

a moderate amount of anti-Semitism. Occasionally one meets a German who is really venomous about Jews in general and Israelis in particular. Some sound as though they're mimicking the Arab propagandist. I've never met a German who admits to having been an active Nazi, nor one who accepts the slightest responsibility for what happened to the Jews.

"I came to Germany full of hope and eagerness. I am leaving soon."

JUNE 19, 1953
Library to BRE

Here is another report from Germany. Along with the Nina Straub story, it will give a personalized picture of certain postwar German attitudes. It is excerpted from a 1951 survey by one of our correspondents and quotes an important jurist.

"The judge is about sixty and lives in Frankfurt. Both he and his father's family are Christian; his mother was Jewish. Two members of her family died of Nazi maltreatment. He himself continued to practice law in Frankfurt under the Nazi regime into the early 1940s; but, having been secretly informed that he was about to be arrested, fled into hiding for the balance of the war.

"He is one of the principal jurists assigned to 'restitution of Jewish property' cases. In this high legal post he associates with many of the same people he did before the war. Although some of these had been pronounced Jew-baiters, he says that he now experiences no overt prejudice personally. In fact, known anti-Semites show him a studied politeness and consideration. He thinks this is partly out of guilt, and partly to make amends. Not that he believes that these bigots have really gotten rid of their underlying hatreds, but that they recognize that showing them does neither their country nor themselves any good."

II Cross-Currents in Germany

JUNE 29, 1953
German Correspondent to AF

You inquire about what significance should be attached to stories like Nina Straub's. I have sent you many similar since 1945. They are, in the main, accounts of unhappy attempts at readjustment. Widespread as their occurrence is, well defined as they are, it is best to remember that they do not illuminate the central issues in Germany today. Anti-Semitism, hidden or overt, obviously exists, but if you ask me what most Germans think about Jews, I would have to answer that most of them don't think about Jews at all; they are too preoccupied with rebuilding their own lives and fortunes.

People outside Germany can have no idea how all-consuming this drive for material security is. And after the personal problem, the East-West struggle for strategic control of the country is the paramount subject of thought. With foreign armies facing each other in a divided nation, in Berlin only a hand-grenade-throw apart, few politically minded Germans consider any other problem nearly so grave or pressing.

JULY 1, 1953
Press Department to BRE

The following summation of an incident that took place in Verden, Germany, last winter should certainly be added to any material you gather on German thinking.

Verden, in the British Zone, was a garrison town under Hitler. It was, therefore, an all too appropriate place to choose for a welfare organization reunion—that is, for a welfare organization made up of veterans of the Waffen-SS, the Nazi Party shock troops. Today they are naturally in civilian clothes; they were labeled a criminal organization at Nuremberg.

1 The Nazi Diehards

The reason this little alumni club exists is, one might say, plausible, even sentimental—to care for those in their ranks who survived and to locate lost comrades. The reunion, their first since the war, brought five thousand men to Verden. Mufti-clad, they marched through the cramped, flag-bedecked streets to the rally with all their famous and former military precision.

Major General Hermann Bernhard Ramcke, an ex-paratroop commander who, though never a member of the SS, had managed to make an impressive record as a war criminal, was guest speaker. His style in public speaking, obviously based on the more illustrious style of his former Fuehrer, was just as obviously aimed at rousing similar responses. He got them. "Who are the war criminals?" Ramcke screamed. And he answered his own question: "They are those who destroyed German towns like Dresden . . . who dropped the atom bomb on Nagasaki and Hiroshima!" From the audience came shouts of "Eisenhower *Schweinehund.*" And back at them came Ramcke with vilifications of the Allied wartime leaders.

SS Generals Herbert Gille and Felix Steiner, who had organized the reunion and would be held personally responsible for its repercussions, frantically tried to stop the tirade. But Ramcke and the SS veterans had gotten completely out of hand. A furious and all too familiar hysteria had been worked up and could not be curbed.

The Bonn government and the West German press were unified in their castigation of the rally. Its organizers quickly disavowed Ramcke's statements, and denied that he in any way reflected the principles and political beliefs of their society.

The incident was reported and analyzed in the world press. The London *Economist,* a conservative British periodical which had supported West German rearmament, called the events at the rally a warning signal, and said, summing up the general reactions:

> Former SS men find it safe to be proud of belonging to that organization, for the grave reason that German public opinion has never faced the truth about it. . . . It is this forgetfulness . . . that can still corrupt and wreck democracy in the Federal Republic. . . .

II Cross-Currents in Germany

Others found clear evidence in the incident that seven years of denazification had been of little consequence. To some it gave the impression of accurately reflecting an important facet of current German mentality. It was not to be forgotten, they pointed out, that except for a few hundred Nazi war criminals still in jail the majority of Nazis—all the other party members—who had undergone denazification proceedings were back in circulation.[1]

JULY 2, 1953
Library to BRE

A survey was completed this January by the U. S. High Commissioner's Office in Germany to determine rightist and nationalist sentiment in West Germany. Two tests were used: the attitude toward war criminals and that toward restitution of Jewish property.

Opinions were solicited on (1) General Ramcke's statements that the German war criminals roster was really an "Honor Roll" and (2) that the real criminals were the Allies who had bombed German women and children. The poll-takers found that 31% of those questioned said he was right; 25% thought he was at least partly right; and 25% thought he was wrong.

On the restitution question, a vast majority of those surveyed believed that the Germans need feel neither guilt for the persecution of the Jews under Hitler nor responsibility for righting these wrongs. Two out of three thought the Federal Parliament should reject the West German-Israeli restitution agreement.

On the subject of the possible restoration of a Nazi regime, 24% of those questioned declared they would do everything in their power to prevent it; 13% avowed they would actively seek such a return; 12% had no opinion; and an additional 26% said they would not like a return of the Nazis but would not do anything to prevent it; 25% said they "did not care."

---

[1] Just one month later *Time* magazine made the following summation: "Since 1949, a million ex-Nazis have been re-enfranchised. A dozen pennywhistle Fuehrers are after their votes."

1 The Nazi Diehards

Even among the young (who had shown a strong desire for Europeanization and for a better understanding of Germany abroad) there was now a strong desire for a "single strong national party which really represents the interests of all our people." Of those polled, the majority were in favor of unrestricted political and business opportunities for former Nazi Party members; and a minority favored giving such opportunities even to former Nazi leaders.

JULY 2, 1953
Library to BRE

With respect to the survey statistics that we sent you earlier today, you should be reminded that their unexpected release some months ago provoked a considerable uproar in Germany. Chancellor Adenauer protested the survey, saying that it was "not a true reading" of the West German mind and that its conclusions were false. He insisted there was no serious or immediate threat to democratic government from resurgent Nazism. It was reasonable to expect that the Bonn government would minimize the significance of findings that put German public opinion in so unfavorable a light.

Most West German newspapers also disputed the conclusions.

In any case, the pro-Nazi sentiment revealed in the poll is not evident in the now developing West German election campaign.

JULY 2, 1953
Research to AF

On January 14, 1953, six once prominent Nazis were arrested by the British authorities in West Germany. One of them was Dr. Werner Naumann, an importer-exporter who had been an SS captain and an Undersecretary of State in Dr. Goebbels' Ministry of Propaganda. Although no specific charges were filed against him, it was announced that Naumann was involved in a conspiracy threatening the security of the state. At the time it was rumored that Naumann was the author, under a pen name, of a long series of anti-government articles, and that he was the "discussion leader" of a secret political group.

Today we received from the Wiener Library in London a detailed memorandum based on the impounded documents in the case. The following charges, unknown to us before, had been made:

1. Naumann and his associates had been plotting to regain power in Western Germany.

2. They had set up a plan, already in effect, to have their followers infiltrate the three established German political parties. Naumann's greatest success in this plan was his helping secure the post of personal secretary and political adviser to the chief of the Free Democratic Party for an intimate friend of his, Wolfgang Diewerge. Diewerge is a former SS colonel, a violent Jew-baiter, and had been a high official in the Nazi Propaganda Ministry.

3. Naumann's group had "pulled wires" designed to capture control of several ex-soldiers' organizations.

4. By careful planning, Naumann has established working friendships among Gauleiterkreis (district leaders).

5. Naumann was in regular, secret communication with many camouflaged factions in extreme right-wing, nationalist groups.

6. Naumann's group had developed a very real influence over the content of *Nation Europa,* a monthly journal of the fascist international. Its editor, Dr. Arthur Ehrhardt, accepted political instructions from Naumann.

Included among the impounded documents was Naumann's diary, which discloses that his present political activities are the result of three years of planning. In the summer of 1950, Naumann talked with the Nazi sculptor, Arno Breker; then reported in his diary:

Of course Breker urges caution. I should not let things drift. He says that of all the people he knew only one was really able to master the situation, and that was I. According to him, I was able to put forward ideas which would adopt the good things of the past and add what the new times required. I should withdraw to a quiet place and work it all out. He is also convinced that only young, new forces can do it. He

1   The Nazi Diehards

advises against using Guderian. Such people were merely a handicap. His demands weigh heavily on my mind, and I have grave doubts whether I shall be able to fulfill his expectations.

In August 1950, Naumann wrote in his diary:

In order to influence political events, the National Socialists shall join the Free Democratic Party, swamp it and take over the leadership.

Another significant entry was made by Naumann in 1950:

You cannot betray an ideal in which you believed from your early days as I have done. Maybe the ruins of the Reich Chancellory hold for us greater values than are dreamed of by rash critics.

As you can see, the evidence, mostly attitude and intent, is not legally the most convincing possible. Let's wait and see what overt acts, if any, come to light.

JULY 3, 1953
Library to AF

Werner Naumann became a member of the Nazi Party in 1928 at the age of nineteen and remained consistently loyal. In command of the Wilhelmplatz Battalion guarding Hitler, he was in the bunker with him when the end came. For nearly six months previously he had actually directed Goebbels' ministry. As a reward for this, Hitler, before his suicide, appointed Naumann to the Doenitz cabinet as a Reich Minister, and nominated him to be Goebbels' successor in his will.

Together with Martin Bormann, and Reich Youth leader Axmann, Naumann escaped from the Reich Chancellory on May 2, 1945. The Russians picked him up but, unaware of his identity, released him; and nothing more was heard of him until 1950, when he appeared in Düsseldorf. Apparently he had waited all that time for the passage of a general amnesty law which would save him from trial as a war criminal.

During his disappearance, he was in the Soviet Zone, and later in the Western Zone, working under an alias as a bricklayer.

II Cross-Currents in Germany

JULY 7, 1953
AF to BRE

From what we know of him, Werner Naumann is a potentially serious figure on the German political scene; he is one of the few top-echelon Nazis free to operate, and he is still comparatively young. He may not at the moment make much impact on the German community, but we have been informed that he is one of the few men in Germany with the leadership qualities and statesmanship necessary to guide an effective fascist movement. Nor should we forget that he has had top-level protocol experience.

Present obscurity is no guarantee against future success; Hitler was far more obscure in 1919 when he and seven followers formed the National Socialist German Workers Party.

I have suggested that one of our German correspondents be assigned to look more thoroughly into his story. We will try to learn whether he has American contacts. Whether he has collaborators elsewhere.

Background material will be submitted to you.

JULY 15, 1953
German Correspondent to AF

Will submit reports as requested on Naumann from time to time. You should realize, by the way, that Naumann is not the only leader in the neo-Nazi movement. One of his important behind-the-scenes mentors is Wilhelm Meinberg. For the present, here are some more facts on Naumann himself.

Until his arrest in January, Naumann's group had been operating secretly and had avoided the more violently outspoken neo-Nazi parties; but since his release from jail some weeks ago, Naumann has been active with the German Reichs Party. Openly.

Two other items: this particular movement that Naumann has asso-

1 The Nazi Diehards

ciated himself with is the first postwar extreme nationalist clique that has the support of Germans prominent in public affairs and the professions. And: Naumann came out of hiding at a time when the neo-Nazis began a serious search for a new leader.

He has important qualifications for the job or, if you wish, role. In his early forties, capable of intense concentration, thrifty of word, using only carefully selected phrases in a quiet, educated way, Naumann has trained himself in the tradition of the intellectual diplomat. The picture is completed by conservative dress and the demeanor of a high Prussian official.

No rabble-rouser could fit as well for what is wanted now.

JULY 17, 1953
German Correspondent to Research

Naumann conducts a profitable import-export business in partnership with Lea Lucht, widow of an old associate in the Propaganda Ministry. Their establishment in Düsseldorf, combining home and business, includes two new substantial brick buildings surrounded by a high wire fence with a sign at the entrance: "The Dog Bites!" There is also a main villa which, in the cabbage-patch landscape, stands out as a luxury dwelling. The villa is furnished in the prosperous German style—oversized rooms filled with overstuffed furniture are further crammed with bronze ornaments and weighted with tapestries.

He has a wife and four children in Stuttgart whom he sees only at rare intervals.

When meeting political visitors, he now is extremely cautious; to Oswald Mosley and other compromising friends, he suggests that they see each other in the American Zone, where surveillance is less political. And where Naumann claims to have some friendly American contacts.

II Cross-Currents in Germany

JULY 18, 1953
German Correspondent to Research

In replying to the conspiracy charge, Werner Naumann displayed his considerable talents before the West German Supreme Court in Karlsruhe. His task was not easy. The neo-Nazis hoped for a courageously lucid apologia for their position. They expect it of a leader. At the same time, Naumann had to guard against damaging admissions that might substantiate the charges against him. His manner was restrained, with the humility of a man being done an injustice so great that he must put aside anger in an effort to understand why such a thing was happening to him. A disarming act. He spoke carefully:

"I stand before you a citizen, trying simply through earnest effort to rebuild his business existence, who can indulge in politics only in his spare time. . . .

"In my small way I have wanted to avoid misleading news items about me in the foreign press which, arousing hostility against us National Socialists, might have endangered Germany's revival even in the slightest way. Also, I have assumed a fair attitude toward those leaders who are responsible for the country, and whose burden I am not eager to share. . . .

"I recognize that I was a faithful worker for the National Socialist state. I did my duty as I saw it up to the last moment. . . . My one wish was that we should not lose the war. . . . My great concern is to block bolshevizing Germany. That consideration outweighs all others. Our leaders must think of the spiritual and biological values of our people. . . . We must make the Western Powers understand that we are all in the same boat. There must never be a coalition as in 1945 [against us]. We must seek to win the sympathies of the West through trustworthiness, through peace and order and hard work. . . .

"There was much of value in the National Socialist thinking. Saying that shouldn't shock anyone. These thoughts were not an invention of Hitler—they existed before and continued after his death. Many rightly share them now, though often under another label. . . .

1 The Nazi Diehards

"I am also charged with wanting to restore the National Socialist system. . . . This is what I really said: 'History does not stand still. There is no repeat performance. We do not want a restoration.' . . ."

AUGUST 2, 1953
German Correspondent to AF

The German Reichs Party has persuaded Werner Naumann to become its titular head.

Wilhelm Meinberg, once a powerful Nazi administrator, is the chief architect of this ultranationalist party which is now aiming to weld together as many of the scattered neo-Nazi splinter groups as it can. He is unknown abroad.

Almost inevitably dressed in tweeds, short and stocky, about sixty-five, Meinberg is what the Germans call a *Kraftmensch*—a strong, tough man, a "go-getter." His bulldog expression accurately reflects his authoritative, assertive, explosive qualities. When he talks, his characteristic staccato Prussian shout is that of a man who expects and gets obedience. Any disagreement provokes an immediate reaction—a flushed face, a lashing violence of vocabulary and manner. At the center of all this immoderate display is the essential Meinberg, a well-to-do farmer with the conservative realism of outlook and moderate hardheadedness typical of his class.

He enjoys great prestige throughout Westphalia, and sees no reason to hide his views. "My outlook on life," he says, "was shaped mainly by the National Socialist Party, by my experiences in two world wars, by two defeats and six years of internment."

Nor has he ever wavered in his conviction of German racial superiority. Nevertheless he has always opposed professional anti-Semitism and expropriation of Jewish property. Never a hero-worshiper, his outspokenness extended even to occasionally criticizing Hitler. Never a dreamer, he scoffs at the mystical jargon of those Nazis who talk of "crusades" and "saving the White Race."

He applies his hard clarity of outlook today to the selection of neo-

II Cross-Currents in Germany

Nazi leaders. Those who do not meet his rigid standards are ousted without ceremony; Naumann has made the grade and won Meinberg's wholehearted support.

AUGUST 3, 1953
AF to Research

Reports are coming in from Germany on the public and secret activities of Werner Naumann. Examine them carefully for hints of domestic contacts. And alert your field men here to be especially on the lookout among the extreme nationalist and anti-Semitic groups for leads to possible American friends of Naumann's.

AUGUST 7, 1953
German Correspondent to Research

Naumann has been chosen by the German Reichs Party as its candidate for the Bundestag from Lower Saxony. Doubtless they consider his arrest good campaign publicity.

The British did not hold Naumann for trial after they suddenly seized him in January. Instead, they detained him for questioning ten weeks and then handed him over to the Bonn government for prosecution. Subsequently he was released by the German authorities, who issued strict orders that he was to be kept under close surveillance. But they could not, of course, prevent him from being news, and from cleverly making capital of it.

Naumann appears to be convinced that neither the British, for all their usual thoroughness, nor the Bonn government can develop a provable case against him. The meticulous avoidance of overt provocative actions typical of himself and his party thus far will, he believes, certainly turn out to have been effective political strategy.

In January, when the British took him in custody, a team of intelligence men raided his Düsseldorf villa, searched everything, and took

1 The Nazi Diehards

away whole cabinets of his papers. But Naumann, though annoyed at this, just smilingly declared that there was nothing that could be termed "compromising," merely business correspondence.

His philosophy, as he expresses it, might, on the other hand, be considered at least compromising by many. He says: "National Socialism is the natural order of the world. Democracy is an attack on this natural order, and therefore an attack on God." He has also declared that National Socialism is the only remedy for "materialism."

The neat restraint of his manner has endeared him to many high-level friends who might possibly be put off by a more bombastic personality in a leader. Or who might think such bombast impolitic at this juncture. Among the "famous" whom he counts as close friends, and who agree with his neo-Nazi thinking, are: Mrs. Pierre Laval, Colonel Otto Skorzeny, Colonel Hans Rudel, and Sir Oswald Mosley.

Patience is another of his winning traits; he always insists that the neo-Nazi movement must be rebuilt slowly and not emerge into open activity "until the right moment." This time they do not mean to make mistakes, to confuse a quick victory with a permanent one. Patience. Restraint. "We Germans," he explains, "should be realistic. We lost two wars to the Jews. Why should we lose another?"

With patience and restraint, you can list dedication.

AUGUST 7, 1953
Library to Research

Here is an outline of the history and setup of the German Reichs Party as well as what we can gauge of its relation to the rest of the German political picture:

Founded in 1948, the German Reichs Party first assumed some degree of importance when it was reorganized in 1951. Its program today follows the usual pattern of European fascist parties, favoring a full-strength German army under its old leadership and a Western Europe governed by the neo-fascists.

Thus far the party has avoided such public activities as might challenge or provoke the Bonn government. The punitive action taken

II Cross-Currents in Germany

against its kindred spirit, the Socialist Reichs Party, outlawed by the government in 1953, has evidently taught it caution.

Although its membership is drawn from all sections of West Germany, the party's main center of activity is in the industrial, rural areas of Upper Rhine-Westphalia. Its major recruiting is done in the more backward Protestant communities where it does not hesitate to play upon anti-Catholic feeling. There is also a great emphasis placed on the recruiting of youthful Germans.

Werner Naumann is now its head; Rudolph von Thadden serves as secretary in charge of foreign relations; Meinberg is its chairman.[2] Under his chairmanship—which is to say, his policy-making and leader selection—the German Reichs Party has already grown into a compact band of more than seven thousand zealots. Their leaders need have no fear about the devotion of these members; they will give an enthusiastic response to any demands of a neo-Nazi brand. The party's aim is to build up a sizable organization ready in perhaps four years' time to test its strength openly.

There are five important parties, four of them in the Adenauer coalition, and one of them, the Social Democratic Party, in the opposition. The German Reichs Party can by no means be labeled one of the larger movements in Western Germany; the majority of citizens today are affiliated with the Christian Democratic Union, the Free Democratic Party, and the Social Democratic Party.

The largest of the parties, the Christian Democratic Union, can be fairly described as made in the image of Adenauer, seeking close ties with the West. Predominantly Catholic, it includes a wide range of opinion, from the orthodox-conservatives—farmers and prosperous businessmen—to Catholic trade union members on the left.

The Free Democratic Party, headed by President Theodor Heuss, can be characterized as liberal-conservative; but it is also infiltrated in several provinces by large numbers of neo-Nazis. This was one of the organizations chosen by Werner Naumann for the placement of his political associates.

---

[2] Meinberg was re-elected chairman of the German Reichs Party on September 25, 1955.

1   The Nazi Diehards

The Christian Democratic Union together with the Free Democratic Party, the All-German Bloc, and the German Party constitute Chancellor Adenauer's coalition. The German Party, strongest in Hanover and in Lower Saxony, is predominantly conservative and agricultural. It is for state rights, a free economy, and strong protection of agriculture. The chairman, Heinrich Hellwege, has accepted the collaboration of some neo-Nazis. The All-German Bloc is the party of the German refugee-expellees from Eastern Europe, now a fifth of the German population. The party is strongly anti-communistic. It has an assortment of extreme nationalists among its members.

The chief opposition party is that of the trade unions, the Social Democratic Party. In its domestic policies it follows pretty much along the traditional lines of other European social democratic parties. It has shown the most consideration for rights of minorities and for restitution to Jews. It has maintained a vigorous anti-Nazi and anti-communist line. However, its foreign policy line has often been old-style nationalistic. A majority of the party leaders favor a neutral East-West role for Germany, placing German unification ahead of coalition with the West.

AUGUST 9, 1953
German Correspondent to Research

It should be realized that the German Reichs Party is not an adequate measure of the neo-Nazi movement's strength, and even less a measure of the extreme nationalist movements getting under way in West Germany. There are more than three hundred big and small groups in this movement. But Werner Naumann, as head of the German Reichs Party, is significant because he today seems to be the one man who can rally most of these small extremist groups to his leadership. Several of the leaders of the eight or so neo-Nazi splinter groups have already indicated that they would be happy to accept this leadership.

II Cross-Currents in Germany

AUGUST 12, 1953
Research to BRE

Initial reports from Germany have already named several of Naumann's foreign links; Sir Oswald Mosley, for one.

Mosley's record of fascist activity dates back as far as Naumann's Nazi Party membership; since 1931, when he organized the British Union of Fascists, his determined espousal of these ideas has been constant. Prior to that, Mosley had been political inconstancy itself, serving in Parliament first as a Tory, then as an Independent, and finally with the Labour Party. After visiting Italy and examining fascism in operation, he found himself. The Mussolini black shirt was adopted as the uniform of his followers; the bolt-of-lightning insignia worn as an arm band was a little adaptation of his own.

At the inception of the movement Mosley's political program was simple and concise—Mussolini-type government, anti-Semitism. There were mass rallies in Hyde Park, parades through the streets of London; and there was occasional violence, especially when they clashed with organized Jewish groups. When the war began, Mosley's ties with Mussolini and Hitler landed him, his wife, Lady Diana, and his first lieutenant, A. Raven Thomson,[3] in jail for the greater part of the war. For the fascist faithful, this only added to their prestige.

At present Mosley's headquarters are in a modest, three-story building on Vauxhall Bridge Road, close to the heart of London. The atmosphere is that of unobtrusive precision, neatness, and dedication, of restrained British bustle; the narrow corridors are no longer crowded, as they had been in recent years, with East End thugs lounging against the walls. There seems to be plenty to do, and the tidy staff goes about getting it done in a purposeful, businesslike way. Even the name of the organization has been tidied up; it is now the Union Movement.

As a type of gentleman fascist, Mosley has much in common with Werner Naumann. It is difficult to assess in either case just how genuine their anti-Semitism is, as Hitler's most certainly was. Before the

---
[3] A. Raven Thomson died on November 8, 1955.

1 The Nazi Diehards

war, at any rate, Mosley's seemed to many observers of the British scene to be a rabble-rousing device rather than a personal conviction. The defeat of fascism in the war, however, may well have intensified an expedient based on prejudice into a hatred based on bitterness. The lesson that the neo-fascist leaders apparently draw from the past is not that they were too brutal but that they were not brutal enough—at the right time and at the right places.

Mosley has devoted the last few years to commuting between England and the Continent, establishing, reworking, and strengthening his contacts. It was with an eye toward this that Mosley has spent much time improving his knowledge of German, so that today he is able to handle the language with facility. His big problem remains resolving the widespread British aversion to everything Nazi. Specifically, one of his main concerns is making his neo-Nazi friends acceptable comrades-in-arms to his British followers, acceptable to the point of enthusiasm. This is basic to all his long-range plans.

This year his plans to visit Germany, particularly to see Naumann, were temporarily canceled at Naumann's sudden arrest, but he intends to go there soon. Surreptitiously, of course.

He also has begun to develop American contacts, a situation that pleases him. "My relations with American officials have been the best, with British officials, the worst," he once remarked. But Mosley's ambitions do not extend to winning over Americans; he simply hopes for a benevolently neutral United States if and when the fascists make an open bid for dominance in western Europe. And he would like to visit the States, perhaps in a year or so.

In the meantime, the important plans continue; the goal is still The Day. And when the day comes, says Mosley, he will be ready, among other things, with his program to put the Jews "in their place."

AUGUST 24, 1953

German Correspondent to Research

Because he had been so long in hiding, Naumann never went through the routine clearance procedure and had no denazification certificate.

Cross-Currents in Germany

After his release from jail, when it became apparent that he seriously intended to seek public office, the Bonn government hurriedly initiated proceedings in the German Denazification Court through the government of North Rhine-Westphalia. Today he was declared a "Category Two" Nazi; he is deprived of civil privileges and barred from engaging in any form of political activity—no right to vote and ineligibility for public office. This of course ends his German Reichs Party candidacy for the Bundestag.

It does not, however, destroy his appeal among Germans already subject to it, nor has it frightened Naumann himself into retreat. He still has many friends in key positions, not only in Bonn, but in public office throughout West Germany. Naturally they have avoided public identification with him since his arrest, but we have no reason to believe they have ceased being friends. What measure of subsequent success he may have can be taken as one yardstick of the German nostalgia for Nazism.

SEPTEMBER 2, 1953
German Correspondent to Research

Here's a lead on some anti-Semitic activity in Germany aided by outside sources.

Last March German police in Hanover and Lüneburg raided the homes of the leaders of the German Rally, a neo-Nazi splinter group banned by the state government of Lower Saxony. They carted away a large collection of Nazi and anti-Semitic literature. The material was assembled in Hanover for official examination, and much of it was found to have been printed in foreign countries, some in the United States.

One of the confiscated pieces was a four-page cartoon pamphlet describing West German co-operation with the United States as "happiness for the Star of David." I have examined it. The cartoon showed West German Chancellor Konrad Adenauer standing in the midst of bomb ruins with former U. S. Secretary George Marshall decorating him with the Star of David. Behind them were grinning caricatures of Stalin and a "Jew." Readers were told to write for more of the same material to the LeBlanc Publishing Co., Box 155, 208 East 86th Street, New York.

SEPTEMBER 7, 1953
Research to AF

The LeBlanc Publishing Co., Box 155, 208 East 86th Street, New York City, is operated by one Frederick Charles Weiss.

SEPTEMBER 7, 1953
Press Department to AF

West Germany's second postwar elections were held yesterday; and the German Reichs Party cannot be said to have done very well. Their total national tally was less than 296,000, a fraction over 1% of the total national vote of 27,541,055. This is an especially poor tally in view of the large number of candidates they put in the field. They won no seats in the Bundestag, the requirement for a seat being 5%.

The Communist Party received 607,413 votes, 2.2% of the total. They, too, failed to win a seat in the Bundestag.

The present trend decidedly favors the moderate business and churchgoing segments of the community.

SEPTEMBER 8, 1953
BRE to National ADL Chairman

At the invitation of the Bonn government's representative in New York City, we have had several informal discussions regarding the feasibility of an on-the-spot Anti-Defamation League study of conditions in Germany. The representative would like us to meet with members of the German mission in Washington. With your approval, I will set up a conference on an agreeable date.

II Cross-Currents in Germany

SEPTEMBER 21, 1953
Research to AF

Frederick Charles Weiss served as a captain of artillery in World War I with the German Army. During World War II he was taken into custody here by the U. S. Immigration authorities, and held on Ellis Island for more than a year.

His father was a prosperous German industrialist, and he himself made a good deal of money selling patents on industrial inventions abroad. However, his substantial resources vanished in the aftermath of World War I.

Since his arrival here Weiss has dabbled in real estate. His main income at present comes from the rentals of an apartment house that he manages in White Plains, New York. He has a farm at Mount Hope, Middletown, New York.

Weiss has never been naturalized. He remains a German citizen.

OCTOBER 14, 1953
Research to AF

Several times during the last few days hundreds of "election" leaflets floated down to the streets around the Empire State Building. We have not been able to determine who dropped them or from where.

The leaflets, mimeographed, are liberally sprinkled with the Star of David and bear the legend: *Vote Jew. We Will Get Our Man in No Matter How You Gentiles Vote.* Above this, in crude caricature, is a hook-nosed "Jew" whose tie clasp is in the shape of a hammer and sickle and who wears two lapel election buttons. One is stamped *Vote Jew;* the other bears a hammer and sickle.

Comparison of the leaflet with various other specimens in our library leads us to believe that this is the work of the National Renaissance Party. We have no proof as yet.

1 The Nazi Diehards

OCTOBER 20, 1953
New York Correspondent to Research

I have spent a number of hours talking with Frederick Weiss.

Weiss is a big, loosely dressed German, with a grayish head of thinning hair. He has a thick German accent which can, on occasion, reinforce an impression of Old World charm that is also backed with an active mind and a Heidelberg-Sorbonne education. On other occasions, when he is angry, the accent further underlines far from elegant invective.

"I haven't been back to Germany since 1930," he said regretfully, "but I am in close personal contact with key nationalist leaders at home and with exiles in other places." When I pressed for the names of these foreign contacts, I soon realized he was not at all inclined to identify them.

Did he have any intention of going back? "Certainly not now," Weiss answered resentfully. "I wouldn't even dare cross the border. My photographs have been circulated among the German police. They even try to keep track of my activities here in the States."

We talked about his ideas. As a long-time dedicated German nationalist, Weiss advocates the subtle exploitation of religious prejudice where he thinks it helps the cause of "Germandom." Anti-Semitism he regards as both a dynamic propaganda weapon and an excellent come-on in the promotion of totalitarianism. It is, he found, one of the most salable elements in his own writings and in those of his fascist friends in this country.

As an example, he cited the case of Keith Thompson. Thompson, who he says works closely with him, once had no genuine dislike for the Jews, "but," Weiss added, "as no one had the slightest interest in his political views on other subjects, I showed him how he could get attention by attacking the Jews. . . . He was a ready pupil." But Weiss obviously looks down on Thompson for having no political ideas of his own, and only getting attention when he borrows startling clichés

II Cross-Currents in Germany

from others in the field. Weiss thinks of himself as the Grand Old Man of clever extreme nationalist pamphleteering, and men like Thompson are apparently taking his experienced guidance.

"Clever" is the key word above, for Weiss is extremely caustic about the blatant anti-Semitic propaganda used by others in his circle. James Madole, leader of the National Renaissance Party, he regards as much too shrill in his anti-Semitism; and he says he deplores the obnoxious caricatures of Jews peddled by street-corner rowdies in New York. These are only bad for the general public, evidently, for Weiss admitted circulating these same caricatures himself in private.

Weiss, square-jawed, clear-eyed, a teetotaler except for an occasional beer, impresses one as a man of great vitality and determination, a man who does not worry much over the personal consequences of his activities. He is deeply involved in neo-Nazi and fascist intrigue on an international scale. He is not a crackpot.

OCTOBER 21, 1953
Research to AF

Weiss's correspondence, like that of so many of his cohorts, appears to be in the quasi-public domain. In Germany, neo-Nazis reveal confidences and exhibit documents to those they would win to their cause. The German government and even occupation authorities obtain such material from centers of seditious political activity. In the United States congressional committees subpoena this type of correspondence and publish findings. Followers on the fringe of the hate movement peddle such information to newspapers. In other words, this kind of material is readily available from all manner of sources.

OCTOBER 23, 1953
Library to AF

You asked for a sketch of H. Keith Thompson.
Thompson, born in Orange, New Jersey, Yale '46, is a young, tall,

1 The Nazi Diehards

soft-spoken, obviously vain, good-looking bachelor who lives with his parents in Chatham, New Jersey, and has a partnership in a wholesale textile house.

His father, a successful New York businessman, provides his family moderately well with material comforts; Thompson seems to have enjoyed a pleasant enough boyhood, later went to Drew University in New Jersey, and then served in the U. S. Navy during World War II. In 1946 and 1947 he served aboard the flagship of the Byrd Antarctic Expedition as a communications officer.

In July 1952 he registered with the Department of Justice as a foreign agent for Germany's largest postwar neo-Nazi organization, the Socialist Reichs Party. Here is his own explanation of his concern for German war criminals and the "German spirit." It comes from a supplement to his registration papers filed with the Justice Department:

"[I] have since high school days surveyed the American political scene and participated in a number of political movements. . . . [I] was once attracted to the political left, but after practical experience in business realized the shortcomings of the welfare state. . . . In regards the foreign policy of the United States [I feel] that a strong Germany is our foremost weapon against communism. To have a strong Germany, we must have a revitalized, enthusiastic Germany who will work with us as a full partner. . . . German nationalist spirit must be encouraged, Germany's union achieved, 'democratic guarantees' guaranteed."

Throughout this document Thompson puts both *democracy* and *war criminals* in quotes, as though he obviously could not take either as a valid concept.

One of our New York correspondents, discussing the recently outlawed Socialist Reichs Party with Thompson last December, denounced the German neo-Nazi groups for collaborating with the USSR. Although the "foremost weapon against communism" argument is basic to Thompson's justification of his neo-Nazi activities, he did not seem in the least put out at the possibility of collaboration between the Soviet and the Germans.

"I have been told that our Socialist Reichs Party in Germany took

II Cross-Currents in Germany

funds from the USSR," said Thompson, "and the information may be right. But I deny it. I say that if the party has taken funds, it was to hold out longer against the pressures of the Bonn government."

"What about the neo-Nazi prattle of undying hatred for communism?"

"With the kicking around that the Reichs Party is getting from Washington," he answered, "and from their stooges in Bonn, I would not blame Ernst Remer and the others if they have taken funds or if they were to take more. They are justified in using any means whatsoever to preach their cause. If now they are forced to work underground, it is because they have failed to get backing elsewhere."

Personable as he is, Thompson is not politically shrewd. A wiser propagandist would have avoided public identification with George Sylvester Viereck, top German propagandist in two world wars and a polemicist for German nationalism for over a half century. Nor would he have affiliated himself with Madole's NRP, and publicly agitated and spoken for them. Thompson did both; and propaganda somehow always looks better if it can give an outward semblance of independent thought.

He also makes very little effort to avoid charges of open anti-Semitism. Jews left prewar Germany in great numbers; that he admits. He does not deny that things happened to Jews who remained. But, he argues, the Jews, as vassals of a world-Jewish conspiracy, could not properly maintain allegiance to a Hitler regime demanding loyalty to the Fatherland. They had, therefore, no right to remain in Germany.

But Thompson's significance is not in the field of theory. He is helpful as an enterprising distributor of hate literature, a very useful transmission belt. He has also helped to give an American coloring to a variety of fascist-type organizations. His present activities keep him in repeated contact with fascist leaders in countries like Japan, Spain, and Argentina; and he is constantly sending press releases and petitioning letters to the State Department and the United Nations, to German-Americans and to Germany.

Thompson claims to be registered as a public relations counsel, pub-

1 The Nazi Diehards

licity agent, and representative for *Die Andere Seite,* a Munich periodical published by Dr. Rudolf Aschenauer.[4]

OCTOBER 26, 1953
New York Correspondent to Research

Weiss has become somewhat more expansive.
"You want to know the big secret of my life?" he asked. "I was on the World War I list of German war criminals, last name from the bottom. For shooting up a French village; I was an artillery captain."
"Were you punished?"
"When the French seized the Ruhr in 1920, I fled. But they caught me in Düsseldorf. I spent eleven months in prison."
After further questioning I learned he was born in Pforzheim in 1886, first came to the United States in 1910, went back to Germany to serve in the army for World War I, and returned to the United States on a visitor's visa in 1930.
Had he run into any difficulty as an enemy alien during World War II? I asked.
"Naturally," he replied, "but not for political activities. They picked me up and held me on Ellis Island for many months—because I know the wrong people." When he was released it was on a $5,000 bond. The bond still stands.
In itself this would be sufficient reason for Weiss remaining in the background. Risk is part of a propagandist's work, however, and Weiss does not seem overconcerned about the added risk of his status here. And, realizing that his activities have hardly remained completely unexposed, it is a shrewd part of his discretion to admit and even to boast about part of his activities. A little open activity serves as good camouflage for more important work.
"But I never joined the Bund and never became a Nazi Party member. That's why the U. S. Government was never able to pin anything

---

[4] He has since registered as correspondent of *Der Weg,* the most important neo-Nazi publication appearing outside of Germany. *Der Weg* is published in the Argentine.

on me even though they held me for investigation many months." He holds a high opinion of his own agility. Of the country that is now host to him, he says: "It has no culture worthy of mention. And if Germany is not rebuilt, European culture will die too."

Weiss uses the LeBlanc Publishing Company as a front for his political propaganda, issuing press releases through it in a variety of aliases, sometimes even in the name of a friend. Since the war he has built up a sizable mailing list of top ex-Nazi military leaders and party members who have been punished for war crimes. Weiss is still anxious to keep his close association with these men secret, still refuses to divulge their names to me. His contact with many of them is a man called Schmidt in Dortmund, Germany.

Cagey as he is, though, Weiss talks freely on other subjects. He has quite freely admitted that he would prefer, under some situations, to see Germany tie in with the USSR rather than with the United States. This notwithstanding his all too frequent tirades against "Jew-manipulated bolshevism" and "Asiatic hordes."

"We Germans must find out whether we can get more out of the East or the West. I've come to the conclusion—and this is disclosing my innermost thought—that we can work out a better deal in going along with the East rather than the West. With our know-how and with our experience, we can get ahead faster with the USSR than with the West. Furthermore, the USSR has much more to offer us.

"The West," he adds, "is still dominated by the Morgenthau ideal, even though it's hidden in 'bread and circuses.' They need us Germans and do not want us to die, but they fear to let us live. They have Adenauer as a stooge. The Bonn government is at the beck and call of Wall Street. True, the West gives lip service to a united Germany, but it really fears a united powerful Germany."

It is Weiss's belief that the Germans, as the one people with "unity of soul," are destined in time to dominate not only the Russians but the world.

He is working toward that end; destiny obviously cannot be trusted to manage for itself.

1 The Nazi Diehards

NOVEMBER 2, 1953
German Correspondent to Research

I have been accumulating a record of Werner Naumann's utterances on several topics from his public speeches and personal statements.

Neo-Nazi political organization: Naumann urges all who are in league with him to infiltrate the existing "respectable" parties, and at the same time to associate in the creation of a political movement which expresses their own special principles.

Organization of the state: Last November, Naumann unfolded his program for creating the basic structure of a totalitarian state within the existing one, in speeches at Düsseldorf and Hamburg.

"There should be large organizations for the farmers, for the several soldiers' associations, for the retail traders, the refugees and the taxpayers. We ought to make ourselves heard in the local councils. Our men should try to become councillors and mayors, then all join hands in a new office for local government, perhaps, too, in a regional branch of this or that political party. Altogether we should infiltrate into all organs of public life in all their branches. And when they—either all or only some of them—have been sufficiently won over, then the hour of a United Front has arrived. Then we should come forward to declare that, in addition to the licensed parties, there is also still an independent Germany.

"This is our aim. Let us work for it tirelessly day by day. Let us close our ranks more tightly than ever; let us form a dedicated fellowship of a few hundred, sworn to keep the faith, and we shall be a power which, though as yet in the background, will one day achieve before the eyes of the world those ideals for which we once were called up and for which our comrades laid down their lives."

The possibilities of neo-Nazi success: Naumann, in private conversations, has expressed great confidence in a European fascist revival. "This can be done," he says, "even in a capitalist society dominated by Jewish influence. Germany, a capitalist nation in the days of the

11 Cross-Currents in Germany

Weimar Republic, was under the domination of Jews, just as the United States was in the time of Roosevelt and Truman. Yet Hitler, a penniless leader of the people, successfully captured the Republic."

Anti-communism and the reorganization of the German Army: Naumann believes that the Soviet Union always needs to be countered and that this need still validates Hitler's military program. The Nazi-Soviet Pact of 1939 he either ignores or pretends to think too unimportant to consider in this context. His argument extends into practical matters:

"There is a formula to get the German Army into the field [against Russia] within a year. Let the once great Tank General, Sepp Dietrich, out of jail and direct him to call to arms his old tank comrades for training in a remote part of Germany.[5] Let more of our Nazi generals out of jail. Tell them that they again have a chance to fight against the Bolsheviks. Let them help to recruit their old comrades and see what a fighting force they could put together in less than a year. . . . Adenauer's methods to build fighting forces are hot air. He talks of creating German military might while preaching pacifism to German youth. . . . This may sound as though I want war. I don't. We know that any such war would be fought mainly on German soil. Also we know that the Americans would be dropping atom bombs and on the way to Russia might by mistake drop a few on Germany."

NOVEMBER 2, 1953

New York Correspondent to Research

More conversations with Frederick Weiss. At his Mount Hope farmhouse we discussed his attitude toward Jews. Weiss is much too well trained and too practical in his outlook to show or to be victim of an emotional anti-Semitism; in fact he emphasized that German Jews had made important contributions to German culture.

---

[5] On October 22, 1955, Sepp Dietrich was released from the United States-governed prison of Landsberg. Dietrich had been sentenced by an Allied court in 1946 for a number of war crimes including the massacre of American prisoners of war at Malmédy during the Battle of the Bulge.

1 The Nazi Diehards

"Jews had a large part in the professions," he said. "At least four of the ten judges on the Leipzig Supreme Court under the Weimar Republic were Jews. There were large numbers of doctors, artists, and outstanding bankers who were Jewish, with higher codes of ethics than most others. One of my closest friends was the head of the Sueddeutsche Bank in Pforzheim. The prospects for Germany today would be better if those Jews were back. Of course, I don't mean by this the Polack Jews."

Shortly after World War II, Weiss wrote a pamphlet, *Germania Delenda Est*. A hundred thousand copies were printed, 30,000 of them in English; and he mailed copies to every name on his list of ex-Afrika Korps men.

NOVEMBER 4, 1953
Research to AF

After carefully examining the documentation on Frederick Weiss that has been coming in, we are able to provide you with a sketch of the network in which he is involved.

Weiss is in correspondence with contacts in virtually all parts of the world, and not merely obscure crackpots in remote corners, but leading fascists, anti-Semites, and extreme nationalists. Here is a partial list: Einar Aberg, Maurice Bardeche, Per Engdahl, G. Amaudruz, Raven Thomson, Arnold Leese, Amin el Husseini, and Otto Strasser.

Aberg, chairman of the Swedish anti-Jewish Combat League, sends Weiss "Nordic Greetings," and inquires for material "which is written in German and is very good; it would be important to spread it in Germany." He adds, sadly, that his publication, *Kretz Nytt*, printed in Malmoe, is the only anti-Semitic paper left in Sweden. Aberg was once Swedish agent for Welt Dienst, the former Nazi world propaganda service.

Maurice Bardeche, of Paris, is chairman of the National French Committee, well known as a writer and a collaborationist. He sends Weiss numerous French fascist publications.

II Cross-Currents in Germany

Per Engdahl is head of the Swedish fascist organization, Nysvenska Roerelse.

Amaudruz, general secretary of the Swiss People's Party, writing from Lausanne, offers Weiss his own services as a clearinghouse for information on fascists in other countries.

A. Raven Thomson, acting for Sir Oswald Mosley in England, asks Weiss to serve as an intermediary in getting around Brazilian currency control on a payment from a citizen of that country.

Arnold Leese, leader of the Fascist League of Britain, exchanges publications with Weiss.

Amin el Husseini, who handles foreign affairs for the former Grand Mufti of Jerusalem, writes Weiss from Cairo thanking him for his friendly greetings.

Otto Strasser, a dissident Nazi who has been living in exile since the early days of the Hitler regime, appears to have lost none of his fervor for the cause. From Canada he writes Weiss asking him for help in obtaining a professorship at the University of Cairo; Weiss is to negotiate this with the Egyptian ambassador in Washington. "With the help of my knowledge of English," Strasser writes, "this post would give me an inconspicuous platform to carry on our common mission with all energy. Egypt needs a propaganda ministry to operate abroad, notably for Europe and America."

NOVEMBER 5, 1953
Library to AF

Here is a more detailed background on three of Weiss's foreign contacts:

Arnold Leese is the English publisher of a newsletter devoted almost entirely to violently anti-Semitic agitation. In 1951, at Malmoe, Sweden, he helped organize the European Social Movement, an international, delegate body designed to co-ordinate the propaganda activities of the European fascists. (Karl Heinz Priester, a former Hitler Youth leader, who runs the German wing of this movement from Bonn, still lives in

1 The Nazi Diehards

a Nazi dream world so fantastic as to commit repeated political indiscretions embarrassing even to his dedicated fellow delegates. It must take a lot to embarrass men like Oswald Mosley, Per Engdahl, and G. A. Amaudruz, names already familiar to you from the Weiss list; but Priester seems to manage it.)

Otto Strasser, now a resident of Bridgetown, Nova Scotia, defined his basic program some time ago in one of his own newsletters:

> We will talk Russian to the East and English to the West, but at heart we will remain Germans.
> Any tactical measure to help Germany will be justified.
> America's and Russia's battle is *not our concern,* except insofar as it helps our comeback.

Einar (Gustav Vilhelm) Aberg, of Sweden, age sixty-four, is a natural to find involved in any campaign to revive Nazism. He first printed anti-Semitic leaflets in 1933, and stuffed them into letter boxes throughout Stockholm. The data for these leaflets, he explained in 1947, were gathered "by communicating with publishers in Nazi Germany and with institutions working for enlightenment in this matter."

His association continued; during the first two years of World War II he maintained a close liaison with the Nazi propaganda agencies in Germany and with the German Legation in Stockholm, once even trying for an official position in the Nazi government.

Next, in October 1941, Aberg opened a bookshop in Stockholm to sell anti-Semitic publications. Perhaps feeling that the titles in his window display were not self-explanatory, he added a placard reading: *Entrance Forbidden to Jews and Half-Jews.* A police court ordered it removed. Aberg's ingenuity may not be boundless, but it is prompt; he substituted another: *Only Swedes Allowed to Enter (Consequently No Jews or Half-Jews, Even If They Are Swedish Citizens).* He has had his tribulations; the venture lasted barely two months.

Then he organized his very own anti-Semitic movement, Sveriges Antijudiska Kampforbund, dedicated to the "total extinction of Judaism in Sweden." There was to be no democratic nonsense in this organization: Aberg elected himself director, and, carefully directing

II Cross-Currents in Germany

his comrades to contribute funds, to give advice, and to offer suggestions, reserved for the director all rights of final decision.

Aberg has by now achieved an international status in his field; his output has turned up generously in Australia, Mexico, England, France, and Holland, among other places. Switzerland, another of his dumping grounds, announced in August 1950 that it had forbidden him entrance.

But along with such minor setbacks Aberg has also made many friends and admirers. The former Grand Mufti of Jerusalem has expressed his gratitude to Aberg in the warmest terms; and he has ardent fans in America as well. Gerald Smith's *The Cross and the Flag* hailed Aberg as "a diligent crusader in defense . . . of the independence of the Gentile World"; *Women's Voice,* official publication of the disruptive We, the Mothers Mobilize for America, Inc., and the *Individualist* of Danville, Virginia, have reprinted his material and run laudatory articles about him.

At home, his fellow Swedes regard him as a crank. Indeed, five years ago a Swedish court ordered a mental test for him; and thereafter he subdued his Swedish activities and concentrated on the export trade. As we have seen, with results.

The Swedish authorities repeatedly hailed Aberg into court, and in 1948 Parliament enacted a special law, "Lex Aberg," which made it a penal offense to threaten or defame a group publicly because of race or religion. While this, too, kept his local bigotries in check, there were still his extensive foreign operations to be dealt with. Finally, in February of this year, Aberg was convicted of violating a Swedish law that governs the distribution of international propaganda.

But only days later members of the Federal Parliament in Bonn received Aberg material mailed from Neuss, Germany. It was a leaflet attacking Eisenhower and General Mark Clark as Jewish. Aberg is irrepressible; he paid his fine and, blithely picking up where he left off, continues to be the world's largest distributor of anti-Semitica. And so his international exchanges continue; in the United States apparently with Frederick Weiss.

1 The Nazi Diehards

NOVEMBER 6, 1953
Research to AF

Every day brings new evidence that the range of Weiss's international operations is even wider than originally estimated. We now have several letters tying him to Robert Williams, the West Coast anti-Semite, and to Dr. Rudolf Aschenauer, the German newspaper publisher. You recall that Keith Thompson claims to be Aschenauer's registered agent in the States. Excerpts from the letters follow.

Aschenauer to Weiss (April 19, 1951):

I am extremely grateful to you for the regular mailings of printed material. The pamphlet by [Robert H.] Williams has impressed me greatly. We also obtained valuable information from *Common Sense*. . . . Again with sincere thanks for your valuable assistance, I am asking you to send me everything pertaining to the problem dealt with by Williams.

Robert Williams to Aschenauer (May 14, 1951):

I am much pleased to have your subscription to my *Intelligence Summary*, sent through Mr. Frederick C. Weiss of New York City. . . .

Mr. Weiss suggests that I try for wide distribution of my publications in Germany, but I am inclined to think that, since they expose the Jewish backing of Communism and Zionism, and since the revolutionary Jews still exercise great power to misrepresent and also to harass your people, perhaps it would be good strategy not to circulate my *Summary* and booklets there till we can elect an honorable, pro-Gentile president. What do you think about the problem? There may be other ways by which we can, at this time, tend to weld the friendship of all branches of the Nordic race—which we must do or risk self-annihilation through more wars.

I wish I could have the benefit of your ideas and information from time to time, but funds are so limited as yet that I could hardly offer you financial inducement. It is not unlikely that I will have substantial backing in the next few months for a monthly magazine, in which case, I shall hope to get you to contribute an article or articles on the Nuremberg trials, revealing the Communist influence behind them and the alien (Jewish) management. . . . I feel that we are just now on the verge of a mass rebellion against the Communist and Jewish nationalist influence . . .

Robert Williams to Weiss (July 9, 1951):

It occurs to me that some or many of the very highest leaders of Germany may not fully understand the present status of Jewish powers. I am therefore anxious to get a copy of *Know Your Enemy* into the hands of each of such men as General H. Guderian. . . .

I believe you have a famous lawyer friend in Germany who could place copies in their hands, have you not? I will gladly send you 10 or more copies for such use, if you care to undertake the project?

NOVEMBER 10, 1953
Research to German Correspondent

The following list is of some of Frederick Weiss's German contacts: Dr. Rudolf Aschenauer, Erich Schmidt, Arthur Ehrhardt, Dr. Hans Grimm.
For policy decision:

NOVEMBER 11, 1953
BRE to ADL Commission

For policy decision:
The German Mission to the United States began making approaches to the Anti-Defamation League, in the late spring and summer of 1953, about a German visit. It is the view of the Mission that the Bonn government under President Theodor Heuss and Chancellor Konrad Adenauer had undertaken a sincere program

1. to make amends, so far as was possible at this late date, for some of the German anti-Jewish crimes by making restitutions to Jewish survivors or their representatives;
2. to combat existing anti-Semitism in Germany;
3. to outlaw the neo-Nazi parties; and

4. to propagate democratic ideals and concepts.

Confident of its government's achievements, the German Mission proposes that the Anti-Defamation League, as a major agency combating anti-Semitism, promoting civil rights, and fostering democratic ideas, view current conditions in Germany and, after studying them, make such suggestions for future action as it might deem fit.

Please give this careful consideration.

DECEMBER 1, 1953
German Correspondent to Research

Three names on the list of Frederick Weiss's German contacts are of not unknown writers and publishers.

Dr. Hans Grimm, whom Weiss does not know personally, is in his middle seventies. He is a long-time pan-German who deplored Nazi violence though subscribing to a basically anti-Semitic philosophy. His "theory" is anti-Semitism. He lives in monastic retreat on the top of a forested mountain near Coburg, and there plays elder statesman and philosopher to visiting groups of literary fascists. Included among the disciples of this modest man is Werner Naumann. Between discussions with the staff of *Nation Europa,* an international monthly published in Coburg, Grimm, hard-working as well as retiring, finds time to write long explanations to foreign friends, outlining the rationale of National Socialist principles.

In a communication to a British correspondent Grimm wrote:

The aversion to the Jews requires an explanation, because of its atrocious consequences. For it seems that the inhuman atrocities committed against the Jews under the later Hitlerism, excuse and justify every sin which has been and is being committed against Germany, and almost to substantiate *a priori* every false and abominable charge that has been and is being brought against the German people. Superstition played a part in this antipathy to the Jews, a superstition similar to that which England cherished against the Germans in the middle of the eighteen nineties. The Jews had flocked in ever increasing numbers from the East into the Reich in the days when Germany was recently united and beginning to flourish and partly by their industry, partly by an unscrupulousness alien to us, and partly by their quicker wits, had sometimes thrived where native Germans had failed to get on. They settled themselves in, elbowing out the old middle class, and yet remained foreigners in sentiment and mentality. . . . It is rightly said that the bane of anti-Semitism is contagious, but it is also true that in its arrogance the Jewish fungus adulterated, disturbed and contaminated the minds and behavior of a people which had not yet found its solidarity, and this was never more markedly and unquestionably evident than in the sorely stricken Germany of 1917–1933. . . .

We saw, after Versailles, the spread of rottenness and corruption, but we also became aware how far our physical, as well as our moral, degeneration had progressed. Degeneration becomes more noticeable in the nation's dark days than in the days of prosperity. There existed a passionate desire for the regeneration of our race, both in physical and moral purity. That was the beginning. It was a crying need, and anything but arrogance. . . .

In the dastardly Jew-baiting of the November night ten thousand Germans throughout the Reich actively participated, and another hundred thousand Germans were probably spectators.

I was unable to obtain a clear picture of this revolting occurrence. There were no Jews in the village in which I lived. The details I heard from outside sources weighed heavily on my heart. I felt myself tormented as a human being and defiled as a German. I saw that this cowardly, un-German behavior would loom larger than the injustice done to our whole nation, and would incalculably magnify and aggravate every hostile misunderstanding of Germany. . . .

More was done in that time, in the years 1933–1939, internally for the health of the nation, for mothers and children, in the way of mutual assistance, than has been done at any time, yes—one may even say—anywhere. . . .

The German people, in its majority, did not instigate the different actions of its government, but there is no doubt that it heartily endorsed them. . . .

I am concerned with the utter wrongness of attributing guilt collectively to a nation or to a community or to any organization.

It was just such a false collective accusation of guilt against a whole racial community—and a great part of the German people realized this to their disgust from 1938 onwards—that the prescribed propaganda of the National Socialist Party tried to inculcate in the minds of our people. Without this indoctrinated belief in the collective guilt of the

1 The Nazi Diehards

Jews for the misguided errors of the "White Man," and for all the muddle and confusion of the Germans in particular, there would never have been the gruesome mass-slaughter of the Jews. . . .

Erich Schmidt is the editor of *Der Reichsruf,* official organ of the German Reichs Party. Like many ex-Nazis, he had to rebuild his life from the very bottom; a delicatessen shop in the industrial section of Dortmund now provides him, who was once an SA major, with the means to carry on his Party work. Schmidt is still faithful to the Nazi tenets of anti-Semitism, and regards all non-Germans as inferior beings. Frederick Weiss, with whom he corresponds frequently, is only one of the many contacts he maintains with fascists outside Germany.

Arthur Ehrhardt, identified on your list as having exchanged literature with Weiss, is a book publisher in Coburg who also owns and publishes the monthly magazine *Nation Europa,* which he has molded into the outstanding fascist periodical in Europe. An extraordinarily large man, with a literary and organizational flair, this sixty-year-old ex-Nazi was the outstanding authority on the techniques of street fighting in the heyday of Streicher.

•

DECEMBER 3, 1953
German Correspondent to Research

Here are the identifications of more Weiss contacts in Germany. It is amazing how wide a range the man covers.

Gunther Bardey is a Hamburg anti-Semite.

Peter Wallraf, of Cologne, a former Nazi governor of the Ukraine, and currently a high-level contact man for neo-Nazi groups, is also a writer of neo-Nazi and anti-Semitic literature.

Three weeks ago I reported to you briefly on Arthur Ehrhardt, publisher of *Nation Europa* in Coburg. Now I have two letters of his to Weiss, testimony of Weiss's helpfulness to the neo-Nazi movement overseas.

Also, you probably recall my mention earlier this month of the anti-Semitic pamphlets seized by the German police when they raided the

II Cross-Currents in Germany

homes of German Rally leaders. Further investigation reveals a Johann Strunk as a German distributor of these. More on him very soon.

DECEMBER 7, 1953
Library to Research

Our files indicate a relationship between Dr. Rudolf Aschenauer, and Benjamin H. Freedman, of New York. Freedman is the wealthy pro-Arab propagandist, and one of the backers of *Common Sense,* Conde McGinley's hate sheet.

Common Sense appears to have its foreign admirers, for Dr. Aschenauer, back in June 1951, contacted Freedman about the possibility of publishing in the U.S. a similar paper in the German language.

I have been informed by Mr. Frederick Chas. Weiss of the decisive share you have in the struggle so important for the fate of the Western world, a struggle which the periodical "C.S." has been waging with increasing success for years. You may rest assured that this work is being observed with great interest also by circles close to me. We are very grateful to you and your friends for your endeavors to energetically and openly approach a central question of world policy.

It was in this letter that Aschenauer proposed "a new periodical in German which shall address the ethnic German public living in the U.S.A. . . .

DECEMBER 8, 1953
Research to AF

Weiss and Aschenauer have thus far not succeeded in bringing out the proposed German-language periodical styled on *Common Sense.* Instead Weiss is utilizing the *Renaissance Bulletin,* put out by James Madole's National Renaissance Party. If anything, the *Renaissance Bulletin* is even lower in tone and repute than McGinley's sheet.

1. The Nazi Diehards

DECEMBER 10, 1953
German Correspondent to Research

There is little to add to the material you already have on Dr. Rudolf Aschenauer; discretion, if not age, seems to have retired him from active participation in the neo-Nazi movement. He found that he couldn't carry on activities as counsel for a high church dignitary and promote an outlawed discredited political movement, or a publication connected with it, at the same time. So politics bowed to business. List him now merely as the *former* publisher of *Die Andere Seite*. His editor, however, Dr. Heinrich Malz, one time an SS police chief aide in Berlin, has become an important behind-the-scenes figure in the movement.

Dr. Heinrich Malz is one of Werner Naumann's top associates; he corresponds extensively with Frederick Weiss, and forwards him Nazi and anti-Semitic material for processing and distribution in the States. I have had several long talks with him.

This small, thin, ascetic lawyer with a hawk nose and keen eyes has never forsworn his fealty to National Socialism. He is now the paid lobbyist for an organization of some fifty thousand former Nazi civil servants. He unhesitatingly admits to having been jailed as a war criminal.

"What did you do when you were released from prison?"

"I went to Nuremberg," Malz said proudly, "to assist in the legal defense of Kaltenbrunner."

"The former national head of the SS?"

"The same."

Ernst Kaltenbrunner—usually regarded as the man most responsible for the wholesale extermination of Jews; he had been convicted and hanged.

"What did you do after he was convicted and the case was all over?"

"I moved on to Landsberg where I became a chief counsel defending the so-called Malmédy war criminals."

"So-called" indeed! The cold-blooded murder of three hundred American GIs. I changed the subject. We discussed his present activities.

As of now, Malz is the big idea man for the outline and preparation of neo-Nazi propaganda campaigns. He has worked up some studies called *The Big Swindle of the Six Million,* which "prove" that millions of Jews were hidden in current world census figures and were not exterminated by the Nazis. This is part of the material sent to Weiss for circulation in the States. I am convinced that Malz collaborated with someone else in the preparation of these studies, but have been unable to learn who it is—a well-guarded secret.

Some of the other studies prepared, or in preparation, under the direction of Malz and his unidentified friend, for dissemination in Germany and abroad, cover the following theses:

1. How in the Weimar Republic Jews overcrowded the professions, particularly law, medicine, journalism, the theater, and finance.

2. How Jews throughout history practiced marginal and unpopular businesses such as moneylending and cattle trading.

3. Jewish hostility to Germans as far back as 1815.

4. Atrocities committed by the Western Powers and the USSR—with particular emphasis on the dastardly execution of Nazi war criminals, and on the pitiful plight of those still imprisoned.

DECEMBER 11, 1953
German Correspondent to Research

In yesterday's report I was able to indicate the working relationship between Malz and Weiss. Here is the exact text of a "getting-acquainted" letter written by Malz to Weiss on April 22, 1951.

I belong to that generation of young Germans who identified themselves with National Socialists for idealistic reasons. I am dealing with this point very openly because I regard it as decisive if one is to make headway along the lines of your thinking. I have experienced the peaks and the depths of National Socialism very consciously. During the war

1 The Nazi Diehards

and afterwards I had activities which gave me a very deep insight into the background of that [Hitler's] government both in its strength and in its weakness. (At the end I was a close collaborator of the Chief of the Security Police and of the SD Intelligence Service, Dr. Kaltenbrunner, who was executed at Nuremberg.)

After the collapse I was interned nearly three years and later collaborated with Dr. Aschenauer on the Nuremberg defense cases. These gave me an opportunity to think over past events and to make a serious analysis of the pro and the con. I took all this very seriously.

Now to your detailed letter. You express ideas that I myself have often had. I have read your writings, those of Mr. Williams, and *Common Sense*. I have read it very carefully and I now see suddenly fully and clearly confirmation of the basic idea which we originally had as our point of departure. We supported National Socialism because it recognized for our people and for the whole white race the threatening Red peril in its whole seriousness and this party alone offered the means of effectively combating it. For this reason we gave up many privileges in our lives which otherwise were basic treasures of the white race. We gave up our unrestricted personal freedom and submitted ourselves to hard political necessities. We worked day and night. We sacrificed our private lives to the Will to dominate that danger.

I do not need to describe to you what taking this position cost us. You yourself know that the arbitrary spirit of revenge of the victors joined hands with the hatred of our own new dominant classes. We were jailed and with our families were made outcasts and today are completely outside the political life of our people.

Now you ask me these questions: where is the German elite? Why do they keep silent? When are they finally going to make an appearance?

If only you knew how these questions churn about in me and how painfully conscious they make me of the whole unholy inner and outer status of my people.

What do you understand by German elite? As far as I have been able to understand American opinion I have no reason to assume that people have turned away from the well-hammered-in idea that all that is National Socialist is black and that all that was against it was white. I hesitate to identify myself with the "German Elite" for this reason. Today's "German Elite" is cut out of other wood than we who earlier had a right to regard ourselves as "The Elite." Today's "German Elite" is mainly recruited out of German resistance groups. That is to say those circles which decisively crippled our war against the Eastern peril.

II Cross-Currents in Germany

Today's "German Elite" sits in all powerful government posts. They are in the office of the Chancellor, and in the other ministries. They hold all key positions. That they were not willing to see the Red peril in all its significance and above all to look behind the scenes and to come out and oppose it is unfortunately the bare fact. They will never be ready to put German prestige in relation with the West foremost. No, the power which alone would make that possible has now been so thoroughly dissipated that it cannot at present be counted upon. The Germans have been so shattered that they can only just keep their heads above water and are in part so upset that they no longer have clear political vision. All that has been done so far in pulling together the healthy elements which to your way of thinking must become active, discloses that fortunately there are still inner forces that are ready to stand up to the danger. Lacking, however, is a strong dominant personality.

Also lacking is a new flaming idea that once again will unite the German people and fire them to deeds beyond personal self-interest. I really do not see, in view of the hopeless inferiority of the West as against the East, in view of the deplorable suicidal policy of America, the people to whom fate brings us the closest, and in view of the complete lack of leadership of the German people, just what will pull people out of their existing lethargy. In a few strokes I give you this pessimistic over-all picture, but this does not mean that the real "German Elite" no longer exists and that they can no longer be counted on. The yearning for a real national revival is there, but one should not look for this, for such a revival, until America creates a clearer situation. Currently Germany is entirely split open and is under the domination of four victorious powers with entirely divergent interests. Our real national forces are entirely helpless. Without a push from outside, the German people—which is different from after 1918—cannot get free.

DECEMBER 11, 1953

German Correspondent to Research

By dint of patient questioning and prodding I managed to get an account of some of the major episodes in Naumann's Nazi career, from closemouthed Heinrich Malz.

1 The Nazi Diehards

Although Malz is not a superstitious man, he did insist that Werner Naumann leads a charmed life. "He frequently risked his skin on the Russian front," Malz explained, "and was wounded a number of times. He was back in the fight in no time."

"Many courageous soldiers lived through such an experience."

"Yes, but not many politicians."

"What do you mean?"

"His association with Hitler nearly cost him his life three times. Way back in the beginning, Naumann was a Brown Shirt officer, one of the four men closest to Ernst Roehm. When the assassination plot came to light, Naumann avoided the first dragnet. He escaped the firing squad but was thrown into jail. He was held four months and convinced his captors of his deep devotion to Hitler. They released him and he was readmitted to the hierarchy."

"Then what?"

"His second escape from death came when Hitler's bunker fell into the hands of the Russians in the Berlin assault. Fleeing across the flaming city, Naumann stumbled and was knocked unconscious. A Hitler Youth leader dragged him to safety and saved him from capture. Had any one of his comrades betrayed him, the Russians would have stuck him up against a wall and blown holes in him."

Malz continued his account—a neo-Nazi legend in the making. "The third escape was from the Nuremberg trials. Naumann is convinced that if he had not been in hiding he would have been hanged by the Allies. That's why Naumann has a feeling that he is destined for great things."

"Does Naumann actually have a sense of charmed existence?"

Malz was indulgent. "Dr. Naumann feels he is destined to play an important role and he is very conscious of the effect he creates. Werner always wants his close friends sitting near him in the audience, to watch the effect he has on us. Sometimes I think his restraint is a calculated technique. He keeps his distance from the crowd, avoids handshaking and glad-handing as much as possible. He wants to give the impression of being a man above the crowd."

I wondered if Malz considered himself as lucky; his record in the early war years might well have brought him Allied retribution. When Berlin was first bombarded, Malz, responsible for the evacuation of 50,000 criminal and political prisoners from the Oranienburg Prison, had them packed into sealed railroad cars for shipment to Magdeburg Prison. For three days, as they were shunted back and forth, the prisoners, with insufficient food and water, were also subjected to a heavy bombardment. But Malz refused to order the cars unsealed. Many suffered and died there, trapped.

DECEMBER 17, 1953
Library to AF

Dr. Hans Grimm and Arthur Ehrhardt propound, Naumann heads, Malz and his unknown friend "document" and plan the propaganda for, the Nazi revival. That is, in brief, the German picture. Einar Aberg in Sweden, Sir Oswald Mosley in England, Frederick Weiss in the United States, and others in other countries, distribute the resulting literature.

That is, in brief, the international picture. And we have here documented evidence that should help clarify the picture at home.

Among Weiss's extensive domestic correspondents, contacts, and associates is Edward Fleckenstein, a lawyer, of Weehawken, New Jersey. Some months ago Fleckenstein visited Germany and, while there, actively campaigned for August Hausleiter, a neo-Nazi candidate in the elections. In June, Fleckenstein wrote to Weiss from Bavaria as follows:

Thanks for your letters of June 20th and 22nd which arrived here yesterday and today respectively. My report on my trip will be delayed a few days. I am preparing to go to Rothenburg to speak before Hausleiter's group. He and I have been in touch with each other by special delivery letters.

Thanks for the Renaissance Bulletin. Your message is magnificently presented. It makes a very good impression. Congratulations on this fine edition! I can see your planning in this bulletin. Introduction is perfect. For months I have been telling [Keith] Thompson the new committee should be a Verband or grouping of societies, a high policy planning group, as you put it. I told Thompson long ago that all groups, including Madole's, should be members of this Verband and possibly appear on the letterhead. . . .

Thank God, you were able to talk Thompson into this practical new approach. Also I am glad that you were able to put "direction" into the ideology here. Makes a very good impression. I don't know when I saw anything so impressive in the nationalist field at home. You have the theory and the practice presented therein.

The Jewish aspect will be a problem. Even Dr. Malz wants no anti-Semitism (open); he wants no use of the word "Jew." Your latest article (from "The Untouchables") is a twilight zone case. The forces we have are too weak. But, if you can put together a separate organization —by itself—this could be a solution. . . . I also suggested to Thompson as a reasonable (very reasonable) compromise on the Jewish aspect, THAT the committee be put together and take in representatives from anti-S. and non-anti-S. groups alike. . . . PLEASE TREAT THIS LETTER AS CONFIDENTIAL. DON'T LET IT FLOAT AROUND. It is compromising. . . .

Obviously the Weiss-Fleckenstein tie-in is a close one. We are preparing the requested data on Fleckenstein and Hausleiter as well.

DECEMBER 24, 1953
Library to Research

August Hausleiter is the organizer of the German Association (Deutsche Gemeinschaft), an ultra-nationalist splinter group started in Munich in 1949. Although it is his main concern to attract the younger ex-Nazi Party members and the former Hitler Youth, his zealous personality and florid oratory have more appeal to the older Nazis, as can be judged by his membership. One of his main tenets is that "Eisenhower is nothing but a front for Frankfurter, Baruch and Morgenthau."

This stupidity extends to practical matters; Hausleiter accepted Fleckenstein as representative of an important American political group and featured him in his election campaign. At his failure to win office, he attempted to join the Naumann group. But, according to our Euro-

II Cross-Currents in Germany

pean sources, Naumann regards Hausleiter as a potential liability and has even avoided meeting him.

DECEMBER 24, 1953
Library to Research

We have a good deal on Fleckenstein in our files.

In July thirty neo-Nazi splinter groups met in Mannheim to form a "National Rally" for putting up candidates in the elections. They dispatched greetings to the convicted war criminal Admiral Doenitz. Among the speakers, many of whom denounced the Nuremberg trials as the greatest war crime and attributed World War II to President Roosevelt, was U.S. citizen Edward A. Fleckenstein. His particular contribution was an assault on democracy as a glorification of mediocrity, and an attack on Adenauer for not having made sufficient demands on the Western Allies. He told the six hundred and twenty delegates he was the president of the Voters' Alliance for Americans of German Ancestry.

Fleckenstein, a thirty-three-year-old of German descent, has long wanted to lead a militant German-American bloc here, so his participation in a German neo-Nazi rally was no surprise to us. His public activities began after the war, when he offered his services to congressional committees considering the German problems. Later he developed a "constructive program" of political action for Germany's rehabilitation and joined a half dozen German-American societies; but he did not attract much attention until he turned up in 1949 as the attorney for the Voters' Alliance, and then took over the presidency from A. O. Tittmann the next year. The group continued its monthly meetings at Yorkville's Rheinland Café without much outward show. "Anti-Semitism," Fleckenstein had said before he headed the organization, "is a dead issue in Yorkville as far as the German element is concerned," and had added that he personally was against any form of racial prejudice; in spite of which, his group made a strangely contradictory impression in the year of the presidential election.

1 The Nazi Diehards

In the spring of 1952 they sponsored a widely publicized German-American Friendship Rally that was held at the Yorkville Casino. Austin J. App, a lecturer and pamphleteer who had once demanded that General Eisenhower be hanged as a war criminal, told the gathering that its purpose was to "rid the State Department of its last traces of Morgenthauism"; and accused "anybody not in harmony with our views" of being either a communist or a "half brother of a communist." There was also no doubt that he was well understood when he denounced "the people who furnished the atom spies . . . who believe in an eye for an eye."

Fleckenstein, who also acted as chairman, after attacking the Truman Administration, referred to Eisenhower as "the John the Baptist of the anti-Christs" who was "allowing the glamour, hoopla and Wall Street money" to boost him for the presidency.

Aside from this public manifestation of what he obviously felt were live issues, Fleckenstein also established close contact with H. Keith Thompson, who in turn helped organize some of the Voters' Alliance meetings. Fleckenstein to Thompson to Weiss.

Then, before leaving for Germany and the Mannheim rally in the summer of 1953, Fleckenstein composed a lengthy "open letter" to Dr. Konrad Adenauer, offering "some observations regarding U.S.-German affairs." Printed, and signed by Fleckenstein as president of the Voters' Alliance, his letter had a wide distribution here and abroad.

The main portion of his "observations" dealt with why the Bonn government should not ratify the Allied Peace Contract and the European Defense Treaty, should not, in fact, have much at all to do with a U. S. Government whose "administration is corrupt at every level." His main premise: "The U.S. form of government is actually a quasi-dictatorship ruled by the hidden tyranny of money and satanic pressure groups. Well meaning bourgeois are still in the majority here but they get nowhere [because] the U.S. Administration is dominated by a secret invisible Government."

Elsewhere Fleckenstein has stated that this "secret Government and its conspirators" put Eisenhower into office.

But if the American government is bad as a "quasi-dictatorship," one whose "secret police" is the FBI, it would seem paradoxically to be, as a democracy, even worse to Fleckenstein. He defined democracy as "the glorification of mediocrity," and further characterized it as a system which allowed "plain trash such as Roosevelt and Truman or rubber stamps such as Eisenhower" to rise to the top.

Fleckenstein is less impatient with the USSR, since it appears to him to show "signs of desiring to cooperate with the West to preserve world peace." Fleckenstein also warned that German-American friendship must be "between the right Germans and the right Americans. The men of the Washington administration are not the right Americans, and you, Mr. Chancellor, are not the right German. . . ." He hastens to assure Dr. Adenauer that this does not mean "we are encouraging an overthrow of your regime by force." And adds, surprisingly enough from an American citizen: "But we do encourage voting you out of office."

And who are the "right Germans"? Fleckenstein has much to say on this topic: "When Germany was destroyed, National Socialism was rooted out and utterly extirpated. . . . All National Socialist institutions were outlawed. The whole of Germany was 're-educated.' The democratic 'reeducators' became masters [and] National Socialism had not one out of a thousand chances to even assert itself.

"If with all these disadvantages and in the face of this one-sided picture there are today large numbers of Germans who want National Socialism, I must conclude that it must indeed be a superior philosophy. . . . Many define National Socialism by its concentration camps. It might just as easily be defined by its Strength Through Joy organizations or its Autobahnen."

Obviously the "right Germans" are those who hold this "superior philosophy."

Fleckenstein's writings and speeches finally achieved notice. After addressing a rally of the National Bloc in Munich on August 8, he was arrested by the West German authorities. Then, charged with meddling in the politics of a foreign nation, his passport was declared invalid by the U. S. Consulate, and he was ordered to return to the United States.

1 The Nazi Diehards

DECEMBER 28, 1953
Research to AF

Another American correspondent of Weiss's visited Germany this year. He is Arthur Koegel, Sr., seventy-six, American-born, a Chicago coal dealer and newspaper publisher, active since the thirties in many German-American clubs, including the German-American Citizens League. His paper, the *Deutsch-Amerikanische Buerger Zeitung,* official organ of this League, has printed anti-Semitic articles; and his speeches reveal a strong sympathy for neo-Nazism. During his recent visit to Germany he made contact with the Naumann group.

As publisher, Koegel has a certain importance in the neo-Nazi propaganda network, for his paper serves as an outlet for Malz's concoctions in this country. Now and then he even prints several thousand extra copies of an issue and sends them free to friends outside the U.S. He is also a busy go-between, corresponding with men like Eberhard Fritsch, head of the Duerer-Verlag and publisher of the Nazi magazine *Der Weg* in Argentina, and other neo-Nazis in that country. In other words, Koegel is a cog in that particular machine, important perhaps, but a cog nevertheless. He is far too dependent on Weiss in the U.S. and on others like Erich Schmidt in Germany for interpretations of the world scene to be a big wheel himself.

But, if his opinions occasionally need clarification, the basic faith behind them remains unshaken. "I am under the impression," he wrote Weiss on December 28, 1951, "that the consensus[6] are seeking to make Germany and the Germans seem despicable and to keep hatred alive. We must fight them and our first objective is to block [the proposal to put up] a monument for the six million Jews. If we succeed in that, then we will have good prospects."

---

[6] The word "consensus" in the lexicon of the group under discussion is a frequently used euphemism for the word "Jews."

II Cross-Currents in Germany

JANUARY 2, 1954
German Correspondent to Research

Johann Strunk, a schoolteacher in Düsseldorf, uses his spare time composing anti-Semitic poems and pamphlets, or traveling through the industrial Ruhr distributing his own and similar compositions, and making speeches. The speeches are violent, the man is a fanatic. Currently he is editing a series of anti-Semitic pamphlets; the most recent, a 40-page booklet called *Demon Money,* traces the source of the world's major ills to the gold standard, an international monetary system of which the Jews, naturally, are the architects.

Another of his books, a collaboration, titled *The Abyss of World War III,* describes "the criminal intrigues of Jews, Zionist and other secret societies" since 1897. Not surprising, then, that he is the man identified by the Hamburg police as the distributor of the mimeographed flier—the crude drawing of Adenauer accepting an award of the Star of David—of which I wrote you.

Strunk has been arrested a number of times for violating press ordinances; once his school salary was docked. Düsseldorf Jews, he says, complaining to the local police, are persecuting him. Which only inspires him further.

It has also taught him a measure of caution. To side-step the Düsseldorf authorities and their "persecuting" press ordinances, he has sent the manuscripts of his 60-page booklet, *The Abyss of World War III,* to the United States for printing in English and German. His proposed deal gives his American contact the right of sale in the U.S., both versions, in exchange for 1,500 free copies and seven per cent of the American profits.

Strunk's contact in the United States is Frederick Weiss.

1 The Nazi Diehards

JANUARY 5, 1954
Library to Research

Our files provide the epilogue to the Strunk story. Here is a letter from the Düsseldorf schoolteacher to Weiss:

> Your handbills are here and are being shipped out at once to friends. They are already delighted with them and are calling for more. Please send us at least 150 copies of each kind. You can be sure that they get to the right people and are fully understood. . . . I am sending you some earlier articles of mine so that you can get an idea of my work. These are the only samples out of my important material. The handbill "Did Hitler Really Destroy Six Million Jews" should be given to thousands of people. The contents of this article are the right answer to the howls of the New York Jews. Also please read the throw-away, "The German People Are Guiltless." If you want to reprint it over there, you have my permission to do so. I only ask you give me a thousand copies of each.

As for the Adenauer-Star of David cartoon, it was prepared here in New York City on order of Frederick Weiss, who paid for it and for the cost of 20,000 copies, which he sent all over the world.

JANUARY 5, 1954
German Correspondent to Research

Strunk may have a fairly low place in the German anti-Semitic setup, low, that is, in comparison with the kind of tone maintained by figures like Naumann, Meinberg, and Grimm; but he cannot be termed rock-bottom when men like Otto Mahncke and Rolf Kempcke are still around. These two, organizers of anti-Jewish street-corner rowdyism, are ex-Storm Troopers from Hamburg, and have been arrested a number of times by local police. But despite this and repeated warnings from the Bonn government, Mahncke has recruited nearly a hundred men into his imitation Brown Shirts in Hamburg, and Kempcke still

II Cross-Currents in Germany

leads a group there, the Verband deutscher Soldaten, in clandestine anti-Semitic agitation.

I wonder if they have United States tie-ups.

JANUARY 8, 1954
Library to Research

Mahncke and Kempcke, according to our files, have relied heavily on the National Renaissance Party here. The two Hamburg Nazis had an arrangement with Madole's NRP whereby letterheads, layouts, and mailing lists were forwarded to New York, and their literature, illegal in Germany, was then run off on the NRP's mimeograph machine and mailed to individuals back in Germany.

Two   The New Foundation

JANUARY 8, 1954
Press Department to BRE

The N.Y. *Herald Tribune* bureau in Bonn asserted this week that the German Reichs Party, as the result of its crushing defeat in the national elections in September, has dropped almost completely out of sight. According to this source, the immense publicity that the party achieved by running Werner Naumann achieved nothing else.

Other experts on the German scene have been filing dispatches suggesting the demise of the neo-Nazi movement because of its repudiation by the electorate.

JANUARY 12, 1954
Research to BRE

It would be fine if the tentative conclusion of the several experts in Bonn were accurate. However, you should be aware that despite laws and repeated threats of police repression a section of the press still exists in Germany devoted to keeping ultra-nationalist and totalitarian

II Cross-Currents in Germany

sentiment alive. Though such attitudes are by no means typical of the German press, we must be concerned about the number of fascists and anti-Semites who, with the lifting of Allied restriction, resumed their National Socialist propaganda activities.

We have here, from our European sources, content analyses of at least thirty newspapers and magazines which appear to be extremely rightist, ultra-nationalist, or outrightly pro-Nazi.

They range from the blatant *Reichsruf*, official publication of the German Reichs Party in Hanover, and the *Wiking-Ruf*, organ of the Elite Guard Veterans Organization, both ardent supporters of Hitlerism, to the more careful right-wing publications of the *Stahlhelm* type, the organ of the Steel Helmet organization.

Of course there were many more than three-times-thirty Nazi newspapers in the days of Hitler's German Reich, the total circulation of which then numbered in the millions instead of the five-figure circulation today.

But the continued publication of this hard core cannot be ignored.

JANUARY 14, 1954
Press Department to BRE

Chancellor Adenauer's comment in an address before the National Press Club in Washington on April 8, 1953, should be read in the light of the press summary you already have. He said:

"Naturally there are still a few die-hard National Socialists in Germany. Indeed, it would be a miracle if this were not the case . . . but a few Nazis do not, by a long sight, make for a German people controlled by National Socialism."

JANUARY 22, 1954
From the Minutes of the ADL Commission Meeting

The German Mission's proposals were considered within the councils of the Anti-Defamation League in the light of

2 The New Foundation

1. Jewish relationships to Germany
2. the Israeli-German and German-American restitution agreements
3. American policy toward the Bonn government, and
4. the part which West Germany is likely to play in the Western alliance as a result of that policy.

After consultation with the U. S. State Department, the League decided to accept the German invitation if we are assured complete freedom of action and public report.

JANUARY 26, 1954
AF to BRE

Called the German Mission's representative and informed him of the conditions upon which we would accept the Bonn government's invitation.

FEBRUARY 23, 1954
BRE to ADL Commission

Since our policy meeting in November, several exploratory conferences were held with the German Mission.

We have been assured by the German representatives that our study team will have complete freedom of action, that we may arrange such conferences as we desire, and that we may make such appointments and investigations as we may independently decide to undertake. We have also been assured that there is no question whatsoever as to our complete freedom of publication in our findings.

Attached are excerpts from the official invitation which came after the understandings set forth above were arrived at, and which we have therefore accepted. The invitation from Bonn, extended by Secretary of State Walter Hallstein to a three-man ADL committee, reads as follows:

Bonn, February 17, 1954
On behalf of the Federal Government I have the honor to invite you

II Cross-Currents in Germany

to a four weeks' study tour of the Federal Republic and Berlin (West).

This study tour is intended to enable you to see conditions in the new Germany for yourself. You will be given an opportunity to acquaint yourself with conditions in the Federal Republic in general and in your special field of interest in particular.

By resolution of the German Bundestag 80 leading personalities in American public, political and cultural life were invited for the first time last year under the Federal Government's America Exchange Programme. In view of the great value attaching to such an exchange programme it has been decided to repeat the America Exchange Programme this year. The participants will again travel in small groups ... assembled according to spheres of interest. The stay in Germany is to last four weeks.

From among a number of nominations put forward by American and German quarters you have been chosen as a participant in the group "Civic Rights." . . .

May I express the hope that it will be possible for you to accept this invitation. I should be greatly obliged to you for an early reply.

With the expression of my high consideration.

FEBRUARY 23, 1954

AF to Research

Continue your coverage of Werner Naumann in Germany; intensify your study of his operations with friends in this country—and correlate the results for me.

MARCH 1, 1954

German Correspondent to Research

Despite the government crackdown last September, Werner Naumann is unmistakably convinced that Der Tag, *his* Tag, though it may not be tomorrow, is only several years away; and if he has no illusions that a return to power will be easy, he is also not at all dismayed.

Naumann continues to chafe under the restrictions imposed by West German authorities; he wants to work more openly. "My arrest helped me more than it hurt me," he says. "I was able to see who my real

2 The New Foundation

friends are; those who stuck with me." Still he does worry about another British move against him.

After years of petty intrigue and government harassment, the neo-Nazi groups have now finally centered about Naumann. The nominal bosses of at least four separate splinter groups, in talks with newspaper correspondents, have acknowledged that Naumann's prestige, personality, and, above all, his dedication to the cause, make him an ideal choice for Fuehrer.

Naumann maintains that, if he were free to campaign politically, within a year he would garner the support of at least twenty per cent of the voters. He insists that the older Germans—many of them former Nazi Party members—are still awaiting a leader with a dynamic program. He remains confident that he will have the support of many former Hitler Youth, who are now of fighting age, and of many old Waffen-SS men.

The failure of his party to win representation in the Bundestag does not disconcert him. Looking back, he wonders whether, in light of the newness of the party's reorganization, its limited budget, and short membership drive, it was wise at all to participate in the September elections. He and the other party leaders are looking three years ahead; three years in which quietly to build up an active membership. They recognize that those who openly join the movement are hard-core followers unafraid of government threats or the loss of their jobs.

While the party seems publicly inactive, its individual leaders are nevertheless busy. General Alexander Andrae occupies himself with pro-Nazi speeches in Hamburg, and other ex-generals in the Naumann group cautiously recruit friends from among veteran organizations.

No wonder that Naumann, supervising this revival, quietly boasts, "I often say that one live German is more effective than ten half-dead ones!" He regards himself as that "live German," dynamic and astute; and the "half-dead ones" are the quarreling, unspectacular neo-Nazi, splinter-group leaders whom he is nevertheless corralling. Down inside, Naumann dismisses them as dullards and fumblers, confident that if and when Germany gets its next Fuehrer he, Naumann, will be that man.

II   Cross-Currents in Germany

MARCH 3, 1954
German Correspondent to Research

I spent an entire day with Werner Naumann at his private villa in Düsseldorf. In the luxurious comfort of his large living room he talked quietly and earnestly of his hopes for the neo-Nazi movement, its plans, its strength, its weaknesses. Leading the discussion around to people and movements in other countries, I mused about the lack of sympathy for his viewpoint in those places.

"I have only a few contacts in the United States," he said. "Pretty good ones, but few."

"Americans generally do not burn with nationalism."

"In England they do," he replied, "at least more than in the States. Yet my following there isn't much greater."

"Mosley and his group; some others. But in France and Belgium I have a vast number of friends—the thousands of people who sympathized and collaborated with us, with the National Socialists. They were so abominably treated afterwards that they are our friends for life. They wait only for the day we return to power."

Naumann insists he will have no truck with former Nazis who support a policy of collaboration with the Soviet Union. Some of these former Nazi pals have taken East German money, others have gone clean over the border. Naumann says he wants no part of them.

Officially Naumann eschews anti-Semitism as of dubious political value at a time when the neo-Nazi movement must move carefully to avoid the further political sanctions of both the Bonn government and the occupation authorities. However, an insight into his personal attitude toward Jews may be gleaned from these statements made to me:

"There was always social anti-Jewish feeling in upper circles in Germany. My father was a judge. We had a Jewish doctor for the family and my father was in daily contact with Jews in the court. But he never thought to bring them home. That snobbish sentiment is still there, plus the impact of ten years of Hitler's anti-Semitic propaganda.

2 The New Foundation

Jews whose families were victims of Hitler's policy have understandable grounds to hate us as long as they live."

Admirable objectivity; but despite his air of sophistication, Naumann is unable to divorce himself from the more tired clichés of his political background. For example:

"I feel that Jews shaped the Morgenthau policy, and that this has done great harm to us. I believe that Jewish influence is mainly responsible for the United States continuing to keep several hundred Nazis jailed at Landsberg. Also, I am informed that over sixty per cent of the money in New York City is Jewish. Naturally, I hope that this dominant Jewish influence will not continue."

Yet Naumann insists he does not go along "with the nonsense of a world Jewish conspiracy, with fantastic notions about the Sanhedrin and with mystic masonic interlockings dominating the world."

MARCH 8, 1954
New York Correspondent to Research

Our investigations have produced additional documentation on the intimate relationships between Werner Naumann's propaganda brain, Heinrich Malz, and Frederick Weiss. Repeatedly Heinrich Malz has stated in letters to Weiss his debt for various services. For example, on the subject of the "co-operation" between Wall Street Jews and Soviet Communist Jews, Malz writes (December 19, 1951):

I know perfectly well that I would be just floating in the air with all my work without you, because it is absolutely clear that it was you, and you alone, who gave me the insight into the decisive relationships and background.

Paying tribute to Weiss's ideas and suggestions, Malz writes (May 18, 1951):

Just received your letter of May 14th. Thanks for your understanding of my situation. After these things are now clarified, I feel much freer to start with my work for you. You will have received my long letter of May 16th. My next undertaking will be an article for C.S. [*Common Sense*]. You may expect it by the end of this month. Enclosed is the

II Cross-Currents in Germany

May issue [*Die Andere Seite*]. You'll recognize some initial ideas from your material. . . .

I owe you, dear Mr. Weiss, special thanks for your willingness to open for me special sources of information. . . . Of course, I shall make available to you all information of which I am sure is within your sphere of interest.

And in gratitude to Weiss for providing him with American contacts, Malz writes (January 3, 1952):

The readiness to absorb our material over there [the U.S.] seems to be very great. . . . I just now need a breathing spell to organize systematically the entire correspondence going abroad. In this respect also you have rendered invaluable services. I am dissatisfied with myself for not having had time to develop your wonderful points of departure.

MARCH 10, 1954
German Correspondent to Research

Special research projects are now being carried out by the Naumann group to buttress the "factual" structure of their propaganda.

Malz and his still unidentified friend are combing the works of Jewish scholars and writers, from the Old Testament to modern times, for material to work up unfavorable reflections on Jews and Jewish institutions.

Their assignment is a difficult one, for they had to start from scratch; under Hitler, anti-Semitic propaganda was raised to the level of a science. Many professors utilized their extensive knowledge and disciplined abilities to give anti-Semitic propaganda an appearance of historical validity. Over eight hundred graduate students in Germany during the Hitler era chose for their doctoral theses subjects dealing with one phase or another of the "Jewish Question."

Several large research institutes and libraries were thus built up, the largest at Frankfurt, called the Reichs Institute for History of the New Germany, with more than a hundred thousand books and pamphlets on the special subject of Jews. Alfred Rosenberg also developed a large anti-Semitic collection for his own use.

2 The New Foundation

This background material is all gone; so the Naumann group, under the direction of Malz and friend, have been secretly and laboriously rebuilding a research library to replace it. And they are slowly building up their newspaper clipping files with the help of Frederick Weiss and other friends abroad.

One of their important projects is the card indexing of prominent Jews and their activities throughout the world, with a separate file for the names and activities of German Jews who emigrated, tracing them to their present domiciles.

I am enclosing herewith a batch of the actual index cards from the growing Malz library which disclose the fields of interest and methods of operation of these Naumann research men. Of special fascination to them—and this is verified by careful analysis of all the cards—is the rise of Jewish nationalism; the writings of Theodor Herzl and other famous Zionists are gravely catalogued. Evidence is classified, "proving" that Jewish bankers (the Schiff-Warburg families, and others) finance both capitalism and communism. Thus, I suppose, any case can be argued from any side, according to what is needed and according to what file is consulted. Detailed notes are also made on Jews who visit Germany as representatives of the American government, private industry, the rabbinate, or educational agencies. Even the results of scanning HICOG's telephone directory for Jewish identifications are specifically recorded.

Busy as bees, and a lot more dangerous than hornets.

MARCH 12, 1954

German Correspondent to Research

Malz and his secret collaborator are making skillful use of their painstaking research in a 134-page study called *The Jewish War Against the German People*. A copy was sent posthaste to Frederick Weiss in the United States for processing and distribution to American fascists and anti-Semites.

This study is written in sensational, popular style designed for mass consumption and, needless to say, great liberties were taken with the

II Cross-Currents in Germany

source material. *The Jewish War Against the German People* is unsigned and purports to be written by an American. Still to be revised and expanded, the document is being prepared as a basic handbook for neo-Nazis and for propaganda abroad. Here are some brief excerpts:

Jewish subterranean influences have played an anonymous but dominant role in world history over the last 150 years. . . .

The number of Jews reported killed was grossly exaggerated. . . . American Jews confiscated the German archives where much documentary evidence existed.

Adolf Sabath [late congressman from Illinois], an uneducated little Hungarian Jew had enough power as an adviser of President Wilson to start the moves which resulted in the break-up of the Austro-Bohemian empire.

In our "Institute for Research on Jewish Question" there were 3,600 cases taken from Jewish secret archives and Free Mason files across Europe. Numerous German scholars worked feverishly to find documentary proof that international Jewish influence and freemasonry should be suppressed. But we did not have enough time to complete the work. Could we have done so perhaps our history books would have been rewritten. . . .

The one mistake of the Germans was that they did not see the real significance of this Jewish plutocracy and failed to protect themselves against its domination. In bringing the Germans to judgment the role of the Jews in inciting the Russian revolution and their part in bolshevik misdeeds must be established. It should not be overlooked that Germany offered the strongest bulwark against a drive from the East. While pinning guilt on the Germans, world Jewish leaders were laughing up their sleeves at having Germany made the culprit. By 1939, Germany was encircled. True the Germans started the war on Poland, but had it not been for Jewish influence, the war could have been localized. Long before Hitler had made any territorial demands the Jews through their diplomatic and business connections were already tightening the ring around Germany. . . .

God who created all peoples must have designed the Jews to serve as a test ordeal for us . . . looking back over recent events, we can

2 The New Foundation

see how the Jews have become a big anonymous world power acting according to their own inner laws. In modern history, there is no form of activity where Jews and their accomplices have not reached out to dominate. . . . The high achievements of different peoples on which European culture rests have been brushed aside by a Jewish conception of the equality of all people through mingling and standardization. Whatever form this Jewish influence takes it ends up in destroying all our nationally developed institutions. The emancipation of the Jews and freeing their destructive instincts are the cause of our disaster today.

In earlier times the common people were plundered by their temporal and church princes, but there were Jews at their elbows as financial advisers, tax collectors, profiteers. . . . In the middle ages, Jews fought to defend their enclosed existence. After emancipation Jews no longer fought to survive but to dominate.

The above excerpts clearly indicate the low and mendacious intellectual level of Malz and his research staff, who are producing propaganda no less vicious than the worst of the Hitler era.

MARCH 15, 1954
BRE to AF

You have our itinerary. Keep in close touch and be sure we receive any up-to-the-minute data relevant to our study.

MARCH 30, 1954
German Correspondent to Research

The visit of the ADL Study Team is in progress; and we have had a different type of visitor too: Colonel Hans Rudel's trip to Germany is just ending and he is re-embarking for Buenos Aires. Rudel's reason for his visit was a mission from President Peron to invite German athletes to the Argentine. Transparent, if you wish, but how he wangled it, we don't know.

As you might expect, the German Reichs Party newspaper, *Der*

Reichsruf, making the best of this occasion, painted Rudel as a victim of petty persecution by the Bonn regime. It also reported that during his stay the famous flier visited two generals of the Waffen-SS, Sepp Dietrich and Joachim Peiper, at Landsberg Prison, and, in bringing greetings to these ex-Nazi generals, declared that he spoke in the name of all ex-German servicemen and all German patriots.

The colonel is the main link between the remnants of Nazism now in the Argentine and the German fascists; his closest ties are with the Naumann crowd. His political ambitions, however, and they are not small, keep him in contact with several other neo-Nazi groups by correspondence and during his frequent visits to Germany. Not only that, but his books, the best known of which is *Stuka Pilot,* are widely circulated in Europe.

In 1952, after devising a plan to raid Werl Prison and set free some Nazi war criminals held in the British Zone, he outlined his scheme to a deputy in the Bundestag, Dr. Erich Mende. Mende told a press conference later that Rudel also tried to enlist the aid of a former general of the Waffen-SS. Both, however, refused to have anything to do with Rudel's proposal.

Such planning and such activity certainly indicate how dedicated a Nazi Rudel is and has been.

APRIL 2, 1954
Library to AF

Hans Rudel, once a Luftwaffe ace and deeply loyal to Hitler, became a Nazi idol when he remained in the air corps as a flier after losing a foot.

He now lives in the Argentine. In addition to his German contacts, he is in communication with Arthur Koegel and Frederick Weiss; he hopes they will promote some of his books here. His contact, however, is not solely on literary matters. Last July 28 he wrote to Weiss:

Thanks for the Fleckenstein letter. I have known Hausleiter for years and we consult one another often. Naumann refused to join him in the election as I proposed. Naumann has by far and away the better head. My running for office cannot take place soon because of economic reasons. That is, I can't afford to take the trip for the election. I have telegraphed and telephoned several times in the last few days to Germany; however I cannot take the trip over because I am $500 short.

According to our files, Rudel has also been in touch with Keith Thompson, the New Jersey friend of Frederick Weiss.

Rudel is the "glamour boy" of the pro-Nazis here, who have been eager to exhibit their darling battle-scarred hero in the United States. The Nazis in Argentina were just as eager to have Rudel visit these shores, and called on Weiss to help facilitate this cultural mission. But none of Weiss's contacts has been able to help Rudel get a visa. Weiss might well be wary of mixing with the immigration authorities, too, considering his own status.

Weiss has, however, kept up an active interchange of services with the Nazis in Argentina. The publishing house Duerer Verlag, headed by E. Fritsch, is the main Nazi propaganda center in all Latin America. Weiss receives the publication *Der Weg* and other Nazi material, including anti-Semitic leaflets in bulk for circulation in this country from this group.

Now you have the tie-up—United States, Germany, and Argentina. We understand Research is receiving final documentation on Weiss's ties to the rest of our domestic political delinquents. That should complete the story.

APRIL 3, 1954

New York Correspondent to Research

I questioned Fred Weiss very closely to understand more fully his relationship with James Madole, head of the National Renaissance Party.

"Madole is just a messenger boy for me," said Weiss.

"But you sponsor him as a leader."

"We use all kinds of characters. We have such a shortage of leaders,

II Cross-Currents in Germany

I would use the very Devil himself if I thought it would help get us what we are after. Madole is basically honest but fanatical and ignorant. I find him convenient to run errands and I also can put whatever I please into his *Renaissance Bulletin*. He sends the publication to a list of about a thousand names. His contributors carry half the cost and I'm saved the bother of distributing."

In other words, Fred Weiss is behind James Madole's National Renaissance Party. It may not be the cleanest façade, but it's a convenient one. Generally, Madole goes through the correspondence addressed to his party and then turns it over to Weiss, who writes follow-up letters when he is particularly interested. Madole's correspondence shows how useful he can be to his necessarily retiring mentor, Weiss. George Deatherage, onetime head of the Knights of the White Camellia, writing to Madole last December 10 from Palm Beach, Florida, says:

I will appreciate it very much if you will keep us advised of things as they develop. At the moment, we are concentrating on research—so that we can supply these many new organizations starting up with ... data. ... Upton Close is here with me and we are issuing Closer-ups from here. ... Things are changing rapidly—are they not? Germany holds the key to the whole world problem and their recovery has been amazing. I hope that some leadership will develop there that will make Germany the controlling force in the whole of Europe. They have control now—if they but realize it, as NATO nor anyone else can accomplish anything without her. This should be the basis for German-Americans, whose loyalty to this country, I think, is tops, to start making themselves a potent force in American life and as opposition to the Jewish communist control. ... Personally we can expect nothing from the GOP or the administration as they are Jew controlled in a greater sense than the Truman administration. This means still a long hard fight—and I am convinced that we will eventually fight the issues out in the streets ... within the next decade. ... Do you have a list of names and addresses of existing German-American organizations? I would like to get them on our mailing lists with the idea that we can get them working again actively.

2 The New Foundation

APRIL 5, 1954
Research to AF

Completed the examination of available Weiss material. Here, over the years, are some of Weiss's numerous American correspondents:
From Gerald L. K. Smith (January 15, 1951):

I find your autograph about as difficult to read as my own, so I guess this supports the axiom that brilliant minds do not produce legible autographs. I want to thank you for the booklet, "The Untouchables," and the liberty you have given me in quoting from same. Some years ago, you wrote a book or two, and I have forgotten the titles. Would you kindly give me same, and do you have any of these books on hand?

A telegram about Benjamin Freedman from Conde McGinley which went to a dozen people (December 16, 1950):

RE ANNA M. ROSENBERG, SMEARBUND ATTEMPTING DISCREDIT FREEDMAN WITH AMERICAN GROUPS FIGHTING FOR FREEDOM. STATEMENTS NEWSPAPERS AND RADIO CONCERNING FREEDMAN RETRACTIONS ABSOLUTELY UNTRUE. FREEDMAN MORE FAITHFUL LOYAL ENERGETIC THAN EVER BEFORE. ACCEPT PERSONAL UNQUALIFIED GUARANTEES FREEDMAN'S FAITHFULNESS FULFILLMENT LOYAL AMERICAN OBJECTIVE. WHAT WE NEED NOW IS MORE FREEDMANS. DIG THEM UP THERE. COMPLETE STORY FOLLOWS. REGARDS.

From Forrest C. Sammons, the direct-mail anti-Semitic propagandist of Huntington, West Virginia (April 8, 1951):

I am asking him [my wife's brother-in-law] to see that these papers are properly placed and to advise you directly the names of any German-American newspapers or magazines that may be published in Cincinnati. Thanks for remembering me and I hope that we get the information and make the contacts you want.

From Edward James Smythe,[1] alcoholic editor of the *Protestant Statesmen and Nation,* Washington, D.C. (April 18, 1951):

Some time ago we sent a bundle of your small books over to England and Germany for distribution over there. I'll be damned if in the past week we have had several requests for more of them.

[1] Edward James Smythe died on August 16, 1955.

II Cross-Currents in Germany

(March 26, 1951):
We have received those brochures. . . . Now what are you going to do with them? And how many have you got? And are you interested in placing them where they will do the most good? . . . If so, suppose we map out a plan for you that will bring you the best results.

(November 25, 1950):
Many thanks for that booklet, it is the best ever. Could you spare about a dozen of them so that we could send them out all over the country and bring about a "Review" of it and a greater circulation?

From professional patrioteer W. Henry MacFarland, Jr., Philadelphia:

You will be glad to know, I feel, that only $125 now stands in the way of releasing "National Progress" as a printed publication. . . . I feel sure that the paper can be speedily placed on a paying basis, and afterward enlarged to 12 pages and a still more newspaperlike size. I hope that it may replace "The Broom" as the Nationalist paper in New York, since De Aryan's publication has, in my opinion, become little more than a medium for personal attacks upon persons with whom he disagrees.

APRIL 5, 1954
Library to AF

Analysis of the content of Weiss's propaganda reveals an interesting fact:

Despite his general anti-communism, Weiss and his foreign associates have taken over the communist propaganda cliché that the United States is dominated by Wall Street and by the international bankers. Their additional contribution is the Nazi equation of international bankers and Jews. This theme has inspired every anti-Semitic pamphleteer in the U.S. from Gerald L. K. Smith to Conde McGinley. If the level of inspiration has not been high, the volume of output has certainly been great.

Weiss has also acted as a muse to his professional followers for their propaganda ideas in attacking the United Nations. The Jews are "back

2 The New Foundation

of it all. They are coaxing us," he says, "to give up our arms and our national safety to a supernational authority. They are the sinister force behind our one-world apostles. They are the extinguisher of our entire Western culture. May we not well despair of the future when we see a mob, misguided, misruled, and misled by this sinister force in our midst?"

APRIL 5, 1954
Library to AF

Here is the final tabulation of some of the people, reputable and otherwise, working with Frederick Charles Weiss:

Germany

   Research and writing: Heinrich Malz and unknown collaborator; Erich Schmidt, editor of *Reichsruf*.
   Publishing: Arthur Ehrhardt, intellectual mouthpiece for neo-Nazism, publisher in Coburg of the monthly magazine *Nation Europa;* W. Schutz of the publishing firm of Plesse Verlag; Erich Schmidt's weekly newspaper, *Reichsruf,* current official publication for Naumann's German Reichs Party; other neo-Nazi party publications.
   Distributing: Peter Wallraf, of Cologne, former Nazi governor in Ukraine—currently high-level contact man for neo-Nazi groups; Fritz Roesler, former leader of the outlawed Socialist Reichs Party; Johann Strunk, a schoolteacher in Düsseldorf; Otto Mahncke and other leaders of neo-Nazi cells.

Great Britain

   Writing: Sir Oswald Mosley, an editorialist for the London-published *The European,* an intellectual fascist magazine; helps shape policy for *Action,* a rabble-rousing hate sheet published in the same city. A. Raven Thomson, Mosley's right-hand man and editor. Peter J. Huxley-Blythe, publisher of *Natinform,* an international fascist infor-

II Cross-Currents in Germany

mation newsletter. Blythe has close connections with Nazis and Arabs. Arnold Leese: For over thirty years has been running the Imperial Fascist League in London and publishing a violent anti-Semitic sheet *Gothic Ripples*.

Argentina

Writing: Colonel Hans Ulrich Rudel; E. Fritsch, head of the publishing house in Buenos Aires, Duerer Verlag, principal German-language and neo-Nazi propaganda center in Latin America—its official publication is the monthly magazine *Der Weg*. Fritsch also sends Weiss anti-Semitic leaflets in bulk for circulation in the United States.

United States

Research, writing, publishing, and distribution: Keith Thompson, Chatham, New Jersey, propagandist; Austin J. App, Boniface Press, Philadelphia, Pennsylvania; Conde McGinley, *Common Sense*, Union, New Jersey; Frank Britton, *The American Nationalist*, Englewood, California; Robert H. Williams, *Williams Intelligence Summary*, Santa Ana, California; Forrest C. Sammons, Huntington, West Virginia; Edward Fleckenstein, Weehawken, New Jersey; Arthur Koegel, German-American *Buerger Zeitung*, Chicago, Illinois; James Madole, head of the National Renaissance Party, Beacon, New York; Mrs. Lyrl Van Hyning, *Women's Voice*, Chicago, Illinois; Russ Roberts, Detroit, Michigan; W. Henry MacFarland, Jr., Philadelphia, Pennsylvania; and a host of lesser operators.

APRIL 6, 1954
German Study Team to Library

Our impressions here after three weeks:
Nine years after Hitler, the traveler's first impression of Germany is shock at the devastation which meets his eye in important sections of almost every city; his second is amazement at the high degree of economic activity and the feverish efforts at rebuilding. But it is the

2 The New Foundation

third, and delayed, impression which really gives him a jolt. This comes after some days or even weeks.

The traveler finds he has met dozens of people—Germans, Americans, refugees from the East, liberals, conservatives, Protestants, Catholics, Jews, even an unreconstructed Nazi or two. He has met people who are perplexed, depressed, resigned, feverishly active, thoughtful, or strictly on the make. He has met liberals who have returned from years of exile—self-imposed or otherwise—who hope that the time has finally come for rebuilding a democratic Germany. He has met a Jew here and there who, unable to adjust to life elsewhere, has come back to what he considers home, hoping to recapture some of the spirit of the once flourishing Jewish community. He has met any number of German patriots who hope that out of defeat and destruction, and the great suffering Germans have undergone, Germany will yet rise to become the leading power in western Europe. (On the other hand, if he meets a Frenchman, the latter will express the same thought, with disapproval, of course; and, if it's an American, the answer will still be the same, but on a note of equivocation.) He has met refugees from the East who hope that at last they can find surcease in a congenial German atmosphere from their forced wanderings. But few of these he has met are happy.

The returned liberal may talk bravely to keep up his courage, but he finds he has returned to a wasteland where the people, still suffering deep traumas, will not listen to him. The returning Jew finds himself doubly isolated by one wall he has erected himself, because he can neither forget what has happened nor know which hand he shakes is stained with the blood of his kin, and by another erected by his neighbors to whom his presence is a reminder of guilt. They'd rather he went away. The German patriots are weighed down by the enormity of the task before them; by the ubiquitous wreckage, physical and spiritual, of their former greatness; by the knowledge that to the East are deadly enemies, and to the West, reluctant allies. The refugees from the East—the eleven million Volksdeutsche—find themselves in a difficult position. This may be their spiritual home, but there isn't much spirit here, and physically they are crowding upon the natives who, because of the destruction, find a twenty-five per cent increase in the population makes life even harder for them. And this is very hard indeed.

APRIL 7, 1954
Letter from Germany
BRE to AF

Last night I attended a political meeting at the invitation of Dr. Waldemar Lentz, whom I had met at a session of the Federal Center for Home Service, the Bonn government's agency for democratic education. It was a meeting of the Bad Godesburg unit of the All-German Bloc party.

Dr. Lentz, as the presiding officer, introduced me with a warm welcome when I entered the room—a meeting hall in a *Bierstube*—explaining to about a hundred men and women that I was an American and a Jew, and that "the Jewish question" was put on the agenda after I had agreed to attend and participate. Everyone was to speak with complete candor, he requested. "That would be the only way," he said, "anything worth while would come of the discussion."

The first speaker from the floor, a gray-haired man, said he believed that the German-Israeli restitution agreement, purely a question of foreign policy, would not benefit Germany. "Israel got everything and Germany got nothing," he added. "The government should have insisted upon something in return."

A young man then sharply insisted that it was hardly a "political" question but a moral one. He emphasized that restitution to Israel would be proof to the civilized world that Germany accepted collective responsibility for what had happened to the Jews, and made reparation as an indication of good faith. "I served in the war and, while I personally did nothing against the Jews, as an individual I share in the responsibility and the 'collective shame' which President Heuss spoke about in his famous address."

A one-armed war veteran came to his feet to say that he blamed the whole Jewish question not only on the government but also on the parents. Somewhat shamedly he confessed that his father had taught him to hate three groups: the French, the Catholics, and the Jews. "I had no personal reason for hating any of them," he concluded calmly, "and only after I matured into manhood did I realize this."

The next speaker first identified himself as a war veteran and an ex-Storm Trooper. "What had happened to the Jews," he said, "was the desire of a small clique of Nazis and not the will of the German people. It was not real 'hatred' that the Germans felt toward the Jews, but rather a kind of *Ablehnung* [rejection]." There were murmurs of agreement.

At this point the chairman, Dr. Lentz, looking at the audience but speaking to me, explained that he thought I should know that this political party had the reputation of having a larger percentage of former Nazis than any other political party. "It numbers only 500,000, but I felt Mr. Epstein would get a more frank and forthright expression from the people in attendance here than anywhere else." These were not "intelligentsia," he added, these were working people and white-collar workers. Dr. Lentz sat down.

A man who was sitting at the head table then stood up and very boldly announced that he had been an officer of the SS and that he lived only a hundred metres from Sachsenhausen, one of the most horrible concentration camps. He had not known what had gone on behind those walls. "All the concentration camps' activities were military secrets, kept from the people and known only to those directly participating. We heard from others that residents of towns where concentration camps were located, such as Dachau, knew nothing of what went on behind the walls. They were aware only of a peculiar odor from the smoke which emanated from the camps."

That unloosed torrents. One speaker said the only thing he had against the Jews was that they separated themselves from the Germans. Several agreed with him. A number rose to tell of personal friends, fine people, who were Jews, and how deeply they regretted what had happened to them. Others recalled that they were horrified by the events of Crystal Night in 1938 when the synagogues were burned by the

11 Cross-Currents in Germany

Nazis. "This was terrible," they lamented, "and most Germans were horrified."

By this time I had had my fill of the "it-was-awful-but-I-wasn't-in-favor-of-it" line. I decided to get a few things off my chest.

I asked for the floor and, talking to the group in German, I explained first that I could not speak in separate roles as an American and as a Jew—because I was both—but as both I offered to try showing the distinction in my reactions to Germany. In sum, I quietly spelled out each step in Hitler's program to destroy the world, and I emphasized that nobody but the German people could have stopped him in time, and that their guilt rested in their refusal to do so.

It was twenty minutes later that, beaded with perspiration, I sat down to mild applause. Dr. Lentz turned and thanked me. Then, in his friendliest manner, he added: "When two fellows fight and one wins and the other loses, the winner should walk to the loser, put his arm around his shoulder, and say, 'Come on, let's make up.' The Germans lost, the Jews won. Now that all of this is behind us, shouldn't the Jews make some gesture to the Germans?" As a Jew, he asked me what the next step should be.

I'm afraid my response was not in as calm a voice as I would have liked; it is difficult to hear murder described in tennis terms—"Love all," might have been his next remark. "The Jews didn't win," I exclaimed, "they lost six million. The *Allied nations* were fighting Germany; it was the *civilized world* versus *Hitlerism*. In a war no one wins."

As regarded Jews taking the first step, I pointed out that our acceptance of the invitation of the West German Government, an acceptance by the largest Jewish organization in the world, to come and visit, was in itself a friendly gesture, a first step.

The group broke into loud applause.

"As Americans and as Jews," I went on, "we want to lend every effort to help build a democratic society in what we consider to be one of the key nations of Europe."

I returned to my hotel room and tried to fall asleep. I wished I were back home.

APRIL 10, 1954
German Study Team to Library

We're leaving Germany at dawn tomorrow—exhausted. Included in the visit were eight of the major cities in Germany—Bonn, Cologne, Düsseldorf, Frankfurt, Karlsruhe, Berlin, and Hamburg—and a number of smaller towns and villages in their immediate vicinity.

After our arrival in Germany on March 16 we spent a month here. A stay of this duration naturally precluded any efforts at independent scientific researches, statistical studies, or opinion-polling. No original work was therefore undertaken in these areas. Our plan of operation was to concentrate upon an interviewing process for determining—against a background of known facts about Germany today—the thinking and the views of its various leaders.

In a period of thirty days we spoke extensively with 115 leaders in public life—in government, in the political parties, in civic work, religion, and education. We consulted with writers, editors, political commentators. Finally we spoke with Americans in Germany, U. S. Government officials and others; and with leaders of the tiny Jewish communities that remain or have been revived. We also had an opportunity to observe the operation of government bureaus, of some of the new communal groups concerned with democratic development, of the official Jewish communal organizations, and of American organizations such as Radio Free Europe, RIAS (the U.S. radio station in Berlin), the America Houses, and the U. S. High Commission itself.

A normal day for us began at eight in the morning and continued into the late evening. In addition to the individual interviews, we were also able to engage in group discussions, organizational meetings, and home visits that greatly augmented our total impressions. Half of our time in Germany was spent in Bonn and Berlin. This is readily understandable—Bonn is the center of German political life, while Berlin has major problems that differ from those in West Germany; Berlin also has the largest Jewish community in Germany today.

II Cross-Currents in Germany

In studying we concentrated on (1) developments in the attitudes of Germans toward civil rights and the democratic processes; (2) conditions among the remaining 25,000 Jews in Germany; and (3) the relationship between this small group of Jews and the rest of the population.

APRIL 19, 1954
BRE to AF

Delighted to be back.

I understand the Werner Naumann investigation is virtually completed. How do you interpret the information you have accumulated about his activities?

APRIL 23, 1954
AF to BRE

Several loose ends must be tied together before the Naumann-Weiss investigation is complete. I am told the needed data is on the way. In the meantime, our material is being collated and studied. When it is finished you will receive our conclusions.

MAY 27, 1954
AF to German Correspondent

You may have the impression in Germany that the National Renaissance Party, on which you have reported from time to time, is a thing of substance. The following incident of a week ago may disabuse you.

It was after six when I arrived on the Boston flyer at Grand Central Station. Ordinarily I would have hastened home immediately instead of trudging back to the office, but it was still daylight, so I chose to run into the "shop" for a quick glance at the day's mail.

The ADL office was unattended except for the cleaning woman, and

2 The New Foundation

as I walked to my desk the telephone rang as though it knew I had just come in. I picked it up, wondering who'd be calling at this late hour.

"This the ADL?"

"Yes."

"You interested in information about the NRP?"

"Who is this?" The voice wasn't gruff, but it wasn't tutored either.

"Never mind. You interested in getting the real dope on the NRP? Don't ask questions. Just answer mine."

I was curious now. "You mean the National Renaissance Party?" I prodded gently, knowing full well he did, and detecting nervousness and uncertainty under his rough tone.

He ignored my question. "Listen, I got everything. The works. But I gotta get paid for it. And I gotta be protected."

"Protected from whom?"

Again he ignored me. "I don't want no double-cross. I have all the correspondence. Original letters. From all over Europe and from this country. Between the top guys. It shows the whole Nazi network, name by name. And I can get you their mailing lists too. Is that worth money to you?"

"That depends," I answered, not especially excited about the data he might turn over. The National Renaissance Party is a noisy Yorkville group whose members garb themselves in replicas of the Hitler Storm Trooper uniform with an added patch of red lightning over the breast pocket. Although they have been active for several years they amount to little—a grubby fistful of exhibitionists ignored by the New York press.

"Why don't you come into the office tomorrow morning and we'll talk?"

"I can't. I'm too important," he snapped.

"What do you mean?"

"I'd be recognized."

"That's silly. If we meet, wherever it is, I'll have to look at you," I said, explaining what I thought obvious.

"I don't want everybody in your office to know about it. Just you. Outside the office. They'd all recognize me."

II Cross-Currents in Germany

Only a handful of our personnel would even know the *name* of his so-called party. Were he its head, James Madole, or the next in command, Mana Truhill, perhaps our staff men assigned to watching domestic lunatic groups might know his face. But they're not a memorable collection.

"Okay, let's meet away from my office." I told him who I was, and agreed to meet him outside the next day at 11 A.M.

At ten in the morning, at my desk a lieutenant of the New York City Police Department listened to the story and agreed to follow me to my "rendezvous"; he might recognize the man. The city police know all the leaders of the National Renaissance Party.

I waited in vain for almost an hour in the midtown hotel lobby and then returned to the office where, thirty minutes later, our stranger obsequiously announced himself to the receptionist. "Send him in," I said.

Nobody in the entire office recognized the slim, short, dark-complexioned, twenty-five-year-old, armed-robbery convict who, out on parole, was the New Jersey state director of the National Renaissance Party. Quite a title.

Attached are excerpts—unessential details deleted—from the statement he gave us this morning. Of course he made the usual offer to inform for us and, as usual, we said no.

I, Larry Sestito, do hereby make the following voluntary statement to . . . the Anti-Defamation League.

Thursday evening, May 20, at approximately 6:30 P.M., I called Arnold Forster. . . . I told Mr. Forster . . . that I was in a position to furnish him and his organization valuable information on the National Renaissance Party . . . we arranged to meet on Friday, May 21, at 11:00 in the morning . . . I appeared at the office of the Anti-Defamation League at approximately 12:30 P.M. . . .

I indicated . . . my real identity as Larry Sestito . . . at one time the New Jersey director for the NRP . . . although I did not occupy this position at this time, I was placed high enough within the organization so that I could provide the Anti-Defamation League with regular information. I indicated that I would be willing to do this for "expenses." . . .

2 The New Foundation

During the year 1952, I was serving out a term in the New Jersey State Penitentiary at Rahway. . . . While in prison, I had read a number of newspaper articles dealing with H. Keith Thompson. As a result, I wrote him a letter. . . . He answered my letter . . . was interested in knowing all about me . . . why I was in prison, when I would be released, and if it were possible for him to come to talk with me. . . . I explained I was up for parole within a month. . . .

I was released from prison October 20, 1952, and went to see Thompson in Chatham, New Jersey. We talked of politics and about his program. At the time, Major General Remer was in jail. . . . He told me he was helping with funds, packages and other things. . . . I had read a lot about Germany and was interested to know from Thompson who these Nazis were, how they worked, what their ideas were, etc. He explained to me the workings of the Nazi Party . . . who the men were in the U.S. . . . said the Nazi Party was dead but something would come up once again. The program itself would be almost the same—but there would be no swastikas, etc.

. . . he was trying to get people to cooperate with him and organize a party. He didn't want it to be known that he was doing this and he was looking only for people he could trust. He told me that he tried to combine a lot of small organizations, but when this was impossible, he stopped. . . .

. . . Thompson was a speaker at several meetings of the NRP . . . he was not a member . . . he turned over his whole mailing list to the NRP.

I asked Thompson about the NRP and he told me to keep away from it because it would cause trouble. He felt that their program was too strong. By this he meant that they were too strong in their attacks on Jews. . . . I used to speak with people like Madole and Weiss. I attended some of the NRP meetings. . . . I received a letter from one Hans Schmidt. . . . He asked me to join the Elite Guard. . . . In November of last year, I spoke to Truhill, who told me he wanted me as director for the New Jersey NRP. This was even before I was a member of the party. . . .

Party discipline was my idea. I approached different people to recruit membership and funds—people I felt might be attracted to my program. The majority of new people did not agree with the NRP program because it was too strong for them. . . .

I asked Madole, about a month and a half ago, why the meeting halls could not be filled if the membership of the NRP was so big. Madole explained to me that they do not want to draw the intelligent people.

II Cross-Currents in Germany

They want the gutter and the dirt. They leave the intelligent people to Fred Weiss. Madole wants to overthrow the government.

I resigned as the New Jersey director of the party about two weeks ago. When I told Madole that I was resigning, he didn't like the idea, but he didn't say too much about it because he knows that I have been handling all the contacts for the party with the MSI movement in Italy. The MSI is the Fascist Party in that country. . . .

. . . the party plans to hold outdoor meetings in different parts of the city. They will use different front organizations for these meetings because no one wants to rent them a hall for a meeting place. . . .

. . . the party is just being used by Fred Weiss. . . . I got to know Mana Truhill fairly well and found that he really acted like two different people. When Madole and other officials of the party were in his presence, he was one person. He acted as a Nazi and a violent Jew-hater in their presence. When they weren't around, he spoke a lot about Communism . . . he has said that Russian Communism isn't any good, but that American Communism is. Although he spoke favorably about Communism many times after I got to know him, he never tried to convert me to Communism. He told me he took several courses at the Jefferson School, but I don't believe that he is a member of the Communist Party. . . .

In the time that I have been active in the NRP, I have come to the positive belief that the party is in existence only for the purpose of helping Fred Weiss. Although Weiss is not a member of the party, he does give money to it frequently. I don't know much about his background or who he is, since I only met him for the first time in December, 1953, or January, 1954 . . . he has lots of contacts with Nazis in Europe. I know that very often people who are going to Europe see Weiss first, and he gives them letters of introduction to the Nazis he knows in Europe. I imagine, from what I have seen and heard, that the whole purpose of the NRP is to have a fascist group here in the United States that can cooperate with the Nazis in Europe who are waiting for the time when they can come back into power. I know that the NRP has received letters of encouragement from these Nazis and fascists in Europe. I know there is some kind of relationship between Weiss, Keith Thompson, Edward Fleckenstein and George Viereck. . . .

The head of the Elite Guard is an Italian by the name of Mustachio. For the last several months, the NRP has been responsible for the scattering of leaflets and handbills in various sections of the city. They have been doing this by going to the top floors in some of the large

2 The New Foundation

buildings in New York and throwing out of the window these circulars and letting them drift down to the street. They then take pictures of the leaflets drifting down and of people picking them up, and then send these pictures overseas to the Nazis in Europe, to show them what they are doing. Mustachio has been largely responsible for this kind of activity.

LARRY SESTITO

JUNE 8, 1954
German Correspondent to Research

Heinrich Malz's secret collaborator is Heinz Peter.

Led by Malz halfway across Germany without an indication of our destination or the person we were to meet, I finally found myself face to face with Heinz Peter—the man, who, during the Third Reich, had been one of the top directors of Dr. Walter Frank's anti-Semitic Institute at Frankfurt, Germany.

After eight days spent with Malz and Peter in the remote village of Neustadt on the Neckar River, where Peter lives now in almost total seclusion, I came away convinced that Peter is one of the outstanding Nazi braintrusters today, doing more thinking and planning, more basic research along totalitarian lines, and more anti-Semitic writing than anyone else in Germany. Walter Frank committed suicide after the Nazi capitulation, a broken, pathological, anti-Semite. His assistant, Heinz Peter, is neither broken nor pathological: he is a coldly dedicated anti-Semite whose life work is war against Jews.

During Hitler's march across Europe, Peter toured the Continent extensively, ransacking libraries and sending all books touching on Jews to the Institute at Frankfurt. Today, a tall, gangling, and stooped librarian-soldier in his middle forties, he no longer travels. He is reserved, with a formal military manner, short of breath due to a chest wound. His face has the lines of a man who has suffered; but if disappointment and defeat have marked him, they have not made him less forceful and articulate, nor dimmed his missionary fervor and belligerence.

II Cross-Currents in Germany

Peter hates the United States. "Americans," he said, "are pretty rough and ruthless in their power politics."

I demurred.

"Bosh!" exclaimed Peter. "Old-fashioned chivalry is dead. In the old days the victor showed generosity and even sympathy for the vanquished. He understood that the fortunes of war might turn another way another time. He extended a hand to the defeated enemy. He could respect the honor and dignity of the vanquished; even drink to his courage. But Americans are needlessly ruthless. First they insisted on total capitulation of us Germans. Then they devastated our cities —many of them where no military objective existed and at a time when our defeat was already certain."

"Defeat is never certain," I interrupted, "until the enemy confesses it."

Seeming almost not to hear the interruption, Peter went on: "After our surrender, America went out of its way to humiliate us, interning hundreds of thousands of us. We were left for months, and even years, without proper judicial procedure. American officers refused to return courtesy greetings from German officers. American soldiers thought it funny to hang iron crosses on their dogs' collars. They pulled our uniforms apart and took our medals as souvenirs. And now they propose to give us weapons, urging us that we are wicked if we refuse to bear them."

"Don't you think it is possible for the United States to help Western Germany?" I asked.

"We can't rely on the United States," Peter broke in vehemently. "American internal politics have always disappointed us. We were happy when FDR died. We thought that his successor might give us a more friendly policy. Truman turned out stupider—and equally concerned with pleasing our enemies, not us. Eisenhower is a Russian-lover and a Jew-lover. We thought Senator McCarthy would be our man, and that he could get a good wholesome fascist trend going in the United States. But McCarthy sent a couple of Jew boys around Europe. His fight with the Army and the Church, coupled with his

2 The New Foundation

secret deal with Jews and his defense of these Jew boys at the sacrifice of his own prestige, convinced us that he is not our man."

Peter went on to indict the United States for corruption, degeneracy, and lack of integrity. "Another hypocrisy we resent," he added, "is the Allies' claim that they have come into Germany to free the German people." Straining his neck forward, he paused and then in sharp, Prussian staccato said, "That's really too big for any German to swallow."

His own thought excited him. "Would you really pretend that we are freer today than we were in the late thirties under Hitler? Look at the picture of that period. Look at the enthusiasm of our youth for creating a bigger and better country. Look at the idealism and hope for the future. The Germans didn't want and do not want freedom to be disorderly. They had much more freedom then than they have now with the country split in half, occupied by four armies, with thousands of our citizens in East German jails.

"Instead of tearing Hitler down today, they should mention the many things he did which were good, of course tell the bad too, and in the end show Hitler a grandiose but tragic figure. Hitler saw the importance of making young Germans familiar with their glorious history. He organized expeditions of German youth to visit adjacent countries that had been the early German frontiers against the barbarians from the East. Young Germans were taught the glories of Germany's past. We are those Germans today, and we know that Germany will come back to a position of power." He had started to say "domination" but caught himself. With determination in his voice, he said—and it was an oath and a promise: "Perhaps it will take ten years, perhaps fifty years, who knows, but back we will come."

I could think of many answers as he hammered on, but I didn't want him to stop.

"America has an easy way of pinning labels," he continued. "They talk about Nazi Party members as extreme reactionaries. Actually there was more pragmatic social thinking in our party than there has ever been in Germany before or since. Germans of all kinds joined in our program for improved national welfare. We had enthusiastic followers from all parties. There were Ludendorff mystics as well as Social

II Cross-Currents in Germany

Democrat realists who were Catholics and Protestants. There were clergymen as well as soldiers. National Socialism, as its name indicates, was really a national movement.

"Of course, everything that was good before our collapse was made to look bad afterwards. Everyone, particularly our ex-professional soldiers, now tries to disassociate himself from identification with National Socialism. It is petty and sordid.

"What a confusion of symbols! First Americans called anyone they didn't like a Nazi. Today they pin on the label 'commie.' The commies call the Americans they don't like 'Wall Streeters.' Bonn Catholics call us former Nazis 'Prussian Protestants.' We Protestants pin the label 'Black Catholics' on them."

It was obvious he had thought all these things many times before, but saying them seemed to relieve him; he was calmer.

Naturally Peter deplored the program of the Adenauer government, and especially its policy regarding Jews.

"I was opposed to the German settlement of claims with Israel," he said. "Israel as such had no claim against us. Also we didn't need to make as liberal a settlement as we did. With the Israel settlement many individual Jews got back their property twice and many got back their property plus indemnity. Thus many of them got a triple compensation. If the deal with Israel had been submitted to referendum, a great majority of Germans would have been against it."

What did he think of the Nazi anti-Semitic program?

"I have a high respect for Jewish intelligence and organizing ability," he answered. "I recognize that there should be a place in the world for the Jews. They should have their living space and we white races should have ours. We should respect each other's zones."

Could Jews throughout the world really work out a single destiny for themselves?

"I won't say I believe one hundred per cent in a Jewish world conspiracy," said Peter, "but I am open-minded and can be persuaded that such a conspiracy does exist."

I wondered if he were open-minded enough to believe his own propaganda.

2 The New Foundation

Peter has apparently been occupied for years in reconstructing the historical background of the National Socialist movement and has worked out a complete defense of the Nazi government's record. Another of his primary tasks is to re-create as far as possible the archives of the Hitler period, particularly the basic material dealing with Jews. Along with his research project, Peter provides the remnants of the Nazi leadership with "information" for the propaganda he hopes will help them return to power and wage successful war against "inferior" peoples.

Peter's present activity, unknown except to a few top leaders in the neo-Nazi movement, is carried on by personal contact only, with Naumann and Malz in Neustadt. Naumann frequently gets into his car, races across Germany, and consults with Peter for hours. The reason the neo-Nazi group has kept the collaboration of Heinz Peter secret: they fear that if Peter is exposed the Bonn government would put him under surveillance and otherwise harass him, thereby depriving the movement of one of its best and most strategic men.

The anti-Semitic material produced by Malz and reported to you from time to time has been based largely on the research work of Peter here in Neustadt. The German picture is complete.

JUNE 16, 1954
AF to BRE

My evaluation of the Weiss-Naumann story:

Compared to his big-time contacts abroad, Weiss is a minor figure. But their traffic with him, as a resident in the United States, is relatively useful, and a lead to American dollars. And if one measures the extent of Weiss's contacts and his energy as a dispenser of extreme nationalistic, anti-Semitic propaganda, he emerges as an operator of some consequence.

In Weiss, too, the neo-Nazi movement of Germany has found a channel for the indoctrination of an important market.

The German neo-Nazi movement is a continuing danger so long as the political situation remains volatile. In the words of a New York *Times* editorial (January 19, 1953):

> It is valuable to be reminded ... that Nazism is not dead in Germany. ... As of today, neo-Nazism is very much of a minority movement. What is frightening is that, given time and ... circumstances, a form of Nazism could again rise to power in Germany. ... Materially speaking, Nazism was smashed into a pulp by 1945, but the firm and vigorous roots remained.

The Bonn government has taken energetic measures to curb the neo-Nazi parties. The problem of extreme nationalism is something else again. But any real solution of the neo-Nazi threat remains in the future development and strengthening of German democracy. In Germany and in Europe as a whole it will take many years to eliminate it. In the United States neo-Nazism thus far is an abject failure.

JUNE 17, 1954
AF to BRE

Here's what the Weiss-Naumann data mean:

A propaganda tie-up exists today, and has for some time, between neo-Nazi leaders in Germany and the professional anti-Semites in the United States. Efforts by these elements in Germany, now held in check by the Adenauer government, to acquire support—including American dollars—from nationalist movements and sympathetic ethnic groups in the United States are continuing in full strength.

The propagandists drawn into this loosely knit movement here are mostly well-known professional anti-Semites, discredited by public opinion and acceptable only to the lunatic fringe, a flaw that has thus far handicapped the efforts of the German groups to achieve effective results. However, the propaganda apparatus of the Germans is still in an early phase of development.

The German side of the alliance, in contrast to the participating Americans, involves important men, men once in the Hitler hierarchy;

and these, the directing influences in the propaganda movement, are very close to Werner Naumann, the leading neo-Nazi politician in West Germany today. They include figures as important as Heinrich Malz, chief co-ordinator of information for the Naumann group, Heinz Peter, Naumann's chief researcher, Erich Schmidt, general handy man and publisher of Naumann's German Reichs Party newspaper, and Dr. Rudolf Aschenauer, one of the principal lawyers who defended the Nazi war criminals at Nuremberg (but he appears to be moving away from them). Closely associated with the movement is Colonel Hans Ulrich Rudel, the main connecting link between the Argentine Nazi group and Germany.

The American clearinghouse for much of this propaganda traffic is Frederick Charles Weiss, a German alien living in New York. He has drawn into this exchange, both directly and indirectly, some of the major producers and peddlers of anti-Semitic propaganda in this country, including such notorious pamphleteers as Robert H. Williams, publisher of *Williams Intelligence Summary,* and Conde McGinley, publisher of *Common Sense.*

The anti-Semitic pamphlets and literature are transmitted on an international scale, with principal centers in the United States, Germany, and Argentina.

AUGUST 9, 1954
German Study Team to Library

There are no simple answers to any questions on Germany today. Although it is still an occupied country, it has achieved much independently, absorbing, for example, eleven million refugees from the East without showing signs of social unrest; this despite crowded conditions and, in some sections, considerable unemployment. It is also, particularly in Berlin, a frontier bastion against communism.

But if their situation is a unique one in their history the political shocks and the terrors of war have caused the Germans to shrink from

II Cross-Currents in Germany

public life, thus leaving new problems to be solved by traditional modes —authoritarian modes. Likewise, many Germans seem to live ambiguously with both a nagging guilt and a compensating sense of their own rectitude, that perhaps explain the government's ability to proceed with its policy of Jewish restitutions despite lack of public support on the issue.

The Adenauer government is committed to a policy of accepting the idea of "collective shame" for the German people; of making restitution to Jews through the German-Israeli pact and through individual compensations; of restoring to those German Jews who remain or who want to return all civil rights they had lost and all pensions and social security which are their due; of granting to the organized Jewish communities such financial help as other religious communities receive; and of fostering social and political ideas that will make for better group relationships in Germany.

Therefore Dr. Adenauer pushed the West German-Israeli restitution agreement through, relying on personal political strength, because he believed it a moral duty. Also a law providing for individual restitutions was passed in the last days of the first Bundestag with little opposition. [The Bundestag vote on the Israel agreement was 239 against 35, with 86 abstaining. The 125 members of the opposition party (the Social Democrats) present voted yes; 68 members of the government coalition abstained; and 15 voted no.] These restitutions are practically completed in West Germany, though many cases were still outstanding in West Berlin at the time of our visit. The federal government continues to carry out its legal obligations to individual Jews and to the Jewish community; the state governments are dragging their feet.

This, alas, does not mean that anti-Semitism no longer exists in Germany. It is true that most Germans are embarrassed by discussion of the Nazi persecutions; but it is too much to expect that a generation subjected to the intensive anti-Semitic indoctrination of the Nazis should so quickly throw it off. Opinion-testing since the war has at no time revealed any great lessening of anti-Semitic feeling, nor do the Germans, despite the war catastrophe, reject Nazism with the same intensity with which they reject the parallel tyranny of communism.

2 The New Foundation

It is somewhat heartening, though, that neo-Nazism as an organized political movement has not taken form or size, and at the last general election failed to elect a single deputy to the Bundestag.

But any personnel, both in and out of the government, engaged in eliminating anti-Semitism are pessimistic about their ability to change the patterns of the adult generations; their concentration is on youth and the children.

The difficulty facing those who seek the democratic re-education of Germany is well illustrated by the attitude inherent in the often-heard remark that "democracy is always ordered in Germany after a lost war." It implies that the greatest privilege bestowed by victory would be goose-stepping. "Things might be different if Germans had as much civic courage as they have military courage," was one man's comment on the political apathy of the average German and his great readiness to follow authority. During one discussion of a rightist movement in certain of the political parties, we were told: "Don't worry, the Reds will keep West Germany democratic!" And discussion of German rearmament too often brought forth the well-worn "In other countries the nation has an army; in Germany the army had a nation."

These are cynical comments on German character, if you will, but acute enough to justify the fear of the German militaristic tradition expressed by all the liberal-minded we met. "Germany needs another ten years without an army so that the old military tradition can first die out." "German armies were always trained for aggression, and if German military minds were given the opportunity, they would naturally do so again." "A German army would give a tremendous new push to German nationalism." "A new German army can readily become a political power."

Yet most German liberals favor a European defense system, recognizing that, as one put it, "only in association with the defensive armies of the other European powers can the aggressive tradition of the German military be eliminated." But it requires the strong hand of Adenauer to keep the military out of politics. One shrewd analyst said: "We can depend upon Heuss and Adenauer. But after them there is no guarantee of anything except that in a short time the Germans may

II Cross-Currents in Germany

become the strongest military element in the West European defense system."

Germans thus find themselves being pushed into the world political scene before their domestic political development permits them to be there with safety. To those concerned with German democracy, it seems that just as the people are beginning to understand how their aggressive military tradition has caused so much trouble for Europe and the world they are being told to forget it and to rearm. So they seek the best safeguards available and hope democratization can keep pace with militarization.

They put some of their hope in youth, many of whom dislike military service and are showing more liberal tendencies than their elders. The most determined protest against the revival of films by the Nazi anti-Semitic movie-maker, Veit Harlan, which became a public scandal recently, came from university student groups. Similarly, the efforts of Erich Lüeth, one of the truly democratic civic leaders in Germany today, for a Peace with Israel movement, designed to build public acceptance for the restitution idea, received its greatest response from student groups.

A new opinion survey called "Youth Between 15 and 24" revealed the fifteen- to eighteen-year-old group as giving the most democratic responses; those eighteen to twenty-one as being less liberal; and those in the twenty-one- to twenty-four-year-old group, who had been in the Hitler Youth, as being least so. However, it is interesting to note that those who had been in the Hitler Youth were the most negative toward national socialism. Their objections, significantly, were largely based upon the compulsion they had undergone in the Hitler Youth.

The survey, nevertheless, showed the continuing strong influence of the military tradition. Fifty-five per cent of the youth thought that a "soldier's life is the best education for a young man." Forty-one per cent answered negatively and 4% had no answer. In a related question, "A man looks better in uniform than civilian clothes," 51% answered affirmatively and 47% negatively, and military heroes continue to be the most admired, with 15% naming Bismarck, 6% naming Frederick the Great, and 3% each naming Hitler, Rommel, Hindenburg, and

2 The New Foundation

Charlemagne. Goethe and Luther headed the non-military names, and they, too, score 3% each. More encouraging was the response to the direct question: "Youth should follow, not criticize." Fifty-two per cent answered "No" to this one and 47% answered "Yes." But to the more specific question, "Shall we leave interest in internationalism to the man in charge of the government?" only 37% answered "No" and 57% said "Yes."

Among educational leaders there is a recognition that the traditionalism of German schools hinders the democratization of Germany. The authoritarianism, the stress on accumulating information rather than discussing it, and the embarrassment with which most teachers approach the teaching of recent history are all important factors.

Some forward-looking school supervisors have sought to meet this problem by using new German texts on the history of the past twenty years in social studies and civics classes, and by employing modern teaching techniques; but these innovations meet great resistance among the senior teaching group and even among younger teachers who have been brought up on the traditional methods. The school superintendent of one major city told us: "The picture has improved since 1945, but it is still questionable how many teachers follow through. I am not optimistic, but I am hopeful that we are moving ahead."

It should be remembered that the Nazis had particular success in winning over teachers; perhaps half of all today's teachers were once Nazi Party members. For one reason or another they tend to avoid teaching about the Jewish persecutions or doing much to combat group prejudices handed down by parents to their children.

The federal government's instrument for encouraging all educational efforts in democracy and citizenship by schools and civic organizations is the Bundeszentrale fuer Heimatsdienst (Federal Center for Home Service). Its work, work of a high order, is governed by a Bundestag committee on which all parties are represented; and on an extremely limited budget provided by the Interior Ministry it provides educational material for schools and community organizations. (It was interesting to find among the many publications of the Heimatsdienst a pamphlet entitled, *Treibjagd auf Suendenboecke,* a German transla-

Cross-Currents in Germany

tion of Gordon Allport's *ABC's of Scapegoating,* published by the ADL in 1948.)

It is significant that such a government body is needed in Germany, but it is equally significant that the Heimatsdienst finds it increasingly necessary to farm out its projects to voluntary civic organizations. Said one of its directors: "The Nazi period has made a large part of the German public allergic to government pronouncements in our field. So we use these indirect methods which have the double value of being more effective and of encouraging more people in organized groups to participate in public affairs."

The work of the Heimatsdienst, the America Houses, sponsored by the U. S. High Commission, their British equivalent, The Bridge, and the French institutes, have had a salutary effect upon the development of voluntary citizens' organizations devoted to promoting an understanding of democratic processes, liberal education, civic affairs, and interreligious co-operation. This development is still in its early stages, but it shows a growing recognition that no democratic society can succeed without the effective participation of its citizens.

Excellent programs on a limited scale have been projected by parents' associations, civil rights groups, and church and ministerial organizations like the Evangelische Dienst fuer Israel (Evangelical Service for Israel), the Freiburg Group (Catholic) and the Gesellschaft fuer Christlich-Juedische Zusammenarbeit (Society for Christian-Jewish Co-operation). We found, too, a strong democratic force among trade unions centered in the German Association of Trade Unions (DGB). Their task is nevertheless formidable, for they are hampered by lack of resources and by the continuing resistance of older people and the authoritarian tradition they symbolize.

The Society for Christian-Jewish Co-operation makes almost as much of a stir about Die Woche der Bruederlichkeit in Germany as we do about Brotherhood Week, but without comparable success. Although the Bonn Constitution and those of the *Laender* or states provide a complete set of civil rights guarantees for all, the average German still understands so little of these basic rights that he rarely questions the orders of even the most petty officials. One official of a civil rights

2 The New Foundation

organization told us: "During the Nazi period, people just forgot what civil rights were. Today Germans must be taught what a civil right is." So far, only the skeletal structure of an effective democratic society has been erected in Germany; it has not yet been made into a house that Germans know how to inhabit at their ease.

Old modes of thought are present everywhere. For example, conservative American business experts told Germans that their long authoritarian tradition hampers them economically as well as politically, and showed them figures proving that their industrial efficiency is exaggerated.

The heart of the matter then is this: that political democracy in Germany cannot succeed without a parallel economic development, and that the overpowering traditionalism which permeates every phase of German life with its authoritarian concepts tends to stifle both. How to loosen the constricting bonds, how to break the chain and start in new directions is the problem of the present generation. And indeed it is a task for a generation, for there are elements here that only time can cure. These elements are reflected in the situation in the schools: how can children be taught democratic concepts if there are few teachers who believe in those concepts? They are to be seen in the political field where, at the moment, apathy is the rule and the problems of self-government understood only by the few.

Indeed, whether the problem can be solved at all, even in a generation, depends upon the existence of two factors: Germany needs democratic leadership of a high order and it needs a proper environment in which to live. It has been demonstrated how frequently the German public lags behind the Adenauer government on democratic measures, but it has faith in him and follows his leadership. The ever recurring question in Germany is: What after Adenauer? Indeed, what? Strong man that he is, he has nevertheless created the structure and followed a policy that can mold a truly democratic society in Germany. But should his successors be less convinced of the democratic idea, then progress will be cut short. Herein lies the danger in the return of so many former Nazi leaders to government posts.

II Cross-Currents in Germany

AUGUST 10, 1954
Library to BRE

This is in response to your question concerning the number of former Nazis in government posts:

In 1951, of the 383 senior officials in the West German Foreign Office, 134 were former Nazi Party members; it is much the same today. Hans Globke, credited with drafting the Nazi legal justifications for the Nuremberg Racial Laws, is in actual charge of Adenauer's Federal Press and Chancellory offices. In 1936, Globke made this official contribution to German racial legislation:

The Jew is completely alien to us in character and blood. . . . The [Nuremberg] Laws will form a permanent bulwark against further penetration of Jewish blood into the German nation.

When the Nazis held firm power, Dr. Franz Massfeller was assigned to write the government commentary on the "Law for the Protection of German Blood and Honor." In 1944, after Hitler had depleted his store of available Jews, Massfeller conferred with other leaders as to whether "half-Jews" should be exterminated or merely sterilized. Today, Massfeller sits as a counselor in the Bonn Ministry of Justice, in charge of drafting new marriage and family legislation.

Waldemar Kraft and Victor-Emanuel Preusker are, respectively, Minister without Portfolio and Housing Minister in the Bonn government. As members of Hitler's personal guard, the black-shirted Allgemaine SS, Kraft worked his way up to SS major, while Preusker joined a motorized unit of the Storm Troopers and became an efficient instructor on "racial questions." His "magnificent" accomplishments later, in "analyzing" Jewish property as an officer of the Dresdner Bank, earned him a grateful testimonial from the Nazi government.

In the Bonn Foreign Office official positions are held by men who ordered the extermination of Rumanian-Jewish deportees; who directed the deportation of Jews from Amsterdam; who organized the pro-Nazi activities of the Grand Mufti in the Near East; who headed the Eastern

2 The New Foundation

European Division of the Nazi Foreign Office, and others of like background. The facts, whatever the dangers they represent may be, must be faced realistically. A government needs trained men, and most educated and trained Germans who continued in active public life after Hitler came to power did so because they had become party members. Opposition Germans had been hounded, scattered, jailed, or killed, and those who miraculously survived are today old and tired. A reviving West Germany thus necessarily reaches into the ranks of former Nazis.

The defeat of the neo-Nazi parties in the last election may, therefore, merely mean that a large section of the public still sympathetic to Nazism is politic enough to support a government that can obtain economic help from the West and absorb many ex-Nazis at the same time. Economic revival is, as we have emphasized, the uppermost thought in the German mind. It is also, under a democracy, even a comparatively young one, the best ground on which that democracy can grow. A complicated, contradictory situation.

AUGUST 16, 1954
German Study Team to Library

In the Freiherr vom Stein Strasse in Frankfurt stands a building of Spanish-Byzantine architecture, lending this fine old residential street a bit of medieval flavor; it is the synagogue of the ancient Jewish community of Frankfurt. The building was erected about fifty years ago; the community itself goes back to the twelfth century. On November 9, 1938, Crystal Night, the interior of the structure was completely destroyed by the Nazis; in 1947 its rebuilding, in modern style—at a cost of eight hundred thousand German marks—was paid for by the state of Hesse. It stands empty—the almost perfect symbol of Jewish life in Germany today, and of German-Jewish relationships.

The building stands empty because Frankfurt no longer has enough Jews to fill it; those who pray attend a little chapel that need not remind them of the ghosts of those who once peopled the great syna-

II Cross-Currents in Germany

gogue. Though the building stands renewed, because the postwar leaders of the city and the state may have felt the need to express their shame—if not their guilt—it remains an unvisited museum because the people—apathetically willing to let their leaders have their way—are yet unwilling to participate actively in such restitutions to Jews or in what might appear to be a public confession of shame.

What is German-Jewish life like today? All told, there are perhaps 25,000 Jews in West Germany today. No more than ten per cent are children or young people. The average age is perhaps fifty-eight to sixty—twenty years higher than the average in the rest of the population. Many are in their seventies and eighties; the old-age home is today Germany's principal Jewish communal institution.

Are these the survivors of the great German-Jewish community of about 560,000 which Hitler destroyed? It should be recalled that a great many German Jews—nearly 300,000—escaped Hitler through emigration between 1933 and 1939. (One hundred and seventy thousand to 190,000 German Jews perished in the extermination camps which took the lives of 6,000,000 European Jews.) What was once German Jewry lives today in the United States, in Israel, and elsewhere. The merest handful of those who did not emigrate in those years escaped destruction; and today, even among the 25,000, only a modest percentage are of German-Jewish stock. The rest are mainly Jews from eastern Europe who found themselves in German concentration camps or made their way into Germany at the end of the war.

In Munich there is a community of 1800 Jews; only 200 of these are German in origin. A great many of the latter are married to non-Jews; they survived solely because the feeders of the extermination camp furnaces had not yet gotten around to their category when the Third Reich collapsed. The situation in this community is typical.

What is German-Jewish life like today? It's like this in the city of Bonn: The sole community institution—the synagogue—is housed in two rooms on the ground floor of an old building a short distance from the railroad tracks. Somehow the building had escaped the bombing which laid waste almost the entire area. We attended Friday evening services there in the company of a dozen men and half as many women

2 The New Foundation

of the community. None, with the exception of the reader and the rabbi, was under sixty years of age. We were fortunate to have arrived on this particular Friday night, because services are held only once a month. The rabbi has a large territory to cover and he can get to each community only on a monthly basis. He is English and has agreed to serve these German communities for one year. The reader comes to the town from Cologne, the nearest large city, where he doubles as a teacher for the fifty Jewish children of that city. Perhaps the presence of strangers—friendly strangers—gave the services an extra emotional charge. But the prevailing spirit was indicated by a plaque in German which faced us from the wall. It reads:

> Out of darkness and terror this house stands restored to God, and in tribute to those who had to die for being Jews.
> April 1947

We had a Sabbath meal in a small hotel nearby with a group from the synagogue. No one spoke much; they didn't seem to have anything to say. There were 105 Jews in the town, we were told—no children. Nearly all lived on pensions, stipends, or relief payments. One man, the leader of the community, had regained a substantial retail business under the restitution laws. They didn't mix much with non-Jews, these people; and, though no one said so, they were happy to see us, happy to see other Jews, other people. You could tell it in their eyes. The next day we asked a leading government official about the Jews in his town. He seemed unaware that there were any.

German-Jewish life is also like this: We visited the bustling Rhineland industrial city of Düsseldorf during the Purim holiday. Three hundred Jews have returned to this city, and in the surrounding area there are perhaps another 300. Together they had planned a Purim celebration in a fine old restaurant set picturesquely on the banks of the Rhine. For at least one evening in Germany, Jewish life looked normal to us. Some 500 well-dressed people were present—even a number of children. For one evening at least, an air of well-being enveloped these people. On the stage, the children presented a Purim

Cross-Currents in Germany

play with charm and humor and, of course, with the triumph of Mordecai and the destruction of Haman. Yet no one said a word to draw the obvious analogy between the play and the history of the people in that room; perhaps the fact that they were able to treat the subject without tears, indeed with good humor, was a mark of the completeness of their personal triumph. It was good to be with them.

German-Jewish life is also like this: West Berlin numbers 4500 Jews in its population—the largest Jewish community in Germany. (The pre-Hitler Jewish population of Berlin was approximately 180,000.) There are perhaps another 2000 in the East Sector of the city and no more than another 700 in all of East Germany. The average age of West Berlin Jews is fifty-five and these people are happy in the knowledge that there are 500 children among them. But the most prominent communal institutions serve the aged. A fine old building, regained under the restitution laws, once more houses the Old Age Home on the Iranische Strasse. Its rooms are occupied by bright-eyed old ladies and ancient gentlemen who somehow survived the terrors of Theresienstadt and other concentration camps. They are grateful for the opportunity to end their days here in the peace they deserve as the heroes and heroines they are—if for no other reason than their survival.

Across the street from the Old Age Home stands the magnificent Jewish Hospital. This, too, was returned to the Jewish community under the restitution laws, and the community took it back with pride. It is, of course, too large now to be of use to them alone; and the effect of this may be helpful. Ninety per cent of the patients served by the hospital are not Jews; German patients clamor to get in because of the high reputation Jewish doctors enjoyed in the days before Hitler. To the sparse Jewish population, badly in need of morale, the hospital is an important symbol.

In Berlin's Kleiststrasse B'nai B'rith's Logenhaus, returned to B'nai B'rith under the restitution agreement, still stands miraculously whole, unhurt by the Allied bombs which created havoc all around it. Under the Nazi regime the building was used by Goebbels' Propaganda Ministry as its film center. It is one of the finest public structures in the

2 The New Foundation

city today, but the ample facilities for public meetings, film showings, exhibitions, etc., stand empty because it is beyond the capacities of the community to operate it; Germany's B'nai B'rith was once the second largest branch of this world-wide organization.

There are six modest-sized synagogues in Berlin. (The huge synagogue on the Fasanenstrasse is a shell hollowed out by the Nazis in 1938 and caved in by bombing in the forties.) The Juedische Gemeinde (Jewish Community) is a well-organized group and conducts a variety of cultural and social as well as welfare programs. The community is a going concern, but where is it going?

This is a subject for considerable discussion among Jews in Germany, for the dominant question is not whether Jewish life in Germany can or will survive, but whether it should. Around a table in the headquarters of the Gemeinde in Berlin sat a group of the leaders of the community and representatives of foreign Jewish organizations; and, for our benefit, each gave his viewpoint. None could possibly forget the past twenty years; one called for the removal of the last remaining Jews from German soil; a second called for every effort to reconstitute Jewish life in Germany in the old tradition, believing that Judaism can and should flourish once more on German soil; a third expressed little faith in the community's ability to survive, but saw no reason for a self-imposed liquidation.

As we listened to these arguments, one fact became fairly obvious: whether the German-Jewish community would survive was not something that Jews would decide. The final answer will be given not by Jews or even Germans but by political developments in Europe. Nor does it serve any purpose to intimate that there is something morally wrong with those Jews who find it preferable, for personal reasons, to remain in Germany rather than to emigrate. It does not matter whether the members of this German community are the proper heirs of the old German Jewry—in that they remained—or survivors from the lands to the east, or people who have come back because they could not adjust to life elsewhere. What did seem obvious is that these people deserve the greatest sympathy from Jewry everywhere.

The survival of a Jewish community is a matter of great importance

II Cross-Currents in Germany

to one other group in Germany. Not a group in any formal sense, it includes those who are concerned with the creating of a democratic Germany and those who feel deeply the sense of shame of which Theodor Heuss, President of the Republic, has spoken. They include liberals and churchmen and important leaders in government. They include, too, many Americans in Germany. These earnestly want a Jewish community to survive.

Americans take a very pragmatic approach. To them, Jews in Germany are natural allies in the efforts to create a democratic Germany, and the complete withdrawal of Jews from Germany—a potentially severe blow to that effort. The whole American policy of rehabilitating Germany they see as a risk to be measured against the greater risk of rejecting the Germans and letting them go their way. Jewish participation in the daily life and work of Germany, they feel, would reduce the present risk and be a service to world freedom and peace.

The German-of-good-will recognizes that there is little to draw Jews back. Said one: "I can't see why anyone should want to return to this overcrowded land, unless there is something specific to draw him here"; and "Only those with pleasant memories of Germany should come back," was an oft-repeated comment. We wondered what German Jew under thirty-five who had not left Germany as an infant this last category could possibly include.

They readily admit that, in a moral sense, a permanent Jewish community in Germany may be more important to Germans than to Jews. "Liberal Germans for their own consciences must make it possible for Jews to come back," said one. And again: "German-Jewish communities would be a great asset to German moral life." . . . "Germans must help re-establish a strong Jewish community." . . . "Jews gave a dynamic impetus to the arts for the cosmopolitan flavor which our big German cities need again." And on a religious note: "We need the Jews to repent to."

However phrased, it comes to the same thing: a feeling that something vital has gone out of German life and its moral fiber with the loss of the Jewish community. In the general population, this thought

2 The New Foundation

is mirrored in the gnawing superstition that all the Nazi failures were rooted in the crimes committed against the Jews.

AUGUST 23, 1954
German Study Team to Library

That anti-Semitism and, to a lesser degree, Nazism in Germany have gone underground has caused a lot of Germans to announce that they are buried for good.

These illusions, for they are that, are encouraged by the fact that there are no conspicuous tension areas where anti-Semitism can erupt. With few contacts between Germans and Jews, there are few opportunities for clashes. Even the refugee camps, focal points for trouble in recent years, have nearly all been liquidated. But when a group of butchers recently undertook a campaign, on humanitarian grounds no less, against *schechitah,* the ritual slaughter of cattle for kosher meat, it afforded the butchers' trade journal and other publications the chance to trot out the whole Goebbels propaganda line on this subject. It had been a favorite of Hitler's.

This was not surprising to that comparative handful of Germans vigorously attacking the problem of anti-Semitism. One such recounted to us a fairly recent incident in which he was involved. He was practically evicted from a school during a lecture, because of his favorable comments about Jews and critical ones of the Nazis. He remarked: "It is still a question of making oneself unpopular to press the matter of Jewish persecution and German guilt."

So it is. Germans want to forget. They want to bury the past. They refuse to talk about it; they seek to ignore what has happened. They publicly reject collective guilt, but they cannot eradicate it from their own souls. In a variety of ways, we had this phenomenon expressed to us by men whose consciences are not easily put to rest: "The whole problem of German-Jewish relationships today is one of extreme emotionalism. It is difficult to enter into a discussion of anti-Semitism with

II Cross-Currents in Germany

Germans because of their feeling of shame and guilt and their psychological rejection of the history of the past twenty years."

And another suggested to us: "Perhaps it would be for the best if the Germans did forget, and if the world would permit them to do so. They failed to forget their hurts and their resentments after World War I, and look what it led to. Amnesia has its healing qualities, and in this instance we can save the world from German neuroses in years to come by permitting them to forget."

But such a suggestion makes sense only if one is ready to accept the thesis that the trauma suffered by Germany at Versailles led to the creation of a Third Reich which was neurotic and not evil. This comfortable theory is held by many Germans. One of them put it very succinctly to us: "What happened under Hitler was all the fault of France." But whatever role France may play as a cruel mother in the German psyche, it cannot make the punishable crimes committed by Nazism less evil. In any case, many Germans, perhaps a majority of them, have no difficulty in forgetting and do not seem to react neurotically to their having lived through the Third Reich. Our personal experiences led us to agree with a noted German political scientist who finds the reactions of his countrymen gruesomely healthy, and their good conscience terrifying. When, among Germans, the subject of the murder of Jews in the Third Reich comes up for discussion, he says, there is almost never anything one could call a neurotic explosion. To them, the murder of Jews in the Third Reich is like a legend from a strange and alien world in the long, long ago.

The heard-no-evil, saw-no-evil attitude has, of course, had some comforting effects. One now encounters little of the blatant anti-Semitism of the Third Reich, the raucous yelps that can be heard today in the United States from the press of our lunatic fringe. Even the Nazi groups recognize that the current climate makes hysterical attacks upon Jews unacceptable, and that as a political weapon it has outlived its value.

But Nazism and anti-Semitism find their expression in less obvious ways. One wise foreign observer commented to us: "There are two handy tests for determining how far to the right any given German

2 The New Foundation

leans. One is his attitude on the freeing of war criminals; the other is the subject of restitution of property to Jews. The results are frequently frightening." There are other indications—such as continued references to the "Morgenthau Plan," to names like Warburg or Baruch, to the "evils" of *schechitah* or refugees, or to the "iniquity" of Israel.

Opinion polls have become a touchy subject in the *Bundesrepublik*: because they have been so uncomfortable for the Germans, and because, frankly, Germans doubt their validity. Too frequently, they say, the interviewer receives answers those questioned think he wants to hear; a hangover from the atmosphere of the Third Reich.

That opinion research in Germany is not very popular with the political parties is understandable. The opposition Social Democrat Party, for instance, has found itself almost invariably far out of line with the general public, and frequently out of line with its own constituency. The government parties have had to face embarrassing results on the questions of nationalism and anti-Semitism.

The polls show, for instance, that nationalism is the most potent political force in Germany today. There is, of course, wide variation in the brands of nationalism that compete for the German mind. There are nationalists who are distinctly anti-Nazi, and there are those who seek a return to something like the Third Reich without the more uncomfortable aspects. There are also those who see Germany rising to greatest power through a pan-European policy and the establishment of a Western European community.

Nationalist—especially pro-Nazi—sentiments have their inevitable parallel in anti-Semitic tendencies. In the 1953 poll conducted by the U. S. High Commission, the tie-up between anti-restitution opinions and pro-Nazi views was so complete there could be no doubt that behind "anti-restitution lies anti-Semitism." Further evidence of the prevailing anti-Semitism lay in the bitter anti-Jewish comments expressed by many of those questioned, despite the fact that anti-Semitism is officially frowned upon—and this to unknown interviewers. In characteristically restrained language the report commented: ". . . it would be distinctly unsafe to conclude that anti-Jewish orientations characterize less than a majority of the West German population."

II Cross-Currents in Germany

In the year and a half since the U. S. High Commission poll was taken, many of the basic trends in German public opinion and attitudes it revealed have been borne out. The report indicated, for instance, a growing movement to the right in major political groups like the Free Democratic Party and a general rise in nationalist feeling as opposed to the internationalism which had shown so much strength at the onset of the Adenauer government. The election of September 1953 may have set back the neo-Nazi parties, but millions of former Nazis are comfortably lodged in respectable parties like the Free Democratic Party, a strong factor in the coalition that governs the country. Hopefully, we may take it as a mark of the success of Dr. Adenauer's government that the rightist forces apparently feel that if they cannot "lick him they had better join him."

Werner Naumann, the neo-Nazi leader, has indicated that, for the time being, the thing to do is to abstain from the government coalition. There are today perhaps 100,000 ex-Nazi functionaries sympathetic to neo-Nazi movements, but the feeling among their strongest opponents is that old-style Nazism cannot rise to power again for the very practical reason that big industrialists shrink from financing such movements. They had hoped to use Hitler; instead he used them. And the present economic revival has joined German industrial leaders to the Adenauer coalition.

The High Commission survey likewise indicated a continuing apathy among many Germans toward political affairs. This apathy had not lessened sufficiently to bring forth any cheers among those interested in the development of a democratic Germany. The fact remains therefore that there are enough Nazi-minded Germans today to start a new reaction if conditions should favor them, and there is enough political indifference to favor the success of such a movement. That a new rightist movement would bring anti-Semitism in its wake is a foregone conclusion, for there is a streak of latent anti-Semitism embedded in many phases of German life. Germans will avoid overt anti-Semitism for years to come, according to experts long on the scene, but the receptivity to anti-Semitism is there if any group that comes to power should want to exploit it.

2 The New Foundation

The Germans themselves, perhaps, do not realize how great the reservoir of anti-Semitism is or can be. Over and over again we were told by men of undoubted good will that there is no anti-Semitism in Germany today. Others would vary the thought a bit with the comment that "surprisingly little anti-Semitic propaganda has stuck with the masses of the German population." To the foreign observer, the evidence is to the contrary.

We sat late one Sabbath afternoon in the home of an elderly Jewish couple who had survived Dachau and had come back to their native city, Munich, where they had been, and were again, distinguished citizens. The hope and wit and will to live that had aided their survival were still theirs. They had been well received publicly and by old personal friends on their return, the old man told us. "You can't drive out the Hitler poison from the minds of people in ten years," he said, "but non-Jews here have received returning Jews well and associations between them are good."

At this statement a middle-aged woman who also was visiting the elderly couple spoke up. Her husband, a Jew, had died at the hands of the Nazis eighteen years ago; she, a Christian, had continued to live in the city, faithful to her husband's memory. "I have suffered much," she said, "I have seen so much hatred and brutality perpetrated by Germans. Yet I believe that most Germans did not know what went on in the concentration and extermination camps. But I know of no other German, not even my own sisters, to whom I can talk today about Jewish matters without their showing their prejudice."

The elderly Jew interrupted softly. "Not by hate but by love shall you conquer."

Many Germans also maintain that there were really very few Nazis in Hitler's Third Reich. After breakfast one morning we heard the "facts" expounded by a man of great personal charm—a liberal, and today the head of a government department.

He had been a judge of a denazification tribunal in the American Zone, right after the war, in a district that had 120,000 people or about 30,000 families. The Nazi Party rolls numbered 1200 members. Each of these had to go through the denazification ordeal and, as he described it, some of it was rugged. But most interesting was his arithmetic: the denazification proceedings showed that, of the 1200 members, the ten ringleaders were vicious Nazis. Two hundred more had joined the party, not because they were convinced of its ideology, but for the political preferment they expected; they were strictly opportunists. All the rest were clearly nominal members, and half were considered "unreliable" by the Nazi leadership. Evidence of this was found by the denazification officers in a retrieved Nazi Party file of these "unreliables." By his count, therefore, in a district of 120,000 people there were only 800 real Nazis.

Such exercises in self-delusion—that anti-Semitism has disappeared in Germany and that Nazism never really captured the minds of the German people—may be part of an effort to employ the therapy of amnesia for the German people, but they are not likely to fill the rest of the world with confidence in Germany. Nor is the therapy of amnesia acceptable to that hard core of Germans who seek the remolding of their country in the Western democratic tradition.

The most prominent public figure in Germany to reject the therapy of amnesia is Theodor Heuss, President of the Republic and eloquent spokesman of the liberal-minded in West Germany today. Jews, Heuss believes, "never can or will forget what was done to them." Germans, he is convinced, "must never forget what was done by men and women of their own nationality in those shameful years."

It is equally characteristic that the West German-Israeli restitution agreement should get the solid support of the Social Democrats, the opposition party, while the government coalition—the Christian Democratic Union and the Free Democratic Party—harbored most of the dissenters from the policy pushed so assiduously by Heuss and Adenauer.

We sat one day in the office of an old friend, the former Social Democratic mayor of Hamburg, overlooking the magnificent Alster River as it broadens out into a lake in the heart of the city. Max Brauer, vigorous and ruddy despite his seventy years, had just completed seven years in office. Beyond his window he looked with pride on one of the best-planned, most completely reconstructed cities in all of Germany.

2 The New Foundation

Having just come from cramped and tense Berlin, the atmosphere of Hamburg seemed freer than anything we had experienced in Germany. Part of that feeling of freedom was generated by Max Brauer, whose white hair and deep voice make him look and sound so much like a German Carl Sandburg. It recalled to us those days in the 1930s when Brauer, in exile, had attacked National Socialism from public platforms in all the major cities of America. He gave us hope then that freedom would yet return to Germany. His voice and his words and his spirit had lost none of their magic. We had come for fifteen minutes; we stayed for hours as he ranged over the entire field of German political problems.

We confided to him our fears that anti-Semitism, dormant for the most part, was still deeply rooted in the nationalism that seemed so all-pervasive in Germany. He brushed our fears aside. "The Nazis," he said, "brought anti-Semitism to such an extreme that it has burned itself out. Germany will in time have less anti-Semitism than any other country in the world because of this."

Coming from Brauer, it sounded convincing. The extreme to which the Nazis went tends to obscure the fact that anti-Semitism as a political weapon was not a Nazi invention. Anti-Semitism has been a force in German politics ever since 1869, when, in the North German Federation, "all still existing limitations of civil and civic rights based on differences of religious creed [were] abolished." In the European polemical literature of the second half of the nineteenth century can be found all of the basic attacks on Jews used by the Nazis.

Bismarck's clerical and conservative opponents used the "Jewish question" to belabor him; and he, in turn, when he found the backing of the liberal parties not sufficient to maintain his policies, manipulated anti-Jewish feeling. For a generation Adolf Stoecker, a leader of the clerical-conservative movement and chaplain of the royal court, made anti-Semitism his chief political weapon. Throughout this period political anti-Semitism drew strength and encouragement from official government sources. Only in the twenty-year period from 1895 to the outbreak of World War I did the anti-Semitic tide recede somewhat in Germany.

II   Cross-Currents in Germany

There are many who believe with Brauer that the extreme to which the Nazis pushed anti-Semitism has burned it out. And there is today this marked difference in German politics, a difference which overshadows everything else: for the first time in the better part of a century, anti-Semitism is not an effective political weapon in Germany. The great Jewish tragedy of the Nazi era was caused by a government-powered anti-Semitism; today it is the policy of the West German Government to make amends for what happened and to eradicate as best it can the residue of hate built up in the German people by two decades of pounding Nazi propaganda.

There are some broad considerations that can be set down at this time. We found conditions among the Jews in Germany today painful indeed. Though there is unlikely to be any great increase in their numbers, there will, nevertheless, be Jewish communities in Germany for many years to come. If these people are to enjoy a reasonably contented existence they must achieve spiritual and social stability. To do this, there must be an enrichment of the Jewish aspects of their lives and an adjustment of their relationship to the rest of the population that will dissolve the psychological wall that now separates them.

For spiritual sustenance and revival, Jews in Germany must necessarily turn to their brethren in other parts of the world, mainly to the Jews of the United States, of Israel, and of England. Help must come to them, not only in financial terms, as it already has in good measure, but through specific educational projects that will provide for them rabbis, teachers, and religious schools to spark a spiritual renaissance. At the beginning it may have to be a "lend-lease" program; in time, of course, the Jews in Germany will be able to train rabbis and religious teachers from among their own people. Since the religious communities of Germany in various ways receive state assistance, the federal and state governments must give fullest consideration to the special needs of the struggling Jewish communities and must render assistance as generously as possible.

A solicitous attitude on the part of government toward the Jewish communities will go a long way toward helping in the necessary readjustment of Jews to their environment in Germany. No trumpets blasting messages of good will can do as much as purposeful efforts on the part of the German government and the German people to help Jews in Germany reconstruct the world they lost. Among these efforts must be the completion of the restitution and indemnification programs. Indemnification, which is concerned not with compensation for material and property losses but with compensation for personal injury and persecution, has been particularly unsatisfactory. The Federal Indemnification Law is not adequate and its implementation has been marked by delays.

Even more important, the Germans must extend the hand of friendship to Jews living in their midst—not with a flourish but in consistent acts of friendship and understanding that will restore the faith of Jews that they can once more live normal lives in that country.

Not the least of the factors that will stabilize the situation of the Jews is one that will also restore the faith of the free world in Germany: a steady progress toward democracy, and a continuing re-education of Germans in democratic ideas and concepts. The task is formidable. It is not easy, as Benjamin Franklin once said of America, to eradicate undesirable patterns in a society and to replace them with better ones. It is no easier to remove prejudices in Germany. Nor is it possible for outsiders to perform such a feat, as the occupation forces have learned. Rather, it is a task for self-re-education.

Means for such re-educational efforts are of course already available as we have indicated in foregoing pages. But these means are far too limited for the great task ahead. The knowledgeability of the Bundeszentrale fuer Heimatsdienst, for instance, is impressive, but its penetrating power is circumscribed by a budget that is far too small for its task. No more serious recommendation can be made than to urge substantial increases in the resources made available to this agency and to others with special tasks in the reorientation process.

Prior to the Hitler period, the German educational system enjoyed a very high standard and was a prime experimenter in modern educational methods. The Nazis changed all that; the schools and the universities became propaganda machines. Germans are hard at work at the reconstruction of their educational institutions. It will, of course,

Cross-Currents in Germany

take many years to make them completely effective instruments of training for citizenship in a democratic Germany.

In our discussions with German educators we marked their particular concern with the orientation of the teaching personnel and with the limited teaching materials suitable for citizenship training in the new Germany. It is undoubtedly easier to solve the problem of creating appropriate materials than that of retraining teachers. The latter is a massive and long-range task which, we believe, can be accelerated by a broadened interchange of ideas and facilities with the countries of the West. An expanded foreign exchange program for German teachers can contribute greatly to breaking the grip of the authoritarian tradition in German schools.

As in the United States, primary and secondary school education is a function of the state governments. We were nevertheless impressed with the need for planning on a federal basis. Education for citizenship is not a sectional but a national problem in Germany. There is need for a pooling of the best educational brains in Germany, who in turn would also draw upon the vast experience and knowledge of educators from other democratic lands. By adopting from this experience that which is applicable, the development of a new and modern German educational program would be greatly advanced.

It will be readily understood by those who have come this far in the report that we have looked at the German scene with American eyes. We have filtered the facts recorded in this report—facts known to students of the German scene—through the frame of reference provided by our own background. Our observations have necessarily been colored by ideals and ideas which are derived from this background. It could not be otherwise.

Werner Naumann and his German Reichs Party are, of course, only one symptom of the lingering Nazism that afflicts Germany. In spite of the relative insignificance of this group at present, the kind of support Naumann received from members of the government coalition parties shows how focal his case is. The defense attorney at his trial,

2 The New Foundation

Dr. Ernst Achenbach, holds a high post in the Free Democratic Party and was just re-elected a member of its Foreign Affairs Committee. And the chairman of the Free Democratic Party's North Rhine-Westphalia Branch, *Friedrich Middelhauve*, in a speech to his party, maintained that the decision to drop proceedings against Naumann shows how unwarranted the original action of the British occupation authorities was. On September 22, 1955, Werner Naumann was told that he could once again engage in politics if he desired. The North Rhine-Westphalian Interior Minister explained to him that, with the restoration of West German sovereignty, the order under which he had been banned from politics was no longer valid. Within a week Naumann made his first new public appearance at a meeting of the German Reichs Party in Hanover.

When one adds to the international propaganda network of which Naumann is the center the obvious sympathy felt for Naumann by key figures in the Free Democratic Party, the sum is a bit alarming. Nor is there much comfort in the fact that Adenauer's Minister of Transport, *Christoph Seebohm*, the main speaker at the German Party's Sportpalast rally in November 1954, has defended what happened there, beatings and all, on the grounds that it was provoked by the "other side." In an election, a week later, the German Party won 4.8% of the vote, an increase of 1.1% over 1950. It may be negligible, but coming so soon after the scandalous rally, it is ominous. A creeping illness is not the less dangerous for being slow, so long as it remains unchecked.

In Bavaria the German Reichs Party was allied to the Refugee Party in the 1954 election. The Refugee Party is generally considered a "good" one; but it is obvious that the political jumble we have noted in all the German parties made it possible for neo-Nazi elements in this party to effect the alliance. The combination, it should be noted, polled the Refugee Party 10.2% of the vote, better than the year before. Also, August Hausleiter's Deutsche Gemeinschaft, an openly neo-Nazi group, led the Bavarian bloc of rightest parties. Happily, they polled less than 1% of the total vote.

Of significance, too, was the Saar Referendum in October 1955, which killed the Franco-German plan to Europeanize the Saar territory and which now opens the door for the return of the Saar to Germany. While the natural nationalism of the Saar voters is understandable, the agitation stimulated by former Nazis living in the Saar territory, who used Hitler-type propaganda at their meetings and in their campaign material, had an ominous note.

In the meantime, symptoms of religious prejudice continue to appear everywhere (there were Protestant-Catholic conflicts at state election campaigns); the German Reichs Party, despite Naumann's eschewal of anti-Semitism as a political weapon, attacked Mendès-France as a Jew; and in the small village of Kurtscheid a bunch of young villagers smashed the doors of an international boarding school there, screaming, "Out with the Jew.... We are going to kill him.... Go and get an ax." The school, not a Jewish institution, was run by a Jew. That was sufficient.

The soil for a growing neo-Nazi movement is obviously still there; and forces are moving in from all over to ensure its cultivation. The New York Times of February 3, 1955, carried a story on Otto Strasser, whose name came up in our investigation of the Naumann-Weiss tie-up. It is datelined Ottawa, Canada:

In Paradise, Nova Scotia, an exiled former Nazi was packing his bags today and laying plans for the peaceful overthrow of the present Government of West Germany. He is Dr. Otto Strasser, who broke with Adolf Hitler in 1933 after having helped the German dictator rise to power. His German citizenship was restored last November by a German court. Today he received his German passport. Dr. Strasser said over the telephone this afternoon that he expected to start the journey to his homeland in about a week. The former Nazi, who is 59, intends to re-enter German politics as leader of a movement to overthrow the administration of Dr. Konrad Adenauer on the issue of German rearmament and German unity. He was leader of an anti-Hitler group called the "Black Front." He asserts that he still has a substantial following in Germany. Dr. Strasser charges that his passport has been held up by joint efforts of the United States and France to keep him out of Germany until after ratification by the Bundestag of the Paris and London agreements on German rearmament and association with Western Europe.

2   The New Foundation

Naïveté is the most charitable label one can pin on a government that allows Dr. Strasser to return. Strasser's long-time anti-Hitler position no more makes him a desirable citizen in a young democracy than it would have made the late Marshal Stalin. The Bonn government will have to learn the hard way. Strasser arrived back in Germany in March 1955. Seven months later, in October, he announced the founding of a new political party.

No doubt his return and renewed activity will also arm the communists with more material for attacking Adenauer. They will, naturally, not mention that at least twenty-five deputies from East Germany's Parliament are former members of the Nazi Party; and all of them were, in effect, appointed by the communist regime itself.

We have in our files a report received from one of our German correspondents in September 1954. The position of the Jews in East Germany may perhaps be gathered from this excerpt of his report:

It was dusk when I crossed from West to East Berlin by staying on the subway to the next stop. The Friedrichstrasse was the hub of life in the old days when the Admirals-Palast and adjoining cafés buzzed with activity. But tonight this part of Red Berlin had the drab grimness of a deserted village. People with their colorless garments pulled tight about themselves were scurrying home. Along a wall stood a line of men and women patiently awaiting their turn to buy sacks of potatoes. The only bright patches on this muddy landscape were large red and white placards on nearby buildings: "Germans Unite Around One Table," "Don't Let Wall Street Make Cannon Fodder of Your Boys."

In the once thronged street an occasional auto or truck rumbled by; and even the subdued sounds of street life were drowned out by two loudspeakers a quarter of a mile away endlessly exhorting, "Down with the American Imperialists."

Most German cities have an air of boom towns; here ruins lay untouched.

I sat on a bench in a newly constructed little park adjoining the station, and tentatively opened conversation with a plainly dressed elderly woman seated at the far end of the bench. I said: "If I had some nuts I'd feed the squirrels I see running around."

"Squirrels? Look again."

II Cross-Currents in Germany

I looked again. The squirrels were fat rats running in and out of the shrubbery as the night settled.

She interpreted my grunt of disgust correctly, and without waiting further broke into a tirade against the East German Government. I matched her indiscretion by disclosing that I was one of those hated Americans that the posters and loudspeakers were talking about. She brightened quickly. As an American, I was an old friend. She only wished we were coming back to Leipzig again. Then she told me she had been sitting on the bench all day and didn't know how much longer she would have to stay there until her husband returned—if he returned. She obviously expected the worst.

This is her story, told me in dull, flat tones: She and her husband had built up a small prosperous business in Leipzig with eight workers. "Although a small outfit, we specialized in a high quality of furs, buying some of the better qualities from Russia and selling to better houses in Britain and the States. But after the Soviets moved in, in spite of the fact that our furs come from Russia, we have been getting fewer and fewer skins. The Russians don't care about us. They positively hate us small craftsmen and tradesmen. We know that they have the skins because we read about their sales in London. They have been giving us fewer and fewer skins. We finally had to switch to rabbit skins, using first, then second, and of late third grade. We find ourselves with no skins at all. Unless we get some at once we must close shop entirely and throw out our eight workers. But all this time our taxes have been increasing. We have no capital or earnings out of which to pay taxes. My husband and I came in from Leipzig early this morning. He left me here while he went to do the rounds of the East German Government offices."

As though this were not enough, she opened up a second chapter of her troubles. They are Jewish. Russians coming into their shop often register surprise at finding any Jews alive in Germany. Occasionally they get off remarks like: "How did the Nazis overlook you?"

"Being Jewish," she continued, "doesn't help us asking favors around these German communists. They seem to hate us because we are tradesmen trying to make a living and brush us off the faster because we are Jews."

I left the despondent woman to keep an appointment in the Press café across the way. Coming out later, I looked toward the benches. The dark figure still huddled there.

This tired woman was facing failure after years of effort and sacrifice to keep a small business going. She and hundreds of other Jewish

2 The New Foundation

merchants in East Germany have found themselves in similar hopeless situations. No merchandise, and a hopeless accumulation of unpaid excessive taxes. The only alternatives are to close shop and become anonymous little numbers in the Soviet trade apparatus, or, in old age, to drift to the West, hoping, with help of the Jewish organizations, to make a start in a small way again in some other part of the world.

CROSS-CURRENTS IN THE MIDDLE EAST

One   The Issue

SEPTEMBER 11, 1954 . . . CAIRO RADIO: IN ARABIC TO THE NEAR EAST . . . "DEAR ARAB BRETHREN, THE VOICE OF THE ARABS WISHES TO SPEAK TO YOU TODAY ABOUT IMPERIALISM'S DREAM OF PROFANING ARAB TERRITORY WITH ITS ARMIES, STEALING THE WEALTH OF THE ARABS THROUGH EXPLOITATION, AND HUMILIATING THE DIGNITY OF THE ARABS BY MAINTAINING ITS RULE OVER ARAB TERRITORY. . . . EGYPT BELIEVES IN THE NECESSITY OF UNITING ARAB POLICY TOWARD THE NON-ARABS. . . . THE POLICY IS ONE OF NO ALLIANCE WITH THE EAST OR THE WEST; THE ARABS ARE THEIR OWN ALLIES. THERE SHALL BE NO JOINT DEFENSE BETWEEN THE ARABS AND THE WEST, AS THE ARABS WILL NOT DEFEND NON-ARABS. THE ARABS ARE THEIR OWN DEFENDERS.

Since 1948, Arab propaganda in the United States has made much of two themes: the "imperialistic" injustice to the Arabs in the re-establishment of Israel and the plight of the Arab refugees. In their exploitation of these two themes the Arabs have had to side-step a good deal of recorded history. And this they have managed quite adroitly, labeling their propaganda "information," and sometimes even "objective information." But what does history itself inform us?
International recognition for the re-establishment of the state of

III Cross-Currents in the Middle East

Israel was expressed in the Palestine Mandate granted to Britain by the League of Nations in 1922. Recognizing "the historical connection of the Jewish people with Palestine and the grounds for reconstituting their national home in that country," the international community of nations committed itself to the realization of this goal, and made the Mandatory (Great Britain) responsible for its achievement. The re-establishment of the state of Israel thus became a matter of right and an integral part of international law.

The League of Nations was aware of the existence of an Arab majority in Palestine when these commitments were made. The League decided, however, that in this case the concept of self-determination, in justice, demanded the re-creation of the Jewish National Home. The Arab leaders agreed with this approach. They recognized the justice of renouncing their own claims to the small area allocated to the Jews in exchange for the liberation of lands covering over two million square miles. The Arab agreement was the result of discussion before the League of Nations immediately after World War I.

In spite of all this, and in spite of the territorial concessions made later to the Arabs, when the United Nations decided to bring the Mandate to its envisioned conclusion the Arab League launched an aggressive war against the fledgling state of Israel. And with war came the Arab refugees. It is plain that there would be no Arab refugees today had the Arab states accepted the UN decision to establish the state of Israel. Instead, the Arab governments decided to try to wipe out the new state of Israel—to drive the Jews into the sea, as some Arab leaders so vividly put it.

The Arabs were convinced that the destruction of the young state would be simple and quick. In line with this, the Arab League ordered the "temporary" evacuation of the Palestinian Arabs to the neighboring Arab states. And these evacuation orders were accompanied by severe threats to those who might stay behind and make their peace with the Israelis. All these plans were naturally in anticipation of the scheduled invasion of Israel. Most of the Arabs who did not leave Israel in time fled after the fighting began. Many left as the armies approached their area. Some, seeing the "easy victory" was not to be accomplished, and that the Israelis were winning, ran in fear of retribution for atrocities committed against Jews under the British Mandate. Those Palestinian Arabs who followed the advice of the Israel authorities and remained

1   The Issue

at home are living in peace. They have retained their property. They enjoy equal rights with their fellow citizens, and, as Israeli citizens, sit in the Knesset as elected representatives to the Israeli Parliament. They are far ahead of their kinsmen in the Arab countries in their economic and cultural progress.

Today some 700,000 Arab refugees live on the borders of Israel, their camps a deliberately maintained political and propaganda weapon of the Arab states. No one can fail to sympathize with them but neither can anyone deny that every attempt by both the UN and Israel to solve the refugee problem has been persistently side-tracked or rebuffed by the Arab states. Nor can anyone deny that under the UN Relief Program the physical well-being of many refugees is better than that of millions of their Arab brethren outside the camps. A joint report in 1952 by the World Health Organization and the UN Food and Agriculture Organization stated that there was "no serious malnutrition" among the Arab refugees. Comparing the condition of the refugees with the lot of villagers in the neighboring areas of the Arab states, the WHO-FAO report added that "the refugees are rather well off because at least they receive a basic ration." As a matter of fact there is much evidence that the number of refugees has probably been swelled by the newcomers who have joined the camps in order to get on the ration rolls. Estimates of the number of refugees are based on the number of persons drawing rations, but no more than 600,000 are refugees from that part of Palestine that is now Israel. The frauds committed in getting on the ration rolls and the opposition of the Arab states to a census of the refugees is a recurrent theme in the UN Relief and Work Agency's reports. The joint WHO-FAO report also pointed out that educational and recreational facilities made available by the UNWRA authorities also compare favorably with those in the Arab states surrounding the refugee areas.

The Arab attitude toward the refugees may be best summed up in the words of Sir Alexander Galloway, a former UN relief director in Jordan, who in April 1952 stated: "... the Arab nations do not want to solve the Arab refugee problem. They want to keep it as an open sore, as an affront against the UN and as a weapon against Israel. Arab leaders do not give a damn whether the refugees live or die." This was also the conclusion of the U. S. Senate Subcommittee on Arab Refugees. In 1953 the subcommittee reported to the Senate that it "does

III Cross-Currents in the Middle East

not believe that the Arab nations can escape responsibility to their fellow Arabs by failing to cooperate fully with the UN in projects designed to resettle refugees and make land available for refugee settlement."

Thus history, Arab propaganda in America notwithstanding. But whatever the themes of Arab propaganda may be, one of its goals in this country is precisely similar to that of every dyed-in-the-wool American anti-Semite. These professionals and their followers are not motivated by any single basic urge; the variety of motivations includes easy money, political opportunism, the emotional need to find a scapegoat for their failures, the dislike of any man different from themselves, self-induced religious fanaticism, or pure personal psychosis. On the other hand, the Arabs are motivated by a single calculation concerning the one certain method of achieving final victory against Israel in the Middle East. This calculation determines the goal of their propaganda here, and that goal is also the over-all aim of the professional American anti-Semite, whatever his motivations: it is the utter destruction of Jewish prestige in America.

In assessing the Arab contribution to the propaganda war against Jews (as distinguished from the Arab vs. Israeli conflicts), the touchstone—the test—is not the extent to which Arab representatives have joined hands with our native rabble-rousers. Rather, the touchstone is the amount of anti-Semitism in the propaganda spread by these Arabs here and abroad. But since so many Arab spokesmen have offered assurances that they have nothing in common with our local bigots, and since they insist that they would refuse to aid or be aided by them, any co-operation between these two forces would be proof of Arab fraud. For this reason we reveal in the ensuing pages the exact nature of such collaboration.

Even if actual collaboration between official Arab agents and America's salesmen of hate were totally non-existent, however, such absence would not constitute proof that the two forces do not, nevertheless, consciously supplement each other. When Arab sources inspire a propaganda argument in their continuing anti-Jewish campaign, its theme immediately becomes a regular part of our native bigots' stock in trade. Typical is the lie that the Israelis have desecrated Christian and Moslem holy places in Palestine. Typical, too, is the now old saw about the

1 The Issue

"*dual allegiance*" *of American Jews, something else the Arabs helped dream up. Perhaps unaware that our country, a nation of immigrant groups, maintains Old World ties and that its citizens traditionally have helped the peoples of their own ethnic origin or native lands, the Arabs claimed to see a failure of American-Jewish allegiance to the United States in American-Jewish charity and friendship for Israel. They beamed the divisive accusation to the United States, and the lunatic fringe here quickly echoed it to all parts of our nation: "Jews have a double allegiance"; "Jews are loyal to another flag"; "Jews are disloyal." The Arabs suggested another: Israel, a part of the world Zionist movement, is oriented to Soviet Russia. The lie was quickly repeated here: Jews equal Zionism equal Communism.*

Prior to World War II not every anti-Semitic agitator had direct connections with Hitler Germany but most of them were deliberate sounding boards for Nazi precepts. Today, not every anti-Semitic agitator has direct connections with the Arab nations but most of them are deliberate sounding boards for Arab doctrine.

While Arab propaganda themes have been taken over completely by professional American anti-Semites, it would nevertheless be inaccurate to equate Arab representatives with native hatemongers. The latter, absorbed entirely by their anti-Semitic fixation, have no interest whatever in any constructive program. The former, viewing anti-Jewish agitation as only one of many aims, are also occupied with winning economic and military assistance, mutual respect and intercultural understanding. But while the Arabs contend that these benign goals constitute the totality of their purpose in the United States, they nevertheless find themselves hypnotized by the ready acceptance of their arguments in openly anti-Semitic quarters. And although they recognize that it sits badly with the American people when Arabs are discovered working closely with known Jew-baiters, Arab officials are reluctant to refuse such unwholesome help. For it is help, after all.

One may well ask whether the American troublemakers' practice of adopting Arab maxims means that these maxims are evil per se. The answer lies in the implications *of the maxims, not in their adoption by local agitators. But their ready use by the agitator is a significant warning.*

The origin and character of Arab opinion-molding in the United

III Cross-Currents in the Middle East

States give meaning to these observations. Until the end of World War II there was no organized Arab campaign on this continent. Before then, Middle Eastern countries, merely colonial stakes in the world's great empires, had little, if any, independent power. By 1945, as sovereignty flowered among the Middle Eastern states, the governments formed the Arab League, binding themselves together politically for the first time in modern history. A little more than a year later, the new association of states set up the Arab Office in Washington, D.C. At about the same time a "cultural" agency appeared on the horizon in the United States for the highly laudable, stated purpose of creating good will between Arab countries and our own. But subsequent perusal of the full record of the newly established cultural agency, called the Institute of Arab-American Affairs, showed that its primary concern was to head off American support for the creation of a Jewish state in Palestine. Thus, from its very beginning, one major undertaking of Arab adherents in the United States was essentially negative.

The Institute of Arab-American Affairs was foredoomed as an effective opinion-winning weapon. The Middle Eastern countries for whose benefit it was created had little in common beyond an intense fear of the impending Jewish state; not enough at the time to hold them together. Unable to agree upon a simple, constructive program for the group as a whole, each Arab state initiated its own individual propaganda operation. As a result, Arab thought-molding activity, although unco-ordinated, increased in intensity as paid agents moved back and forth across the United States, addressing quasi-religious conferences, speaking from civic and cultural platforms, participating in radio forums, and distributing literature and carefully thought-out news releases.

With the actual declaration of the existence of an Israeli state in 1948, the Arab world knew that it must heal the breaches in its own ranks and get down to a serious drive in the United States or permanently suffer a new, modern national entity in its medieval midst. The totality of Arab propaganda thus far had been a curious mixture of legitimate pleas for economic assistance and sordid collaboration with the native bigots.

In the winter of 1950, with the arrival in the United States of Abdul Rahman Azzam Pasha, then Secretary General of the Arab League, the idea of a fully co-ordinated propaganda machine was unfolded to Arab

1 The Issue

embassies in Washington and to the six Arab delegations at the UN in New York City. No longer would each Middle Eastern state be left to its own opinion-making devices, be limited to its particular American contacts, be concerned solely with its own national problems, or be curtailed by its meager, special budget for these purposes. All would be co-ordinated and Egypt would foot the major portion of the bill. Of course, each state could carry on additionally as it pleased, just so long as there was a singleness of purpose.

What was that purpose? It was the absolute elimination of the new state of Israel. Why, then, was operation to be centered in the United States? Because, they argued, the greatest single factor in the creation of the new Middle Eastern democracy was situated right here in the United States—the American Jew. Weaken him and you weaken Israel. Isolate him and you isolate Israel. Destroy him and you destroy Israel.

Azzam Pasha stayed in the United States only three months to whip up enthusiasm for his idea, and then departed for Cairo to report back his accomplishments in this country. Judging from the warm reception Azzam was given by men in American government, by delegates at the United Nations, and by men in American commerce, journalism, and religion, Azzam's accomplishments were indeed substantial.

But Azzam Pasha, experienced and knowledgeable though he was, did not fully comprehend the narrowness of the seven Arab nations' representatives he left behind; nor did he fully appreciate the extent of the political frictions that existed among them. At his departure, enthusiasm for his idea departed with him. Only a few of those who remained to work in the United States believed profoundly in the desirability of a unified Arab propaganda program in America. One of those men was Kamil Abdul Rahim, Egyptian ambassador to the United States, who, in a matter of days after Azzam returned to Cairo, suggested to his home office that the idea be made a reality. Rahim, too, wanted a full-fledged propaganda structure, located in New York City, operating as a central information bureau much, as he put it, like the British Information Office. That was in the winter of 1951.

Exactly four years later it finally came to pass. In January 1955 the Arab League opened its new Arab Information Center at 445 Park Avenue in New York City. Its initial budget—$400,000. Its purpose—as outlined by Azzam Pasha. Its executive director—none other than the former Egyptian ambassador, Kamil Abdul Rahim.

III Cross-Currents in the Middle East

During these years of the Center's gradual formation a number of Americans were drawn into the Arab propaganda orbit. Some of their names will be familiar, some new. And in the Arab countries propaganda geared for the Middle East continued on the Arab radio and in their press.

This series of events, touching as they did on the problem of anti-Semitism, was regularly observed and recorded by the Anti-Defamation League, and in February 1955 resulted in the publication of an ADL memorandum that immediately drew a letter of protest from Kamil Abdul Rahim. Arriving at our offices on March 15, 1955, the letter, with an attachment, said:

ARAB INFORMATION CENTER

Director, Anti-Defamation League
My dear Sir:

Radio Station WNYC yesterday, I understand, carried a newscast based upon an Associated Press dispatch, as follows:

"The newly established Arab Information Center in New York is accused of running a propaganda operation with the aid of anti-Semites. The charge was lodged by the Anti-Defamation League of B'nai B'rith."

I enclose a copy of my letter to WNYC declaring this charge to be completely untrue. I am writing a similar letter to the Associated Press.

This charge, I say to you without qualification, is completely untrue. It is furthermore a baseless defamation of the character of this office and a stain on the members of its staff.

I have not seen the text reported in this broadcast although the seriousness of the charge ought to have prompted the writers to inquire before it was released. I request you now to send me a copy of your charge. I expect to ask you promptly for a detailed repudiation.

Sincerely yours,
Kamil A. Rahim
Ambassador

Encl.

ARAB INFORMATION CENTER

Gentlemen:

WNYC, I am told, in its morning newscast yesterday, March 14, broadcast a charge attributed to the Anti-Defamation League of B'nai B'rith that "the newly established Arab Information Center in New

1 The Issue

York is running a propaganda operation with the aid of anti-Semites."

As the permanent representative of the League of Arab States at the United Nations and as the official responsible for the policy direction of the Arab Information Center, I state categorically that this charge is false.

No one connected with this information center is engaged in anti-Semitic propaganda or is knowingly in contact with anti-Semites or their organizations.

As soon as it begins its informational services and distributes materials, the Arab Information Center can be judged by the American public on what it says and does. Its entire output will be promptly available to public scrutiny in accordance with its registration at the Department of Justice. It will operate to increase understanding and friendship between the American and Arab peoples on the basis of their mutual interests. And it will function in a "fish bowl."

Any charge, which prejudges in advance of its opening what the information center is doing, will do or plans to do, is best answered by this statement of basic policy:

All those associated with the Arab Information Center deplore the defamation of persons on religious or racial grounds as inhuman and vicious.

We will slam the door in the face of any anti-Semite or racial bigot known as such to us. This goes for the back door as well as the front door.

Such is the position of the Arab Information Center.

Sincerely yours,
Kamil A. Rahim
Ambassador

In view of Ambassador Rahim's denials and protestations, let us examine the memoranda and the pertinent facts. . . .

Two   The Side Door

FEBRUARY 15, 1952
Research to Library

Note in your records, please, that Gerald Winrod had lunch today at the Egyptian Embassy in Washington, D.C. Ambassador Kamil Abdul Rahim tendered the luncheon; several of his associates were also present. The private meeting came as a result of the publication in Winrod's *Defender* magazine (September issue) of the full text of Ambassador Rahim's recent speech at Princeton University. Winrod wrote to the ambassador at the time, telling him that this would be done.

JULY 10, 1952
Chicago Office to Research

A malevolent assault on American aid to Israel was leveled by Merwin K. Hart before the platform committee of the Republican Convention.

III Cross-Currents in the Middle East

Attacking American foreign policy as unplanned and badly conceived, Hart argued that it has aided the Soviet, insulted Spain, and "stirred up civil war in Israel; 800,000 Arabs, previously friendly to us, have been driven out." He urged the United States to switch its support to the Arab side, the correct side of the Arab-Israeli dispute, and complained to the committee that our nation had already loaned Israel $100,000,000.

Hart's attack was so harsh, members of the press queried this office on his background. Reading through his long record, they began to understand. One reporter, in the light of what he found, thought the following statement by Hart in the February 1950 issue of his Council bulletin must have been tongue in cheek. Hart wrote:

> Now let's see about this business of anti-Semitism. The Semites include two groups, the Jews and the Arabs. In the controversy between Zionists and Arabs, which led to a bitter war, the Council expressed sympathy with the Arabs. So far as the Arabs were concerned, therefore, we were *pro*-Semitic.

NOVEMBER 6, 1952
Middle Eastern Correspondent to Research

Last month the Arab press devoted considerable editorial space to the German payment of reparations to Israel. This month the editorial writers have shifted their interest to the American presidential election. Perhaps "shifted" isn't the best word, because you will see in the following excerpts that the two events have not been considered separately.

Al-Hayat (Beirut), October 7, 1952, labels reparations the "crime of Adenauer," and states:

> ... the time has now come for the Arab states to remedy this injustice and endeavor to induce Germany to refuse to pay compensation to Israel.
> The Jews were responsible for the annihilation of many Germans.

The Jews were responsible for the instigation of many air raids on German cities during the war. After the war, the Jews who were with the occupation forces caused great moral and material loss to the Germans.

The Jews have cashed their compensation through revenge on the German people, and they have no right to ask for more. Germany may even have the right to ask Israel to pay her compensation for the loss incurred by the Germans due to the Jews.

From *Falastin* (Jerusalem, Jordan), October 7, 1952:

If any German during the Nazi regime ever thought that time would come when Israel would be born and ask Germany for compensations, then that German, be he Nazi or not Nazi, would have gone further in his persecution of the Jews and would not have let a single Jew survive in Germany.

From *Ad-Difaa* (Jerusalem, Jordan), October 12, 1952:

Ben Gurion used all Jewish influence in the White House to put pressure on Dean Acheson, who in turn put pressure on Dr. Adenauer, to pay 350 million pounds sterling as reparations for Israel. Ben Gurion's reward was in the shape of placards carried in Tel Aviv describing him as "Hitler's partner."

Truman's turn remains. His help to the Jews exceeds by far that of Britain and of Ben Gurion. For this reason, the Jews will choose for him the foulest epithets that will match his unprecedented services to Israel.

From *Albena* (Syria), November 6, 1952:

Our interests lie in the fact that the former President who was hostile to us in exchange for Jewish votes has left the White House. . . .

We would like to point out that both Truman and Eisenhower were aware of the attitude of the Jews of New York. The Jews support lies and sell their votes on the black market. . . .

We are interested that the President should not be like his predecessor and lie in the palm of the hand of World Jewry. The Jews reacted in America just as they did in other countries in which they settled—by a knife in the back and by selling vital secrets to the country's greatest enemies. . . .

In the past we suffered from the Jewish control of the White House.

III Cross-Currents in the Middle East

NOVEMBER 13, 1952
Research to AF

Allen Zoll is scheduled to speak to a group of Arab diplomats tomorrow at the United Nations.

Omar Haliq, acting in his diplomatic capacity as the alternate Saudi Arabian representative to the United Nations, met with Zoll late last summer to discuss German reparations to Israel. Always interested in frustrating any benefit that might come to Israel, the Arabs have been using their utmost influence to dissuade the Adenauer government from approving any payment whatever. This is what brought Haliq together with Zoll. The American propagandist came with an offer to publish pamphlets explaining the Arab point of view; Haliq reacted sympathetically.

Zoll is obviously setting plans to ingratiate himself with top-ranking Arab diplomatic representatives and Arab League officials in the U.S. in an attempt to sell his services as a public relations expert.

NOVEMBER 14, 1952
Research to AF

Earlier today Issa Korachi, a correspondent for the Arab press, introduced Zoll to a number of Arab diplomats at a luncheon at the United Nations. During the five-hour session with this group (including several Arab foreign ministers and the Arab League's secretary general, Abdul Khalek Hassouna), Zoll held forth on the implications of the American elections for the Arab nations. He predicted that President-elect Eisenhower and his Administration would be generally sympathetic to the Arabs despite obstructive efforts of some pro-Zionist Republicans. Therefore, Zoll went on, the time was now ripe for the creation of an Arab propaganda office in the U.S. which would help American agencies, including his own, to destroy Zionist influence in American politics and to stave off the influence of a "communist-Jewish world conspiracy."

2 The Side Door

Going far beyond the proposals he originally made to Omar Haliq, Zoll suggested the following themes to be advanced in an Arab propaganda campaign: (1) a demand for cessation of U.S. economic aid to Israel; (2) a campaign against German reparations to Israel; and (3) a boycott in the Arab countries of American products manufactured by Jewish-controlled companies to compel the owners of these firms to stop aiding Israel.

NOVEMBER 19, 1952
Research to AF

Zoll apparently impressed his luncheon companions sufficiently to enable him to arrange other meetings. Today he met with Ahmed Farrag, Egypt's Foreign Minister. This time Zoll added another wrinkle to his scheme. He suggested the establishment of an Arab desk in the New York office of his own National Council for American Education whose function it would be to prepare pro-Egyptian and pro-Arab propaganda for distribution to Zoll's mailing list of American schools and universities. Such an "Arab desk," Zoll indicated, could be of value when Egypt or the Arab League itself opened propaganda offices in this country.

Farrag invited Zoll to visit Egypt at the expense of the Egyptian government. Zoll gave no sign that he is interested in the Arabs financing his trip.

NOVEMBER 20, 1952
Research to AF

Zoll is pursuing his goal assiduously. Today he conferred in New York with Abdul Khalek Hassouna, secretary general of the Arab League. Tailoring his sales talk this time to fit Hassouna's requirements, Zoll discoursed on the need for an Arab League propaganda office in the United States and went so far as to suggest that he be appointed by the League as its special representative to handle the problem of American

III Cross-Currents in the Middle East

Zionist activities. In addition, Zoll presented the League's secretary general with a ten-point program to improve the United States' attitude toward the Arabs and revise it with respect to the Israelis.

Hassouna expressed an interest in Zoll's suggestions and asked for a detailed budget on the cost of the propaganda apparatus he envisaged.

Incidentally, Hassouna also had forty-five minutes with Benjamin Freedman the other day in the delegates' lounge at the UN. Freedman tried to sell the secretary general the idea that the Arab League could make good use of the October 15 issue of Conde McGinley's *Common Sense* which "proved" that "Marxist Jews" ran the United Nations. Hassouna expressed interest but made no definite commitment.

APRIL 24, 1953
Research to AF

Through an aide, Abdul Khalek Hassouna received a rather complete statement about Zoll from representatives of American intelligence sources. It was quite bad. The aide suggested to the secretary general that this should not prevent co-operation with Zoll so long as discretion was exercised, and no open or public support of Zoll shown.

After careful consideration, Hassouna scribbled across the face of the Zoll report: "Confidential: To be answered politely—no promises ... official collaboration should not be instituted for the time being. Preferably as a very private advisor on Jewish affairs in the U.S. and Congress tactics." Hassouna then dated the memorandum—April 24—and filed it under Arab League Document Section as follows: American Affairs —Zionist Activities—Allen Zoll—#456/L.

JUNE 4, 1953
Middle Eastern Correspondent to Research

Allen Zoll yesterday told Arab foreign correspondents in New York City that he is planning a two- to three-month trip through the Moslem

2 The Side Door

world, and that he had already had favorable reactions to his anticipated visit from representatives of the Saudi Arabian, Pakistan, Iraqi, and Yemenite governments.

SEPTEMBER 26, 1953
Middle Eastern Correspondent to Research

Allen Zoll arrived with his wife in Cairo a fortnight ago and spent two hours last week with General Naguib. He checked into a $30-a-day suite at the Semiramis Hotel, the most fashionable in town, and has met with the former Mufti of Palestine, Haj Amin el Husseini, and several highly placed Egyptian government officials, including the chief of Army Intelligence, Colonel Zakaria Mohei El Dine.

Enclosed are clips from local Egyptian papers. Included are two news photos of Mr. and Mrs. Zoll conferring with Naguib. The third picture shows Zoll meeting with Arab news correspondents. The *Al Ahram* news story says:

Investment of American Capital in New Egyptian Projects

Mr. Allen Zoll, one of America's tycoons in finance and industries is at present visiting Egypt. He met with General Mohammed Naguib and other Egyptians in charge of the new big projects in Egypt.

American Money for Egyptian Projects

A press conference was held yesterday in the Hotel Semiramis, where it was announced that Egypt intends to enlarge her industrial enterprises and it is believed that Americans will invest in the new projects which will bring profits to both.

Mr. Allen Zoll declared that he was ready to invest in Egypt and promised to persuade some of his friends to follow in his footsteps.

He also hinted that some businessmen in London advised him, before coming to Egypt, that the situation in Egypt was not stable and that life was not secure there. In spite of all this he decided to come and see for himself the new regime and developments therein. He was surprised with what he saw—the construction and the modern buildings; the streets he found were cleaner and more beautiful than in any of the

III Cross-Currents in the Middle East

European capitals. He said: "Egypt has a reputation of being a primitive country. From what I saw it is quite modern and progressive."

He said he was much impressed by Mohammed Naguib, when he met with him. He was convinced of Naguib's sincerity and patriotism, which is a good omen for Egypt's development. He felt the same about all those he met who serve at present the new regime.

He mentioned the bad publicity which is being propagated against Egypt by its enemies—who are well known and compared it with what he saw in reality. Such propaganda is the cause for persuading tourists not to visit Egypt or potential investors from investing. He also made the observation that it would be wise for Egypt to increase its campaign and propaganda abroad in order to refute the allegations made by its enemies. He also said that it was a mistake to confine the tourist season to winter months only. He pointed out that Egypt could be attractive to tourists in summertime, which is the customary traveling season, while winter is the traveling season for older people who are interested only in archaeological sites.

Mr. Zoll established an Arab-American foundation to better relations between the Arabs and the American people. One of the benefits to be derived from such an institution would be to assist the Arabs in improving their social and professional abilities.

The foundation also supplied the relevant department in the Health Ministry with samples of vaccines which would be useful in the treatment of trachoma. After testing the vaccines, it will be used for mass treatment for the Egyptian people.

Mr. Zoll left today for Syria and Lebanon and will proceed from there to France and America. He promised, though, to return and visit Egypt again.

OCTOBER 10, 1953

Middle Eastern Correspondent to Research

Several days ago Omar Haliq responded favorably to a proposition he received through the mails from Robert Williams. In September, Williams contacted the Arab League with an offer to prepare a 12-page pamphlet on various phases of the Israeli-Arab controversy, including a report on the alleged pro-Israel activities of the Anti-Defamation League and the American Jewish Committee. Williams offered to do the complete job, furnishing suitable names from his mailing list to aid distribution, for the "bargain price" of $2000.

Haliq asked Williams for an outline of the proposed brochure for submission to Cairo. Haliq hoped that the suggested project would be approved and he offered to assist Williams in its preparation in any way he could.

But Haliq does not make the decisions; his approval alone is meaningless.

OCTOBER 11, 1953
Library to Research

This is to remind you that the tentative Haliq-Williams deal is not the first time Williams has tried to do business with the Arabs. In the spring of last year, before the political conventions, Williams got in touch with Abed Bouhafa, correspondent for the influential Cairo daily, *Al Misri,* and pointed out the danger to the Arab cause in a "Zionist-supported" candidate receiving the nomination. Williams had, he said, a scheme to spike such a move which deserved the support of Arab newspapers and suggested getting together with Bouhafa to talk the matter over.

Williams' strenuous efforts to sell his services to Arab representatives in the United States is a long-time thing. Read the following letter to Bouhafa from Williams after the latter sold the Syrian Minister a bill of goods:

ROBERT H. WILLIAMS
P.O. Box 868
Santa Ana, California

May 13, 1950

Mr. El-Abed Buhafa
Al-Misri Bureau
221 West 10th Street
New York, N.Y.

Dear Mr. Buhafa:
   The Hon. Faiz El-Khouri, Minister for Syria, writes that he has

talked with you about my unfinished manuscript *A Gentile Looks at the Jewish Problem* and that your paper might possibly be interested in publishing the book in Arabic, when it is finished.

I think I would be greatly interested in such a proposition.

The book really is finished, but requires much revising and reducing. It now stands at something over 500 pages of double-spaced typed manuscript and should be reduced to not more than 300 pages, I should think. Furthermore, on the chapter dealing with the destruction of Rome and the two chapters dealing with the destruction of Russia, I must do some more research.

I doubt that the book can be ready before fall.

Meanwhile, it occurs to me that your paper might want to publish in Arabic one or both of the two booklets which I am sending you separately: *The Anti-Defamation League and Its Use in the World Communist Offensive* and *FEPC and the Minority Machine*.

If your paper wants to publish them, in book or booklet form, I would be agreeable to the customary royalty arrangement. If, in addition to the booklets, or without publishing them as booklets, your paper should want to print them serially in its columns, then I would welcome a reasonable offer of remuneration.

May I hear from you at your convenience?

Sincerely,
Robert H. Williams
Major, MI-Res.

PS—I believe I shall send both booklets herewith instead of separately.

OCTOBER 26, 1953

Middle Eastern Correspondent to Research

Abdul Khalek Hassouna, secretary general of the Arab League, has been reached by Myron Fagan, of Hollywood, with a fervent plea that the Arabs get out of the UN. Its actions, says Fagan, are absolutely dominated by "Jews and Communists."

Fagan has offered to print, according to need, from fifty to a hundred thousand copies of an impressive pamphlet in behalf of the Arab cause.

APRIL 19, 1954

Middle Eastern Correspondent to Research

Several members of the Arab delegations have been asked by Myron Fagan whether they are interested in his book, *Red Treason on Broadway,* which, he claims, proves the existence of a Jewish-spy network in the United States. A few days ago he was cordially answered, and copies of the book were requested.

AUGUST 22, 1954

Middle Eastern Correspondent to Research

Egyptian Premier Gamal Abdel Nasser is helping to spread the Arab version of the "Jews equal Communists" formula. This week he said in a speech:

"I have previously told you that it has been definitely established that the Communists in this country are working with Zionism. . . . It was established this year and in previous years that they work as hirelings for Zionism."

The "Zionism equals Communism" line is routine stuff in official Arab propaganda in the Middle East. Last June 29 the Iraqi Home Service, broadcasting over Radio Baghdad, declared:

"We have often dealt in past commentaries with the unity of objectives connecting Zionism and Communism and their menacing nature . . . all pointing out that Zionists are brothers to Communists and vice versa."

OCTOBER 28, 1954

Library to BRE

The current issue of Frank Britton's monthly newsletter, *The American Nationalist,* includes this very significant item:

III Cross-Currents in the Middle East

"If you read Arabic you will be interested to learn that an Arabic translation of our book, 'Behind Communism,' is now available from the Farajalla Press, Box 1012, Beirut, Lebanon."

It means that for the second time, at least, this young professional anti-Jewish agitator has worked a deal for himself with the Arabs. The November 1953 issue of his slick-sheet publication featured a piece on the Kibya incident, purporting to show how "the parasitic state of Israel added another murderous chapter to its already blood-spattered record. . . ." In January, Britton got his reward for the article—money from Arab sources.

The pay-off was for services rendered; the article had been drafted by Omar Haliq of the Arab League, then shipped to Britton for publication. With the check went an order for more copies of the Britton publication, ten to twenty thousand, which the Arab League will underwrite.

The Arabs cannot wriggle out of this one. A quick perusal of the Britton newsletter reveals that it is one of the worst anti-Semitic rags in the United States. On a solid basis of co-operation with most of the older professional Jew-baiters, Britton conceals nothing. To him, Gerald L. K. Smith is "the magnificent . . . founder and leader of the Christian Nationalist Movement"; Robert Williams is "the gallant . . . author of *Know Your Enemy*"; and Conde McGinley is "the fire-brand editor of *Common Sense*."

Hate propaganda seems a strange occupation for an American not quite thirty-three years old, a veteran of World War II and a former student at the University of Southern California. But it has paid off. His first pamphlet, *Atom Treason,* a 24-page document charging that communism is Jewish and that the "Jew-ridden" Atomic Energy Commission sabotaged the nation's H-bomb program, brought him substantial orders for copies. That year Smith paid Britton $924.62 for literature.

Britton apparently has still other deals pending with the Arabs at this very moment. Earlier this month he was invited on behalf of Abdul Khalek Hassouna, secretary general of the Arab League, to come East as a guest of the Arab League, all expenses covered, for a

2 The Side Door

private conference. In extending the invitation it was explained to Britton that no final commitments could be made to him via mail pending the arrival of the new director of the Arab League propaganda office (Kamil Abdul Rahim) from the Middle East.

OCTOBER 29, 1954
AF to BRE

Now we understand why Frank Britton is preoccupied with rewriting for his magazine much of the Arab propaganda coming out of the Middle East. His stories include charges that Arabs suffer second-class citizenship in Israel; that Israel has been blackmailing Germany with demands for reparations; that all Jews give their first loyalty to Israel; that Jews are mistreating Arab refugees; that Israel's immigration laws are harsher than the McCarran-Walter Immigration Act; that Israel pursues an anti-Gentile policy more ruthless than Nazi Germany's Nuremberg laws; that Israel is an aggressor nation, a perpetrator of atrocities, a deadbeat on its obligations to Arab refugees, etc., etc.

It is not strange, of course, that many of the same stories, and others even worse, have also appeared in Conde McGinley's *Common Sense* and in Gerald Winrod's *Defender* magazine. These men certainly are faithful parrots for the basest Arab propaganda.

Three   The New Director

OCTOBER 29, 1954
Middle Eastern Correspondent to Research

The Egyptians are being treated to an increasing campaign for eventual war upon the Israelis. Premier Nasser has missed no opportunity to declare that there will be no peace with Israel. During the past three months Major Salah Salim, the Egyptian Minister of National Guidance, went from one Arab country to another, meeting the rulers and the ruled, and announcing in the name of the Egyptian revolution and its Command Council that Egypt cannot even contemplate the idea of peace with Israel, as this would mean the destruction and collapse of all Arabs, both economically and militarily.

None of this is secret; all details are spelled out in the press and over the radio. Examples attached:

September 17, 1954 . . . Cairo Radio: Voice of the Arabs, in Arabic to the Arab World: ". . . we repeat Salah Salim's slogan: 'There would be no Egypt, no Egyptian revolution, and no Egyptian Army if Egypt would make peace with Israel.' Let all of us, O Arabs, repeat

III Cross-Currents in the Middle East

it once more: 'There would be no Egypt, no Egyptian revolution, and no Egyptian Army if Egypt would make peace with Israel.'"

September 20, 1954 . . . Cairo Radio: Voice of the Arabs, in Arabic to the Arab World: ". . . millions of Arabs and Moslems long to sacrifice themselves for the protection of Al-Aqsa Mosque and its Holy Land from the Zionists. This is going to happen without any doubt or argument. Sooner or later, Palestine will be for the Arabs. The countries which are interested in peace and tranquillity in the Middle East should understand this fact. Nowadays no Arab can consent to the conclusion of peace with Israel or call for any kind of understanding or co-operation with it, as long as the Palestine Arabs are dispersed from their homes and as long as the Western Powers in the United Nations support the Zionists."

September 21, 1954 . . . Cairo Radio: Voice of the Arabs, in Arabic to the Arab World: "The UN General Assembly opens its new session today. Each time we examine the UN Charter, we read its seemingly plausible effort to free peoples, to bring them happiness through peace, and to protect them from destruction. . . . The Voice of the Arabs wishes to tell you today not to believe in the United Nations, not to be deceived by its charter, and not to expect any good from it."

OCTOBER 30, 1954
Washington, D.C., Office to AF

Evidently the leaders of the Arab states realize that the American public would be shocked by the bluntness they display at home in discussing Israel. The Press Department of the Egyptian Embassy in Washington this week issued a bit of *Background Information* which included the following:

Egypt does not intend to solve the Palestine question by force, and has declared more than once that it has no aggressive intentions whatsoever. Only a few days ago, Prime Minister Gamal Abdel Nasser repeated that assurance after the agreement with Britain was signed.

3 The New Director

NOVEMBER 9, 1954
Library to BRE

The second issue of a new magazine, the *Egyptian Economic and Political Review,* published in Cairo in the English language, has just arrived from overseas. Our Middle Eastern correspondent advises Research that, although the periodical appears to be an independent organ, actually it is subsidized by both the Arab League and the Egyptian Ministry of Propaganda, and is intended for wide distribution in America to government officials, libraries, travel agencies, radio and TV people, etc.

It is a well-presented magazine and, as an official voice of the Arab world, has some revealing things to say about Arab points of view in the Middle East. Its lead editorial contains these candid statements of Arab policy:

That Israel is more than anxious to achieve a settlement with the Arabs is common knowledge, and hardly surprising. . . . Obstacles to agreement with the Arabs are many. . . . Were all these obstacles to understanding successfully disposed of, one would still have to convince the Arabs of the value of an agreement. . . . To contemplate, at this stage, an agreement with Israel which would bring with it the lifting of the Arab blockade, might amount to virtual economic suicide on the part of the Arabs.

In a full-dress article reviewing Arab League activities, written from a frankly Arab viewpoint according to its author, there appears this paragraph:

Another argument for Arab unity is that of the common attitude toward Israel. Arab defeat in the United Nations debate over Palestine, followed by a military defeat in the field, was, after the initial shock had been absorbed, to become one of the principal factors welding Arab unity. Here the Jewish aggression and the establishment of the Israeli bridgehead, were to become, as indeed they still are today, a challenge to Arab ability to remain united, and a menace continually threatening the political and economic security of the Middle East.

III Cross-Currents in the Middle East

The test of Arab unity cannot be better shown than through the fact that in spite of defeat, and disillusionment, and the constant pressure of almost every major power, *the Arab states have resisted and still resist any arrangement with Israel.* [Italics ours.]

NOVEMBER 20, 1954
AF to BRE

Kamil Abdul Rahim, Egypt's former ambassador to the United States, returned to this country this morning, this time to assume the duties of executive director of the long-planned Arab League propaganda office in the United States.

NOVEMBER 22, 1954
Research to AF

Rahim made some interesting, off-the-record comments about American Jews to friends the day he arrived. If the Arabs in the United States were to minimize their anti-Semitic agitation, said Rahim, many American Jews might then lose interest in Zionism and Israel. But, added Rahim, this was not the solution; there is a better answer. Most Americans do not distinguish between Zionists and Jews. This, he added, is "something we have to exploit carefully." Understanding American public opinion as well as he does, Rahim concluded, it won't be very difficult—although delicate.

NOVEMBER 23, 1954
Library to BRE

One of the professional agitators with whom the newly arrived Rahim has been in touch, at least through intermediaries, is Gerald Smith.

In 1952, Smith sent out a number of letters to prominent Arabs concerning various aspects of the "Jewish problem." Among those to

3 The New Director

whom he wrote was Kamil Abdul Rahim, ambassador from Egypt at the time, and when Rahim's representative, Colonel Mohammed Abdel Halim Khalifa, attended the 1952 Republican Convention in Chicago, he had an hour's conversation with the Christian Nationalist leader.

In his report to Rahim, Khalifa indicated that he had been very favorably impressed by Smith, whom he characterized as one of the principal fighters against Zionism and Jewish influence in the United States. Always the salesman, Smith boasted to Khalifa of the "wonderful co-operation" he had been receiving from various representatives of Syrian-Lebanese American clubs. Believe it or not, Smith promised Khalifa that he would exert great influence to see that the platforms of both major parties pay respect to the national aspirations of the Arab states. For a discredited rabble-rouser like Smith to palm off successfully such a patently phony promise, Khalifa must be a man who is quite ignorant of the American scene.

But apparently Smith has a way with the Arabs. Back in January 1953, Dr. Ahmed Galal Abdelrazek, Egypt's permanent representative to the United Nations, ordered Smith's pamphlets for his legation and found *The Cross and the Flag* so stimulating that he purchased a hundred subscriptions and expressed an interest in personally meeting its editor, Don Lohbeck.

It is interesting, also, to note that the Saudi Arabian delegation, subscribing to ten copies of *The Cross and the Flag* at a subscription rate of $2.00 each, sent Smith a $120 check for the purchase; the $100 gratuity obviously reflected Saudi Arabian gratitude.

Smith must really have put his best foot forward in Arab circles. Our files also show that back in October 1951 he was the subject of extended comment during a meeting at the home of Mahmoud Fawzy Bey, permanent Egyptian representative to the United Nations. Six very top official representatives from the Arab world attended, including the Iraqi, Syrian, and Saudi Arabian representatives to the UN, and Charles Malik, Lebanese ambassador. The Iraqi delegate, Awni Khalidy, was holding forth. Here is the substance of his remarks:

My brothers, my activities last week were concentrated mainly on reports from Iraqi students in American universities. I had given them the task of carrying on an intensive agitation against the gangsters of Tel Aviv. I received eighteen letters from my correspondents in which they reported distributing a considerable number of pamphlets and prospectuses in favor of the Arab cause at universities in Michigan, Massachusetts, California, Washington, and at Syracuse and Philadelphia. In these universities my correspondents work quietly and secretly so that Jewish students do not learn about their activities or report about them to their espionage agencies. I sent my correspondents 1800 copies of a pamphlet which I received from my very good friend Gerald Smith. The sum of it was that the cause of the Arabs is our cause; that we must try to understand it; that we must try to fight for it and learn about it day and night; that we should understand that the cause that the Arab world defends is real anti-communist democracy, and that the Jews are the inventors of communism and are its largest supporters; that we must study the Arab world and understand it; that the Arab world is a world founded by honest people, sincere, frank, and cherishing democracy. I believe that such a pamphlet will touch the hearts of young Americans. Last week I also succeeded in obtaining from my government an appropriation of $2000 which I will spend exclusively to finance our friends organizing a number of meetings. . . .

DECEMBER 27, 1954
Research to AF

An Arab League plan, nursed for five years, to organize a major, centrally directed, opinion-molding apparatus in the United States, becomes a reality with the opening by the League of its propaganda center at 445 Park Avenue in New York City.

According to the current plan, this will be the main co-ordinating point for nationwide dissemination of pro-Arab, anti-Israel, and anti-Semitic propaganda; and here various activities will originate to rouse public feeling against Zionist and the "all-pervading Jewish influence" on American opinion.

3 The New Director

To attain these ends, representatives of the Arab Center will seek the aid of the nation's well-known professional anti-Semites, such as Gerald L. K. Smith, Merwin K. Hart, Robert H. Williams, Frank Britton, Allen Zoll, and others.

Dr. Omar Haliq, Arab League representative in New York, in a comprehensive report submitted last August to his superiors in the Middle East, outlined the suggestions and offers of assistance he has already received from Freedman, Britton, and Williams. On the question of how and under what circumstances the Arab Center could proceed to work with these people without provoking accusations of anti-Semitism, Haliq strongly advised "steady" contact, carried out in secrecy, so as not to hinder or "deeply impair" the work of the new Center.

Outlining the co-operation the new Arab office could expect from these men, Haliq said his conclusions were based upon talks he himself had with them; with Freedman last June; with Hart in July; with Smith and Zoll some time later.

Haliq suggested in his report that to rule these men out of the Arab propaganda effort, as recommended by friends in the American Friends of the Middle East, would be unrealistic, because the Arab Center's mission with regard to Jews is identical with that of the anti-Semites.

DECEMBER 28, 1954
Middle Eastern Correspondent to Research

If you would like to make an educated guess as to the private attitude of Rahim's new office in New York City on the subject of the United Nations, read what one of his bosses, Premier Faris el-Khoury, of Syria, had to say in a speech at home last month:

"It is wrong to expect justice from the big or small nations who are members of the United Nations. The small countries are tied to the wheel of the Big Powers while the Big Powers submit to the Zionist influence. . . . Under these circumstances, what can we expect from these Big Powers? We should rely only on ourselves."

III Cross-Currents in the Middle East

Faris el-Khoury's remarks were broadcast in the Middle East for local consumption only. The Arabs hope that others won't take notice of it.

JANUARY 4, 1955

Middle Eastern Correspondent to Research

Following his arrival in New York from Cairo to take over the Center's directorship, Rahim outlined his program of action to a group of Arab diplomats. He announced that his office would be an aggressive group, operating in all fields where "Zionists and Jewish groups" are functioning—government departments; Congress; the United Nations; universities, colleges, high schools; educational and cultural groups and clubs; TV, radio, and press; and big business circles.

He intended one day, said Rahim, to be able to keep "on the toes" of every important Jewish organization in the United States, "coping" with them in every field of their activities. But, he added, this is a far-reaching task, which will take years of steady, patient work and millions of dollars. We'll get both, Rahim said flatly.

Rahim said he has a budget of some $400,000 for the first year of operations.[1] He added that this did not include important salaries or rent for the office in New York and branches all over the United States and probably Canada.

This budget is also exclusive of special, periodic contributions that can be expected from American groups and business firms having interests in the Middle East.

JANUARY 10, 1955

Middle Eastern Correspondent to Research

The newly established Center in New York is to be formally known as "League of the Arab States, Permanent Delegation to the UN," a title

[1] Before the year was out, Rahim obtained an additional $300,000 from the Arab League, and from Egypt and Saudi Arabia.

3 The New Director

calculated to cloak its political propaganda with official dignity. The office will also be listed under "Kingdom of Yemen, Permanent Delegation to the UN," and "Arab Information Center."

Director Rahim got himself appointed Yemen's representative to the UN, in order, as he reported to Arab League headquarters in Cairo, to secure "diplomatic immunity" with the rank of ambassador. He informed Cairo, however, that the Center's information section would be required by law to register with the U. S. Department of Justice as a foreign agent—that there was no way of evading it.

JANUARY 11, 1955
Research to AF

Behind all the window dressing, the "information" section is the heart and purpose of the New York Arab Center. Director of the Department of Research and Information is a Dr. Fayez Sayegh, a Palestinian of Syrian nationality, who is now working for the UN but will resign in the near future to join the Arab office. The Public Liaison Department is to be run by a onetime lecturer at the University of Chicago by the name of Dr. Ali Othman. A Bureau of Lectures is under the supervision of Miss E. D. Kempt, who was previously associated with American Friends of the Middle East. The Press Department is presently being operated by an American newspaperman, Fowler Hill, who has worked for the New York *Times* and the New York *Herald Tribune*. Chester Williams, a public relations counsel and former member of the United States Mission to the UN, has been retained to act as a general adviser to Rahim.

JANUARY 11, 1955
Library to BRE

Rahim is extremely touchy about any implication that his current mission involves propaganda. He was particularly disturbed that even the

III Cross-Currents in the Middle East

Arabic press had been insensitive enough to attach just that label to his undertaking.

Typical was a piece in the *Egyptian Gazette,* October 25, 1954, reporting that the new Arab Center "will be staffed by Arabs and American experts on propaganda." The Cairo newspaper added that "it will have a section for United Nations affairs and will help the Arab delegates in the preparation of their cases."

And Rahim has had his troubles on the same score at the United Nations too. Once, just before the close of the last General Assembly, he was nettled by a group of Arab diplomats; and, in a voice betraying great pique in its high pitch, declared: "I am not a propagandist. . . . I am an ambassador for the League. . . ."

JANUARY 12, 1955
Library to BRE

You are quite right in assuming that Rahim's record gives him every reason to be sensitive about the tag of "propagandist." As Egyptian ambassador to the United States for nearly four years, the last post he held here, Rahim revealed considerable diplomatic talents. He is personable, a smooth linguist, and a gracious host; he is tall and imposing. Now in his fifties, he has had broad experience in the Egyptian foreign service, including a stint as Undersecretary of State for Foreign Affairs prior to his ambassadorial post in Washington.

Among his other personal qualifications is the respect he commands from his diplomatic colleagues as a devout Moslem, a strong Arab nationalist, and a slow but excellent and thorough organizer. Among his personal traits, one of the most outstanding is his exaggerated concern for protocol in matters involving his prestige. After his post in Washington, he resigned from the foreign service on being named ambassador to Bonn; he considered the appointment a demotion. In his present capacity here, he lost time getting the Information Center started, waiting to receive an appointment as the Yemenite ambassador in order to have diplomatic immunity.

3 The New Director

As Egyptian ambassador, he enjoyed considerable freedom in shaping policy; and he also facilitated the entry of numerous Arabs into this country, and supported their activities here. These men came as business people or journalists. Rahim co-operated closely with the Arab League, which also dispatched agents to this country at the time. Typical was Yusif el Bandak, son of the mayor of Bethlehem, whose activities as an anti-Jewish troublemaker were disguised as a charity mission to aid the Arab refugees.

As ambassador, Rahim acquired numerous contacts, in and out of government circles. He also acquired a familiarity with the American scene outside of Washington, including the operations of our native anti-Semites. Smith, as you know, contacted him; and there were others.

JANUARY 20, 1955
Middle Eastern Correspondent to Research

The Arab Information Center has worked out a formula for co-ordinating its activities with that of Dr. Ezzat Tannous, director of the Arab Palestine Office. This is the office which has been distributing illustrated pamphlets in the United States about alleged atrocities against Arab civilians. These civilians are described as victims of an "Anglo-American-Jewish-United Nations conspiracy." Tannous, who is now in New York, will soon open an office in Washington.

The Cairo newspaper *Al Ahram* reported (January 13) that "Dr. Tannous has received financial aid from Saudi Arabia and Iraq for the explicit purpose of creating propaganda in the United States in behalf of the Arab refugees."

This explains Tannous' dissemination of the pamphlet, *The True Facts,* in the United States. Published in Beirut last October by the Arab Palestine Office, the booklet charges, among other falsehoods, that "The American nation as a whole are suffering today at the hands of the American Zionists who have misled American Public Opinion."

Questioned by the *Al Ahram* reporter as to whether his new office in Washington, D.C., would duplicate the work of the new Arab Information Center, Dr. Tannous replied that he would take on only a small staff but would use Arab Palestinian refugees as lecturers to plead the Arab cause in the United States and would use bright Arab exchange students to accomplish the mission on American university campuses.

Maybe the title, *The True Facts,* is intended to be ironic, but Tannous reported to his cohorts recently that he found his meetings with friends in the U. S. State Department most encouraging—and he said it with a straight face. They assured him, he says, that the present climate in the country is different from what it was in 1947 or 1948. Tannous claims they said that when the threat of communism is used as a justification for a policy it always clicks. When he told them that communism is "sweeping" the Arab refugees, Tannous says, they urged him to point this out as often as possible, since this threat—he quotes them as saying—would justify many United States policies and prepare public opinion for their favorable reception.

How exaggerated or distorted these claims of Tannous are is not known.

Four   The Front Door

JANUARY 24, 1955
Research to AF

Rahim has been exchanging views with the American Friends of the Middle East, to explore various areas of co-operation. Some AFME officials, however, have been critical of the new Arab office and view its propaganda enterprise with reservations, as a kind of challenge to their own function and existence.

In a memorandum last November 19 to Dr. Ezzat Tannous, AFME Executive Vice-President Garland Evans Hopkins deplored the fact that the Arab propaganda effort seemed destined to become "more a general information program than an effective lobby."

"It would, in my opinion," said Hopkins, "be more effectively used in the establishment of a political lobby. If, as now seems likely, the Arab League is going to try to operate a general information agency for the whole English-speaking world, with little regard to the advice of friends who know American public relations and who have nothing to gain personally, then the money had just as well remain in the vaults of Cairo's banks.

"I therefore propose," Hopkins added, "the formation of a new or-

III Cross-Currents in the Middle East

ganization which will attempt to educate and gain the sympathy of congressmen, high government officials, top leaders in churches, labor, industry, education and women's organizations. To try to influence these persons indirectly by a program aimed at the general public would be at once too costly and too long-time a job. At this late date, what the Arabs need is a direct approach to the Americans who make decisions."

And Hopkins suggested that fifteen "known true friends of the Arab cause be asked to come together to form a committee to be known as the Committee for a Just and Durable Peace in the Holy Land. . . ."

JANUARY 25, 1955
Library to AF

Garland Evans Hopkins is a man who privately argues that his major aim as head of the American Friends of the Middle East is to bring peace and understanding between the Arab nations and Israel. Perhaps so. But if that be his purpose, he wastes precious time trying to bring Dr. Ezzat Tannous around to the same constructive view. Tannous is the diplomat who asserts that "the outside world must keep in mind that the Arabs refuse to accept the principle that the Zionists have any territorial claim in Palestine."

What rapport is possible between the two opposing forces if the Arabs insist, as Tannous claims they do, that the price of peace with Israel is its self-liquidation?

Although it is pleasant to accept at face value Garland Hopkins' self-proclaimed role as peacemaker, perhaps a description of other comments he has made on the Middle Eastern situation, and the record of the organization he represents, is in order. A "peacemaker" would not contend, as Hopkins does, that the United Press and Associated Press are two wire services which refuse out of fear to tell the truth about the Middle East. Nor would he refer to the New York *Times* as "a Zionist newspaper." These are the words of a disputant, not an impartial conciliator. But they are Hopkins' words.

Blinking the obvious implications, Hopkins, too, is the Middle East expert who, speaking to several luncheon guests in February 1953, supported the Arab threat that "unless the United States goes along with Arab wishes, the Arabs will turn communist." It was at this same luncheon that Hopkins said in effect that Jews could *not* rely on the American people's sense of justice and fair play in the event of a war in the Middle East brought on by "Israel's intransigence." In such event, he said, perhaps unintentionally making it sound more like something other than fear, there would be a wave of unprecedented anti-Semitism in the United States, with probable excesses.

Last October 30, using the exhausted cliché that Arabs cannot be anti-Semitic because they themselves are Semites, Hopkins staunchly defended Saudi Arabia and its King, Abdul Aziz, against the charge of being anti-Jewish. "This widespread fallacy," said Hopkins, "came tumbling down to the ground during an audience granted a young American Jewish writer, Alfred Lilienthal," by the King of Saudi Arabia. Completely oblivious that he was proving exactly the opposite, Hopkins went on to corroborate his argument this way:

"Lilienthal is currently touring the Arab world for the second time in two years. He and Rabbi Morris Lazaron *are the only American Jews, perhaps the only Jews* who have been permitted to travel freely in those countries since the Arab-Israeli War in Palestine. He [Lilienthal] is the author of the widely read *What Price Israel?* . . ."

JANUARY 26, 1955
Research to AF

What Hopkins forgot to add is that Lilienthal, in the considered judgment of American Jews, is totally unrepresentative of Jewish thinking. This "young American Jewish writer's" passport to the Arab world is, indubitably, the book to which Hopkins referred, *What Price Israel?* But what kind of book is it? So completely biased in favor of the Arabs that immediately after its publication it became one of the most promoted books throughout the Arab Middle East. Translated and pub-

III Cross-Currents in the Middle East

lished in Arabic by a Lebanese firm, it carries on its Arabic cover a cartoon resembling some of the old Julius Streicher caricatures of the Jew. The cartoon shows a Jewish stereotype, with long, hooked nose and claw fingers, being served a piece of meat shaped like Palestine. A waiter, also clawed, in the process of handing it to him, has one of his cuffs decorated with the American flag; the other with Britain's Union Jack.

As for the second visitor (to the King of Saudi Arabia) named by Hopkins, Rabbi Morris Lazaron probably won his spurs in the Arab world by helping to lead the American Council for Judaism, a very tiny, militantly anti-Zionist organization composed of American Jews. Lazaron is also on the board of Hopkins' organization; and it is one of Hopkins' boasts that his success as a conciliator can be shown by his having "forced" Arabs to meet with Lazaron and the other Jews on his board. Rabbi Lazaron, who is by no means malicious, has been moving further and further away from his original extreme position.

JANUARY 26, 1955
Library to AF

Benjamin Freedman, as a volunteer "adviser" to the Arabs, had his own queer reaction to Lilienthal's tour of the Arab Middle East. Omar Haliq thought Freedman's opinion important enough to present it in writing to Abdul Khalek Hassouna as follows:

His Excellency, the Secretary General of the Arab League
Cairo

On the occasion of inviting Mr. A. Lilienthal by the Arab League to visit the Arab countries, I had a talk with Mr. B. Freedman who made the following remarks:
1) the greatest mistake entertained by the Arab world is the belief that Jews are divided into two groups, one for and one against Israel, and that the majority are one and all for the imposition of their devilish ideology over the world. There is no doubt that most Jews are parasitic and should be treated as such.

2) any cooperation per se between the Arab League and the Jews is liable to create various difficulties for the Arabs in many parts of the Arab world. Do not believe or trust Jews, whatever be their external mien.

3) there is ample proof that the world crises in the present circumstances are caused by Jews, and only by Jews. There will be no peace or stability among nations—Arab or non-Arab—as long as the Jewish race exists in the world.

4) the division of Jews into opposing factions is something to be despised but which is very well exploited by them for diminishing the efforts of their enemies against them.

I have thanked Mr. Freedman for his useful suggestions and promised him to relay this information to you.

Yours sincerely,
Omar Haliq

JANUARY 27, 1955
Library to AF

The organizers of the American Friends of the Middle East are all Americans: prominent writers, ex-government officials, educators, and clergymen. Members of its National Council fall into four categories: 15 writers and lecturers, 15 connected with churches, 9 former ambassadors or ministers, and 9 lawyers and business executives. Six are of Arab origin.

AFME carries on a wide variety of activities including: pamphleteering; issuing a newsletter, clipsheets, news releases; organizing group discussions; presenting TV shows; producing films; operating a lecture bureau and a travel bureau; providing travel funds to and from the Arab countries; awarding scholarships and prizes; and promoting numerous student activities, art shows, and social functions.

AFME, forming in June 1951, took full-page ads in the New York *Times* and the New York *Herald Tribune* to proclaim its objectives. They were, to be sure, of the very highest: to thwart communist aggression in the Middle East, and to strengthen the bonds of "culture and religion, of literature and education," between Americans and the

III Cross-Currents in the Middle East

Middle Eastern peoples. All information spread on the Middle East was to be objectively presented. The founder of the group was the noted journalist Dorothy Thompson—later its president—and the roster of charter members included Garland Evans Hopkins—later AFME's executive vice-president; Dr. Phillip Hitti, of Princeton; and Dr. Millar Burrows, author of *Palestine Is Our Business*. Thus, with a welter of vague and fairly expensive verbiage, this "committee to increase appreciation of common spiritual values" was launched.

The purported aim of the American Friends of the Middle East to tear away "the curtain of obscurity and distortion" about the Middle East seems somewhat belied by the insistent pro-Arab and anti-Israel positions and activities of the organization in question.

If, contrary to its spiritual and humanitarian claims, AFME were admittedly a pro-Arab propaganda organization, admittedly an apologist for Arab deeds and misdeeds, admittedly a supporter of Arab nationalist claims against Israel, and admittedly an opponent of the right of European governments to be in Moslem countries, it would be perfectly within its rights. There is nothing improper in special pleading or in appealing for American public sympathy and support. The opportunity to promote causes is a part of our democratic process. But by the same token the American people are entitled to know what the real aim is, what real interests are being represented, and who puts up the money.

Actually, AFME is a propaganda organization for the Arabs and Moslems, doing a job along modern public relations lines that for years the Arabs had demonstrated they were unable to do for themselves.

The membership, the financing, and the character of its contentions reflect AFME's narrow partisan nature. In its four years of existence the organization has actually enrolled only about 2000 members; their combined dues would hardly defray operational costs. Since the general membership contributes only a small part of the organization's funds and since it has little to say about policy, it is misleading to assert that the agency has a grass-roots base. The real strength of AFME is in its budget of nearly half a million a year, mostly from a few oil companies with interests in the Arab countries and from the Dearborn Foundation of Chicago, Illinois.

Whether AFME is an unbiased educational and cultural organization or a propaganda outfit can best be determined by its output. Does AFME present both sides of an issue fairly? Is only one side presented, favorably, with a view to winning public support?

A content analysis of the materials of AFME made recently by a University of Chicago graduate student is revealing. Analyzing about 1000 pages of AFME verbiage, released in a seven-month period in 1953, he found that roughly two thirds was clearly pro-Arab propaganda and one fourth was anti-Israel. The plight of the Arab refugees received most attention. The anti-Israel items were concerned with alleged Israeli indifference toward the Arab refugees, aggressive territorial ambitions, atrocities, and the like. A rare favorable comment about Israel was usually the preface to a much larger criticism.

In a letter to the New York *Times,* printed July 29, 1951, Miss Thompson demurred that her group was "not directed against Israel. . . ." It was merely "determined to try to see to it that the problems and achievements of the other Middle Eastern States are not totally ignored."

In the light of AFME's original statements stressing the vast importance of the Middle East to Americans, the newly defined aim of publicizing the "ignored" countries obviously meant that Miss Thompson's original press release, on June 23, insisting that "we are *not* a propaganda organization, and we are *not* out to grind axes for anyone," was not as accurate as it might have been.

While claiming impartiality on some occasions, at other times Miss Thompson justifies AFME's exclusive concern for the Arabs by explaining: "I consider it one of the principal tasks of AFME at this time to help in breaking down the tendency on the part of the American press and radio either to disregard everything friendly to the Arabs or to print only distorted and even untrue statements about them."

On August 20, Miss Thompson sent a letter to AFME members charging the American press and radio with an anti-Arab bias, and enclosing a copy of a letter written by Vincent Sheean, the American novelist and autobiographer. Mr. Sheean was a charter member of AFME, and his views—the views of a noted man—were presumably to be taken by the membership as representative of what the founder herself endorsed. But if Miss Thompson was out to inform the broad public about the Middle East, she was also reticent about informing the same broad public what a distinguished member of her group had to say on the Middle East.

". . . I believe you will agree with me," she wrote coyly, "that it would be unwise for us to give it to the press."

"It" was a letter addressed to the then minority leader of the House of Representatives, Joseph W. Martin, in opposition to a pending bill to grant economic aid to Israel; and Mr. Sheean also reproved Mr. Martin for his praise of Israel's army as a possible addition to democracy's arsenal. For one thing, Israel, he asserted, has "one of the most active communist organizations in the Middle East." The important thing, though, was that "rightly or wrongly, the Arab States are . . . convinced that the Israeli army is designed as the instrument of an expansionist policy with boundless ambitions. . . ."

To do the gentleman justice, he himself did not advance the "expansionist" argument; he simply presented it as an Arab viewpoint, "rightly or wrongly" held. But even if this were not his personal opinion, Miss Thompson was, from her point of view, quite correct in being coy about its release to the press: to advance an argument as valid *whether or not it is true* is the very essence of propaganda. And we have just seen how sensitive Miss Thompson is to *that* word.

The "cultural" value of AFME was soon appreciated in the proper quarters. Omar Haliq, on September 30, 1951, acknowledged in a memo to Cairo that the organization and its founder had been giving the Arab League invaluable aid. And by the end of 1951, AFME was showing signs of great economic vigor; it moved into new and luxurious penthouse quarters. Then, in April 1952, American Friends Thompson and Hopkins set out for the Middle East.

They hit the sheep's-eye there: a founder of the Arab League, Abdul Rahman Azzam Pasha himself, confirmed his approval of AFME's objectives; and the Syrian government awarded Friend

4 The Front Door

Thompson its Medal of Honor for defending the Arab cause in the U.S.

Then came AFME's first annual conference at the Hotel Delmonico in New York City. This was timed to coincide with the beginning of the Eisenhower term in January 1953; AFME's lecture bureau began to function at about the same time too, sending out both American speakers and visiting Arabs. We may take as fairly typical of what the culture-hungry audiences were fed by the visitors the assertion made by a Jordanian lawyer, Anwar Nashashibi, on his tour. Communism in the Middle East, he maintained blandly, "is directed by Red underground movements in the Arab States and the legal Communist Party in Israel."

At the conference itself, with any Israeli representation conveniently shuffled out in advance, the representatives of thirty organizations and about two hundred members of the general public heard a panel of speakers that included the late Dr. Stephen Penrose, president of the American University of Beirut, and ambassadors and UN delegates from Arab countries. The theme of the two-day meeting was "Partnership in Meeting Needs of the Middle East." Evidently the young Jewish state was considered, at best, a silent partner.

The speakers, to be sure, demonstrated an impressive unanimity of opinion. On one question, however, Dr. Malik, Lebanon's UN delegate, seemed strangely at variance with the Syrian speaker, Farid Zeineddine. The Lebanese diplomat exhorted "Americans who trace their origin to Lebanon and Syria . . ." and who "take an active interest in our destiny and development" to "deepen and develop their activity" in their many organizations. But the Syrian attacked Zionists as members of "a movement which develops loyalty to Israel, destroying loyalty to the individual's own country." Perhaps what seems like a disagreement here can be explained by the premise that, to the Arab world, "dual loyalty" works on a double standard.

One wonders what Dorothy Thompson, who in December 1951 told the Jewish Graduate Society at Columbia University that being a Zionist impaired a Jew's relations with his fellow Americans, felt about Dr. Malik's speech. It must be that she had never considered a similar im-

III Cross-Currents in the Middle East

pairment possible when Americans of Syrian or Lebanese descent are active on the behalf of countries other than the U.S. Nor, it is to be hoped, has she ever considered the possible harm she might effect in the American community by the obvious implication—that Jews are a special case—of this double standard. Yet Miss Thompson must be politically experienced enough, one imagines, to realize that her logic smacks of "ghetto-ism."

In any case Miss Thompson appeared to be well satisfied with the results of AFME's First Annual Conference when she summarized its obvious orientation in one of her regular news columns. In her words: "The consensus expressed was . . . that the favoritism showed by America to Israel is disastrous to American influence and even to the improvement of Israel-Arab relations."

But all of AFME was not as content as it might have been. For one thing, Executive Vice-President Hopkins did not feel that the press had been just with the conference. And it was in the course of his complaints that he made the remarks quoted in an earlier memo. It also emerged that two of his board members had resigned because they felt AFME was not pro-Arab enough. Hopkins explained that he was in the position of a middle-of-the-road conciliator in the organization.

If Hopkins is indeed at the center of AFME's opinion range, it can hardly be imagined what the extremists are like. His opinions on American press and radio, his references to possible pogroms in America, his warnings that Zionist attacks on his organization would not be taken lying down (can he believe such attacks are unprovoked?), and his statements to the effect that American Jews should know that Truman has been replaced by an "American Administration" that the Zionists cannot lead "by the nose," do not bespeak a man of moderate viewpoint.

Nevertheless, the extremists, such as they were, seem to have generated damaging rumors. At about this time the Armenian correspondent, Levon Keshishian, sent a dispatch to the Middle East indicating that some of the Arab embassies here were dubious about supporting AFME because it seemed the group was out to effect an Arab-Israel accord.

4 The Front Door

So Hopkins, the professed proponent of Arab-Israel accord (yet also the man who had warned that in an all-out AFME "war" with the Zionists, the Zionists would be dealing not with a crackpot bunch but with a well-prepared and organized group), rushed off to the embassies to quash the rumors. One can speculate safely on which of the two Hopkinses described above he relied upon in getting AFME back in favor.

The substantial financial contributions reportedly coming in from American oil companies and wealthy individuals sympathetic to its aims kept AFME riding high; the AFME Tourist Program glowed proudly over the "excellent liaison" it had established with Middle Eastern consulates; AFME's Phoenix Lecture Bureau sent its cultural envoys out over the country; college students, with lectures, conferences, and essay contests featuring Middle Eastern tours as prizes, were kept interested in the Arab line; the Phoenix Newspaper Service provided, at a modest fee, "news" and "objective" articles on the Middle East ("objective" in AFME talk appears to mean "pro-Arab"); AFME expanded, opening several regional offices here; and a new Middle Eastern Branch was opened, with representatives in several Arab cities.

There is a striking similarity in selection of propaganda material by the Arabs and by AFME. While AFME does not go in for violent name-calling as the Arabs do, there is always a polite deprecation of everything connected with Israel. The graduate-thesis writer concluded, significantly, that AFME should really be called American Friends of the *Arab* Middle East.

AFME never touches upon subjects which the Arab governments and the Arab League shy away from: notably, recognition of Israel, restoration of normal business relations, mutual development of waterways, and the like. In the numerous AFME publications there is also a notable absence of sympathy for the impoverished farm tenants and others working under intolerable conditions in the Arab countries. Mention of arbitrary domination by Arab petty kings and dictators is, of course, taboo in AFME literature.

AFME, aside from its periods of comparative caution, has always

III Cross-Currents in the Middle East

been careful to make ninety per cent of its noise on perfectly respectable subjects. Who, for example, could quarrel with any project designed to educate and inoculate the mass of Arabs and to ameliorate their living conditions? But that is not our concern here. We are primarily concerned with that ten per cent of AFME's activity which is objectionable because it is divisive.

In December 1954, Dorothy Thompson, speaking at a Washington, D.C., AFME meeting, said that Israel's evolution "was not compatible with what was humane or even democratic." She also remarked that though she herself had once been Zionist because she "was touched by the tragedies which befell European Jewry under the Nazis," a visit to Israel years later had convinced her that she had been "misled on basic assumptions."

The extent of Miss Thompson's "conversion" from Zionism can also be measured by her observation that she found Mohammedanism in some respects a superior faith to Judaism and Christianity.

The president of AFME has apparently made a pretty good adjustment to submersion in the Arab world. And AFME, with its respectable humanitarian front and the respectable names on its board—including the Rev. Dr. Edward L. R. Elson, pastor of President Eisenhower's Washington church—is succeeding in a propaganda field where more blatant organizations like the old Arab Office and the Institute of Arab-American Affairs failed.

JANUARY 28, 1955
Research to AF

Rahim, the new Arab Center appointee, conferred at length with Merwin K. Hart on the feasibility of creating an American foundation which could collect contributions, deductible from taxes, to aid Arab refugees, and at the same time serve the Arab propaganda effort. Apparently Hart considered the idea good, for he volunteered that he had influential and powerful friends in Washington who could help establish such a foundation. Of course these people would require money for

4 The Front Door

legal expenses; but Hart promised, for his part, to submit a report on the problems involved in establishing a foundation.

Rahim's talk with Hart was not confined to the subject of a foundation; they also discussed how the Arab League Center's activities in this country could be operated more efficiently.

Hart made many suggestions, including the following:

1. That the League's Center prepare a regular newsletter, distributing thousands of copies all over the country (Hart said he might consider making his own mailing list available).

2. That the Center retain a top-flight lobbyist to work with Congress, a very important field of action (Hart said, Rahim willing, he could suggest some names).

3. That the Center concentrate on educational and church groups throughout the country, the heart of the nation (once you hit these groups, said Hart, you can swing a lot of influence).

Rahim was particularly impressed with Hart. But Hart's ideas were suggestions Rahim had already turned over and over in his own mind.

JANUARY 28, 1955
Library to Research

After his return from the Middle East in December of 1953, Hart prepared a "confidential memorandum" of his trip. It makes fascinating rereading in light of his recent conversations with Kamil Abdul Rahim. Excerpts:

In November and December 1953 I visited Lebanon, Iraq, Syria, Jordan and Egypt in the Middle East, returning by way of Athens, Rome, Madrid and Lisbon. . . . Through the Spanish Foreign Office which had notified its missions in the Near East . . . I was able to make a good deal of the time at my disposal.

Although there are many Communists in the Middle East I heard less talk about the threat of Communism than in European countries like France or Italy, or even in America. . . . A highly informed Iraqi told me . . . only 5% of the Arabs there can read and write. . . . He said there is a branch of the Tudeh party in Iraq and that Communist

III Cross-Currents in the Middle East

strength is growing, not only among the rank and file but among intellectuals. Many of these latter returning from the completion of their education in Europe or the U.S. cannot get good jobs; and so they sit around the coffee shops and bewail their condition and become susceptible to communist influence.

The American government is disliked by many of the people of these countries, who seem prepared, however, to like Americans. . . .

Most people in the rural parts of Iraq live in mud huts—structures that a Westerner would hardly recognize as human habitations. . . .

Britain is especially disliked in Jordan. Nearly everyone I talked with mentioned this—Americans as well as natives. . . . Some Arabs reserve their first dislike for Britain; others for the United States. This dislike seems if anything more intense than their feeling toward the Zionists themselves. They hold both Britain and the United States responsible for partition. Several Arabs asserted that an Arab never forgets. He will get his land back—if not in this generation, then in the next. He can wait. My visit to the Middle East has more than ever convinced me of the possibilities for mischief of the United Nations. For the UN was the tool with which partition was achieved.

The Arabs in all these countries have successfully boycotted a number of American companies which had opened branches in Israel. Some of these boycotted companies have subsequently closed their Israel branches whereupon the Arabs have removed the boycott. Among these latter companies I heard mentioned was Fairbanks, Morse & Co. . . .

Many times I asked Arabs what they thought to be the solution of the problem. The answer most often was that America should merely withdraw support (both public and private) from the State of Israel; then everything would work out naturally. . . .

It would seem that a crisis is fast developing in Israel. As a nation she might collapse at any time. This would offer the American government an opportunity partially to rectify the tragic mistake of 1948 and thus regain the good will of the Arabs. . . .

The position of women in the Middle East is striking to any Westerner. A woman is treated as an inferior creature. . . .

In concluding this memorandum on my trip to the Middle East, including the brief stops in Italy and Spain, I wish to re-emphasize the debt owed by the Western world to the Arabs.

Five   The Back Door

JANUARY 29, 1955
Research to AF

Our library has just dropped on this desk the current issue of *The Cross and the Flag* containing a malicious piece entitled: "The New Crucifixion in Palestine." Smith prefaces his very detailed story with an admission that it is actually based on a memorandum which came to him "from Jerusalem." Our files, however, indicate that Smith's admission is somewhat of an understatement. This is what we mean:

Some months ago, Smith met with Ezzat Tannous in Washington about the possibility of publishing Tannous' propaganda material in his magazine for a fee. The cost would be on a "per line" basis as though it were advertising matter. Tannous agreed; but since the cost was high, $10 a line, he has been careful about the quantity forwarded to Smith. By Tannous' own admission, there is only one story in the current issue of *The Cross and the Flag* submitted by him.

In all of Smith's distortions about alleged desecration of Christian holy places he finds no room to report the appreciation expressed by

III Cross-Currents in the Middle East

leaders of the Christian communities to the government of Israel for having safeguarded their property and for making prompt repairs to damage which occurred during the course of fighting. Such statements are available by the Latin Patriarch in Jerusalem, the Greek Orthodox Patriarchate and the Greek consul general in Jerusalem, the Greek Catholic archbishops of Galilee, the special delegate of the Lutheran World Federation, and many others.

And, of course, Smith has maintained a very careful silence about the failure of the Arabs to show the same consideration for Jewish religious property in the Old City of Jerusalem. Twenty-seven synagogues were razed to the ground. The historic cemetery on the Mount of Olives where Jews had been laid to rest for generations was sacrilegiously plowed up and the headstones reduced to dust.

JANUARY 29, 1955
Research to AF

When we first learned of the Gerald Smith-Ezzat Tannous arrangement, we asked our Library to run through recent issues of *The Cross and the Flag* and mark off the pro-Arab material. Of course we do not know whether the following two items are the result of the Smith-Tannous arrangement, but their substance fascinates us:

In the August 1954 issue we find the following:

We [Gerald Smith] were received by the Ambassador from Egypt and his staff. They are the ones who represent the new government of Egypt in the United Nations. There are Jews in Egypt, but the Jews are not running Egypt. It is the intention of the internationalist clique, directed by Jewish and British politicians, to starve Egypt out by denying her the proper world trade facilities. The trick is to force her to trade with Russia, if possible, so that propaganda can be put out in the U.S. that Egypt is pro-Russian. Then the American people will be taught by the Jews to hate Egypt thus exploiting the American antipathy for Communism. . . . Egypt refuses to recognize the Jew-Palestine Government on the grounds that it is an invasion. The Ambassador, whose name is Abdel Hameid Ghaleb, is a Moslem. . . .

5 The Back Door

In his June 1953 issue, Smith's "Letter No. 6," addressed "Dearest Mother," reads in part as follows:

One of the most outspoken delegations concerning the world situation is the delegation representing Lebanon, which is one of the Arab states. We interviewed this delegation and confirmed many important and sensational facts which we already knew. Jew-Zionists captured Palestine with the help of England and the United States, driving a million Arabs out of their homes and their places of business to suffer and die in the desert. Many of these people were refined and cultured people living in lovely homes. The Jews not only came in and stole their homes and their farms, but they froze the bank accounts, looted their safety deposit boxes, stole their cattle, swine and orange groves, using the prestige and power of the United States and Western governments to support their lootings. . . .

If Smith's allegations seem vaguely familiar to you, there is good reason for it. You have read these statements many times before in Arab propaganda, the difference being that for the most part Arab literature uses less blunt language than Smith. But I suppose Smith feels impelled to rewrite all his source material; he has earned the right to consider his style inimitable, after all the years he has spent on it.

FEBRUARY 3, 1955
Research to AF

Gerald Smith is only one of many professionals who have hitched their money wagons to the Arab star: his former vice-presidential candidate, Jack Tenney, just one year ago this month, got in on the joy ride. The Arab League agreed to underwrite the distribution of Tenney's booklet, *Zionist Network,* to members of the American Congress, government officials in Washington, UN delegations, and libraries throughout the U.S. As part of the deal, the Arab League insisted that no mention of its sponsorship be publicized.

Tenney was a man of his word. Announcements from Tenney about

III Cross-Currents in the Middle East

Zionist Network, which he first published in July 1953, were received by American congressmen and other government officials soon after he made his arrangements with the Arab League. Not only did Tenney avoid involving the Arab League, he actually wrote his letter on the official stationery of the California legislature; described his booklet as "political dynamite."

The booklet itself—with an introduction by Franklin Hichborn, inveterate writer of anti-Semitic letters to editors—is Tenney's personal report on Jewish organizations in the United States. He describes their activities as un-American and as part of a world-wide network whose "hope for dominance is geared to the rapid decline and destruction of Western Christian civilization."

Ten thousand copies were purchased with Arab League funds, these for distribution throughout the Middle East as well as the United States. Arab governments, too, took for their domestic use a sizable share of the purchase. One energetic salesman of Tenney's *Zionist Network* was an Arab ambassador to Washington, who urged other Arab diplomats to get their governments behind a mass distribution of the book both in the United States and abroad. The Ambassador's circular letter to Arab diplomats and ministers was in far bolder language than diplomats ordinarily employ:

Here is a golden opportunity for us to grab in order to show not only to the U.S. public opinion but to the world opinion at large, the mischievous policies and trends of world Jewry in its attempt to run the world. . . . Let us all join efforts and buy "hundreds of thousands . . . of these books" and have them as widely distributed as possible throughout the U.S. and the world. . . . None of us can speak so frankly about a subject so controversial for the U.S. people. It would have been preferable to buy the rights of reprints for the book, and maybe our Arab League can undertake this function, so as to prevent embarrassment to this patriotic American who dares to face the American Zionists and to tell them in his now-famous letter "If, I, as a Republican State Senator representing more people in the California Senate than half of the U.S. senators represent in the nation, dared write this book, I am sure that you will dare to read it. . . ."

5 The Back Door

JANUARY 31, 1955
Library to Research

An examination of recent issues of Smith's *The Cross and the Flag* against propaganda emanating from the Arab Middle East shows that he has echoed a very large part of it, viz., editorials attacking the "Israeli Invasion of Palestine" combined with pleas for Arab refugees and charges of church desecration by Jews; articles accusing Israel of peddling opium; stories accusing the Jews of using the United Nations to create war upon the Arabs; items claiming that the Jews want peace with the Kremlin but war with the Arabs; editorials in behalf of the Arabs and endorsing such booklets as *The Palestine Refugees,* etc., etc.

Most of these items in Smith's magazine appeared previously in substantially the same form in Arab literature, radio broadcasts, or official releases. Those that Smith thought of first appeared later in Arab propaganda.

FEBRUARY 14, 1955
Washington, D.C., Office to Research

The Egyptian Embassy today released a publication entitled *The Story of Zionist Espionage in Egypt,* a booklet designed to prove that no valid basis existed for the request of the American government that Egypt stay the recent execution of two Jews in Cairo.

Not since the Nazi propaganda apparatus was ousted from the United States at the onset of World War II have we seen such an anti-Semitic brochure distributed here by any foreign government. Attempting to document the assertion that Zionism is building communism in Egypt, the pamphlet also seeks to win the sympathy of non-Jews in the United States by spelling out once again alleged desecrations committed several years ago upon Christian holy places.

Says the pamphlet: "Zionism and Communism are two distinctive

III Cross-Currents in the Middle East

forces with one political objective—world domination. Both powers cooperate secretly and in public without friction since the power in the end will eventually go to Zionism."

If none of your friends received copies of this pamphlet in the mail, you can have all you wish, free, by simply visiting the Egyptian Embassy in Washington, D.C. Tall stacks of them rest on a table in the reception room under a "Take One" sign.

FEBRUARY 18, 1955
Research to AF

The answer as to why there is such a deadly parallel between the propaganda of official Arab representatives in the United States and local American anti-Semites lies in the close behind-the-scenes cooperation between the two groups. The fact of such co-operation is absolutely documented by such letters as the one Dr. Tannous wrote from New York to a colleague three days ago. Indicating with apparent regret that he will have to register in the United States as a foreign agent, Tannous goes on to describe "the pro-Arab Americans" with whom he will have to deal on the domestic scene:

These Americans can be divided into two categories. The first consist of decent and honest Americans who do not know enough about the Jewish plot in Palestine and who could be well influenced. They are not aggressive but honest. They will not help us in any "big way," but their influence on the US public opinion is steady and important. They include Church people, some relief organizations, and others. The second category consists of what the Jews call anti-Semites. I have seen some of them and although I cannot say the same thing of all of them, there are some who can do a lot of things to our cause. I have met people like Benjamin Freedman, a converted Jew, Gerald Smith, a strong anti-Zionist, with a tremendous following, (who helped us in his publications by some articles we have sent him), Allan Zoll, a wealthy influential man whose connections with the Congress are well known, etc. Our contacts with them have been careful to avoid accusations by strong Jewish organizations, like the Anti-Defamation League (which is called here the Gestapo of the Jews). But we remain

5 The Back Door

always on our defensive to prevent wrong interpretations of our actions.

Complaining about the unstable budget allotted to his office, Tannous expressed the hope that eventually this problem would be resolved by substantial regular financing in order to enable Tannous to accomplish "two important aims." Tannous spelled them out this way:

1. The defeat of the well-organized Jewish propaganda and all its evils and dangers.
2. The understanding of the real basic elements of the Palestine Question by the American people.

It will amuse you to know what else Tannous regards as a difficulty in addition to his fiscal shortage. Let us give you his exact words:

Regarding the office, I am still trying to organize its basis but I am faced with many difficulties which are increased by the lack of methods of the new director of the Arab Information Center, Kamil Abdul Rahim who was the Egyptian Ambassador to Washington. While he is a good man, he lacks complete experience in the job he is supervising and is extremely confused. I wonder whether he will ever be able to meet his duties with the necessary strength and ability. Thus, my failure to establish a good relationship with him.

MARCH 17, 1955
AF to BRE

Even if we discard all proof to the contrary and assume that Rahim is passionately sincere when he denies Arab intention to use anti-Semites or anti-Semitism in connection with the Arab Center, I wonder how he could pursue this laudable course and still fulfill what seems to be required of him.

You will recall a report about two and a half years ago concerning conversations Hassouna, Rahim's superior, held with Zoll and Freedman. Now we have a memorandum, marked secret, sent by Haliq to Hassouna that further implicates those old American friends of ours. What it has to say on Rahim's mission is particularly interesting. As for Hopkins, the "conciliator" . . .

Here is the translation:

SECRET

MEMORANDUM

Mr. Abdul Khalek Hassouna
Secretary General of the Arab League
Cairo

With reference to your letter dated April 11, we have the honor to call your attention:

1. I met this week with Mr. Benjamin Freedman and discussed with him the question of the establishment of an Arab propaganda office in the U.S. and he showed his complete disposition to extend his full co-operation with us no matter how many difficulties the Jewish organizations in the U.S. might create for him, particularly if this co-operation is public and official. When I called his attention to the importance of secrecy for known reasons, he answered me literally: "My dear sir, the Jews are criminals, do you expect any justice from them? I am perfectly ready to co-operate under any condition the responsible authorities in the Arab League see fit."

Mr. Freedman did not show any desire to get a salary but said that he was ready to extend to us all co-operation without any salary, but he expects that the Arab League pay him all the extra expenses which his patriotic task toward the Arabs might involve. I did not find any objection to accept his view, but I even told him that this question could always be examined and no doubt settled when Mr. Kamil Abdul Rahim arrives in the USA.

2. I have the pleasure to enclose herewith 5 copies of a magazine which has a great influence on the American people and its name is *American Nationalist*. You will find in it an article written about the Arabs and the tragedy in wounded Palestine. You will be glad to learn that this letter was written after a close co-operation between Mr. Britton and your servant. A sum of $500 is required now to be able to continue the publication of articles of that type in these and other friendly magazines.

3. Mr. Zoll talked to me and said that he was very glad to have received the letter you sent him and he will do the necessary things in the near future.

4. Jewish propaganda remains at its height here, and we still are in great need of a strong office to clarify the minds and we are waiting with great impatience for the arrival of Mr. Kamil Abdul Rahim and

it is important to know before he arrives that the task is extremely difficult and that the Jews still control all information and propaganda services. As Mr. Hopkins told me recently, "The situation is very serious but the American people have started to understand the reality of the Jewish conspiracy and it is necessary to co-operate closely in order to find the opportunity to defeat it."

Accept the sincere respects,

Omar Haliq
Arab League Representative

New York, April 26, 1954

MARCH 20, 1955
New York Correspondent to Research

James Madole of the National Renaissance Party has been consulting with the Arabs about his propaganda work. During a visit to the new Arab League Center, Madole described his organization, its general activities, and his special point of view about Jews; he even exhibited his scrapbook to Center officials.

Despite an undeniably anti-Jewish record, documented for them by his scrapbook, or maybe because of it, Madole was treated kindly by his hosts, who informed him, however, that their new office was interested in "cultural affairs" rather than "political activities." But he went away happy, carrying with him an armful of complimentary copies of *The Story of Zionist Espionage in Egypt*.

Madole also called at the Egyptian Consulate. There he asked about the possibility of guest speakers for his meetings, and he was promised effective co-operation. Given at no cost a large quantity of "literature," including *Zionist Espionage, Questions to a Moslem, The Christian Legacy in Egypt,* and Nasser's *The Egyptian Revolution,* Madole was graciously told he was welcome back for additional copies if he wished them.

The Renaissance Party now has a new source of income. Madole has stamped the covers of all the Arab pamphlets with his party label and is selling them for twenty-five cents apiece.

III Cross-Currents in the Middle East

MARCH 27, 1955
Research to AF

Despite Dr. Tannous' impatience with Rahim, and in spite of the separate office he carefully maintains, any friend of the Arab League is nevertheless a friend of Tannous. You of course remember Zoll's various contacts with Arab leaders and his little good-will tour in the Middle East. Judging from a recent communication by Tannous to Zoll, the American propagandist is still well thought of. Writing from New York on February 15 to "My very dear Mr. Zoll," Tannous, in a letter which he signs as general secretary of the Arab Palestine Office, opens with a show of great gratitude:

> Let me first thank you very much for the feelings you have always shown to our cause. I know that every Arab patriot feels a great debt of gratitude for your generosity and kindness. I have read already in Beirut, Lebanon, many articles about your contributions to the Arab cause, and particularly your struggle against Zionism.

Tannous then goes on to explain his own arrival in this country, his hopes and plans in his new assignment:

> I have come to this country with the hope to organize an efficient office which would be able to conteract the vicious Jewish propaganda in the U.S. and to enlighten the American people about what has happened in our poor old land of Palestine. I have come here, convinced that as long as we could depend on esteemed friends as you, we may hope for the day when our Cause will be, at last, heard and understood.
> I was told of your many contributions to our Cause. What we need is not money, but good will and understanding. What we need is not financial assistance, for the time being, but cooperation with all those who have at heart the preservation of the Christian spirit in the Holy Land. What we need, last but not least, is the feeling that we can depend on people without whose assistance our work will never reach its aims. This is why I hope that we can depend on you.
> We are perfectly aware of the many vicious campaigns which the Jewish organizations will, undoubtedly, unleash against us, accusing us of all sins and plots, of all sinister aims and intrigues. But our books are widely opened and our hearts are equally as white as cream.

5 The Back Door

I do hope that I will have the opportunity to meet you at an early date. Please accept my highest esteem.

MAY 16, 1955
Middle Eastern Correspondent to Research

The Cairo radio is beginning to report to Egyptians the work of the Arab Information Center in the United States. The following, verbatim, was on today's radio:
"The information office which was opened several days ago by the Arab countries in New York is the first step. . . . There is no doubt that Zionist propaganda and influence in the United States is strong. The new Arab bureau in New York should expose all Zionist plots and propaganda to the American people. We must not squander any more time in agreeing on a policy for that bureau."

JUNE 4, 1955
New York Correspondent to Research

James Madole held a "cultural" meeting of his organization last night and his guest speaker was Abdul Mawgoud Hassan, press attaché of the Egyptian delegation to the United Nations. The Arab official, present with three other Middle East representatives, arrived in time to hear Madole vilify and ridicule Jews in an opening statement to the small audience. Flanked by an American flag and the National Renaissance Party insignia, Madole also bitterly flayed President Eisenhower as a traitor for "selling out" to the Russians when he was Supreme Allied Commander during World War II.

Warning that communism would emerge victorious in the Arab world if the United States continues its dangerous support of Israel, and attacking the "Jewish International Bolshevik forces which run America," the Renaissance Party leader then proudly introduced Mr. Hassan. The Egyptian official talked quietly for fifteen minutes about "Jewish atrocities," about the "unfulfilled promises" of the Allied Powers to the Middle East, and about general Palestinian problems.

III Cross-Currents in the Middle East

Hassan, apparently concerned about his diplomatic status, kept his remarks well within the bounds of propriety, if not accuracy, for a partisan speaker; but Madole's follow-up speech made up for it. All reports about the fate of the six million Jews in Europe are false, Madole said, because the whole obnoxious lot of them can be seen any day in the garment center in New York City. Describing those who oppose public school racial segregation as "refugees from the Warsaw ghetto," he wryly added that they have noses so long you could hang your laundry on them. But he is no bigot, said Madole for himself, because it certainly would not matter to him even if the Jews had noses twenty feet long.

Hassan left for another speaking engagement before Madole's second speech. A Syrian attaché, attending the meeting and pleased by the experience, promised that he would return in the future to address the organization.

All the Arab literature that had been accumulated by Madole was on sale at the back of the room, stamped with the words: "Distributed by the National Renaissance Party, Box 137, Planetarium Station, New York."

JUNE 6, 1955
Library to AF

The only thing surprising about the memo on the Madole meeting is Hassan's comparative restraint. On May 13, Hassan was the Arab speaker in a round-table discussion at a Quaker institution, Earlham College in Richmond, Indiana; he was not so moderate there.

On the subject of Palestine, Hassan contended that the Jews stole the land from the Arabs and that the Jews massacred the Arabs, driving them from their homes and out of Palestine by force or intimidation. They left, he said, about a million Arabs to die in refugee camps. When you are robbed, he argued, the only solution is to snatch back your property. He concluded that many Arabs believe the Israeli should be driven into the sea.

Six   The Touchstone

June 8, 1955 . . . Cairo Radio: Voice of the Arabs, in Arabic to the Arab World: "This Israeli State is a religious state, protected by Zionists and Jews all over the world. It is protected by big Christian powers which are controlled by the Jews through their capital, trades and industries."

JUNE 10, 1955

Middle Eastern Correspondent to Research

Sunday's editorial in the Jordanian newspaper, *El Jihad,* is blunt:

There is no Arab in his right mind who believes that there can be peace, stability and security in the Middle East, until Israel is wiped off the face of the map of the region, and Palestine is returned without reservation to its former status. No one in the Arab World disputes the fact that the Arab nations are in a state of war with Israel and with *World Jewry*. This state of war will be maintained until justice is restored in spite of the artificial agreements of the armistice which have been imposed upon us.

As you see, speaking in the Middle East in its native tongue, Arab officialdom is not reluctant to state bluntly that the cold war which

III Cross-Currents in the Middle East

they are carrying on is directed not only against the Israeli state but also against world Jewry. Outside the Middle East, of course, the Arabs pretend that their war is only against Israel and Zionism.

You may question whether the above editorial expresses Arab consensus in the Middle East. Anticipating your question, I offer the following typical utterances, culled easily from the abundant record of recent months:

Last November, Jordanian Premier Tawfiq Abu al-Huda, at the opening of Parliament, declared to his nation that Jordanian policy on the question of Palestine had been kept consistent with the principles established by the Arab League. And then he added: "It has thus frustrated the repeated attempts by the Jewish side in the international field to lure us into separate direct or indirect negotiations ... our policy in the Palestine question, in accordance with the basis adopted by the Arab states—is that there will be no peace or negotiations with the Jews."

The passing days of this year have seen a constant intensification of the demand for war with Israel. Because they think that radio broadcasts make less of a permanent record than newspaper editorials, their radio statements are blunter. In January of this year the Madrid radio quoted Raif Abu al-Lama, assistant secretary of the Arab League, on the subject of Arab-Israeli relations. He said: "If the matter were left entirely between the Arabs and Israel, nothing more would need be said. No Arab government would dare sign a peace treaty with Israel. If it did, it would not last twenty-four hours."

In May the Damascus radio, addressing itself to Syria and the Near East, declared: "The Arabs did not lose the war in Palestine but only the first battle. The Arabs should be ready for the second battle and should recall past mistakes to avoid repeating the tragedy. . . . Let us persuade imperialism that the Arab countries will determine the end of the battle. Let us persuade those who support Israel that the Arab people have awakened to revenge themselves. When we believe in this it will be inevitable that the battle will begin."

A very important part of the Arab cold war against Israel is the economic boycott—by means of which it is hoped that the new state will be effectively bankrupted. As you know, each of the Arab states has established the most severe penalties, including death, for entering any business transactions with citizens of Israel. In January, this year, the Cyprus radio in a broadcast beamed to the Arab world reported: ". . . the Arab League Secretariat is now discussing with the member states the establishment of Offices for the Boycott of Israel in London, Washington, and Paris. These will contact the European and American companies to show them the extent of losses to which they will be exposed should they deal with Israel—the loss of the Arab markets. It has been decided to establish a branch Office for the Boycott of Israel in Kuwait."

Syria, too, is typical. On February 22 the Damascus radio reported that Premier Sabri al-Asali, in a statement to the Syrian Chamber of Deputies, declared: "My government rejects any peace with the Zionist authorities. It likewise refuses to enter into any relations with them whatsoever. It will always energetically endeavor to tighten the economic blockade on the Zionists. . . ."

There is no difference of opinion among the Arab states on the wisdom of the boycott. On April 19, over the Cairo radio, the Voice of the Arabs gloated that: "The Lebanese Al-Jarida said . . . the Boycott of Israel was the only question on which there was unanimity on the part of the Arab states. . . . The economic boycott of Israel is no less important than the rearming of the Arabs . . . its . . . implementation is of our concern alone."

We have made it the practice constantly to compare what Arab official representatives say to the world from their United Nations platforms in New York as against official Arab statements in the Middle East; the two are completely contradictory. At the United Nations they talk of international good will and peace, but at home they poison the atmosphere, accusing the Western Powers of bad faith and of fomenting strife. On February 3 the Voice of the Arabs, talking of course in Arabic only to the Arab world, said: "They tend to forget that Gamal Abdel Nasser shouted at the top of his voice . . . that no alliances are to be concluded with the West, with non-Arabs. . . . Salah Salim toured the Arab world . . . to acquaint the Arab governments with

III Cross-Currents in the Middle East

the policy of Egypt which maintains that no alliances are to be entered into with the West, with the imperialists, or with non-Arabs. . . . Egypt refused, and is still refusing, a true gold mine of ammunition and arms from the West because its Arab policy does not allow alliances with the West, with the imperialists, but only alliances with our Arab brethren."

And on April 28 over the Cairo radio the Voice of the Arabs had this to say: ". . . The three Western Powers are primarily responsible for Israel . . . and for the impossibility of finding a peaceful settlement between the Arabs and Israel. . . . We, therefore, do not expect the meeting of the three Western Foreign Ministers to protect our rights in Palestine, for it is they who robbed us of Palestine and gave her to Israel. Nor do we expect them to settle the problems between us and Israel because, as the creators of a usurping state in our land, they cannot remove it from existence—the only settlement satisfactory to the Arabs."

JUNE 11, 1955
Library to AF

By official action the Arab states—and Arab agitators by sustained verbal and written propaganda—continue to intensify their attacks outside of Israel against Jews as Jews. In the United States these attacks are manifested by attempts to strike at American businessmen of the Jewish faith. Since 1953, American concerns have received demands for "certificates of non-Jewish origin" from Saudi Arabia. On September 22, 1953, a letter was sent to a New England concern by a Saudi Arabian importer who wrote as follows:

[Saudi Arabian] merchants . . . know that it is forbidden to deal with a Jewish company or with a company whose any of its workmen is Jewish or has branch in Israel, and if a merchant intended to deal with a company and knows that the same company is not Jewish, should also be asked to submit a letter of certificate issued by the Chamber of Commerce certifying that neither of its workmen is Jewish nor has branch in Israel.

Therefore we will request you to furnish us with a certificate issued by your local Chamber of Commerce to that effect.

Please note that if your consignment arrived here without being accompanied by the certificate called for, the merchandise will be confiscated; not only that, we will have to sustain many other expenses related to it.

If your firm is coinciding with the decree passed by our government, we shall . . . request our banks to redirect the goods to Bahrain . . . where we shall arrange disposal. Otherwise, it is necessary that we will have the order cancelled. . . . We believe you agree with our suggestion so that we avoid any unforeseen consequences that would prove fatal.

Another tactic devised by the Arab states to discomfort and impede Americans of the Jewish faith has been to refuse visas to Jews traveling through the Middle East. This policy has imposed grave disabilities and hardships upon Jewish travelers. An American physician of the Jewish faith attempted to travel from Karachi to Istanbul. Because the plane in which she was traveling was scheduled to stop at Iraq where she would be subject to immediate arrest as a Jew, her reservation was canceled. As a result she was left stranded in Karachi until a route was finally worked out to take her to Istanbul by way of Abadan and Rome. This kind of incident is a daily occurrence.

JUNE 13, 1955
Library to AF

While you are on the subject of Arab double-talk, keep in mind that this deceitful practice is pursued on many issues; on the concept of democracy, for example. To the Western world the Arabs offer themselves as believers in democracy, but at home they tell a different story. Their totalitarianism is not only practiced, it is also bragged about. Last November the Cairo radio reported verbatim Major Salah Salim's speech to the Egyptian Lawyers Association. This is what the Egyptian Minister of National Guidance had to say about democracy in the Arab Middle East: "Low voices rise here and there, now and then, and

III Cross-Currents in the Middle East

high voices rise outside Egypt against this regime, and condemn it. We are told: 'You announce now and then that you desire sound democratic life. What about these concentration camps? Why do you arrest the innocent? Why do you put them in prison? Why do you destroy the parties? Why do you restrict the freedom of the press?'

"I tell them, 'Yes, we have imprisoned hundreds of people. We have restricted the freedom of the press. We firmly believe that without taking such measures we would not be able to achieve the greatest freedom and the liberation of the country. We were similar to any army fighting a life or death battle. We could have relaxed these restrictions. We could have left the parties intact, we could have let the press speak and publish as it wished. We could have set up a parliament of some kind. All of you realized that by doing this we would not have been able to solve any of the country's problems. . . . We were of the firm belief that by having freedom of the press in the circumstances in which we were living in the past and are living now we could not have reached our greater freedom."

JUNE 19, 1955
Research to AF

The Arab League is leaving nothing to chance in so far as the Arab students in this country are concerned. AFME has, of course, been a great help, with its student conferences on the Middle East, conferences from which Israeli students were carefully excluded. But conferences are not enough; these students obviously represent a full-time propaganda investment for the Arabs. In line with this, last month they were sent a directive from the Arab Center offices in New York.

The directive is titled: "Observations about How to Fight Zionism in the USA." It was preceded by a letter, signed by Rahim, asking all Arab students to work and fight for the cause of their nation in the U.S.A.

The "Observations" themselves are what you might expect: the usual polite palaver about the political menace that Zionism represents to the

Arab world, and the "tragedy" of Israel's formation as a state. The students were also informed that the Zionists have directed the bulk of their propaganda to America because "America has the greatest number of Jews." This, of course, was to underline for the students the importance of their counterefforts.

The directive, therefore, after its background notes, provides the students with arguments and suggested tactics. Everything is very discreetly managed. Two examples will suffice:

Nowhere is Judaism referred to, but the students are urged that: "You should always prove your love for democracy and freedom and your respect for the US people, and you should always show the close relations between the spiritual religions of Islam and Christianity."

This little gem of propaganda by omission is all the more significant in that the students are also directed: ". . . the most important point is to stress the difference between Jews and Zionists." And they are to point out that the "struggle against Zionism is a struggle against an imperialistic movement which has occupied an Arab land and which is trying to grab other parts of the Arab world, not actually a fight against a religious community."

In the meantime, the directive clearly implies, better not mention the "spiritual religion" of Judaism. Judaism—which gave the initial inspiration to Christianity and Islam.

Then, too, the students are to argue that "the Arab nations have announced their disposition to conclude peace with Israel on the basis of the implementation of the UN resolutions." Surely the Arab Information Center and its head are familiar with the real Arab position, which has been stated time and again at home, and which was summed up in one sentence last December by Major Salah Salim, the Egyptian Minister of National Guidance: "... *the Egyptian policy is not to accept peace with Israel in any form and by any means even if Israel complies with the UN resolutions.*" Surely Rahim knows this intransigent opposition to any settlement with Israel. He knows that the above "argument" is misleading, to say the least. This is hardly in keeping with another part of the directive, which states:

". . . the Arab Information Center was opened in New York not in

III Cross-Currents in the Middle East

order to conduct a merely empty propaganda effort but to give the true facts to the U.S. people about the exact nature of the Arab world."

Empty or not, the Center is certainly overlooking nothing and nobody in its efforts. Rahim is a busy man.

JUNE 21, 1955

Middle Eastern Correspondent to Research

Kamil Abdul Rahim's reports to his home office, the Arab League, are being summarized over the local radio in the Middle East. Today's report revealed that the Arab states are conducting talks with the United States government for the purpose of stopping American aid to Israel.

JUNE 26, 1955

Middle Eastern Correspondent to Research

Kamil Abdul Rahim has prepared an "analysis" of the March ADL release about his new office in New York City, which has been broadcast throughout the Middle East in the last three days.

Yesterday the Cairo radio said that the Arab League received a report that hostility against the Zionists in America is growing day by day. The report was further quoted as maintaining that the Zionists had been compelled to take organized countermeasures through an organization called the "B'nai B'rith." It was also reported that the Americans resent this behavior on the part of the Zionists and are taking all possible measures to combat this power that is attempting to control them.

From the Ramallah, Jordan radio, at the same time, came a statement that the Arab League had received information from reliable sources in the United States that the Zionists in that country had been increasing their attacks against the Arabs during the last fortnight: they are accusing the Arab Office in New York of racial discrimination (anti-Semitism). The report advises that a well-known American news commentator said that the Jewish campaign against the Arabs indicates for the first time the fear of the Zionists that there is ever increasing apprehension among Americans concerning Jewish control in different economic fields. And the Zionists have threatened television companies, the radio, and the Jewish press that they will stop advertising through their media if they do not increase their propaganda against the Arabs.

On the other hand, some Americans have come to the Egyptian Embassy and to the Arab Office, the report went on to say, and have offered their services for the distribution of pamphlets against Zionism. The deputy director of the Egyptian desk in the American Foreign Office (State Department) stated, according to the report, that in his opinion the Zionists are afraid that there may be a possibility of solving the tensions along the armistice line, since Israel is exploiting these tensions to achieve unity among the Jews and for fund-raising purposes.

Three days ago the Voice of the Arabs said that the Arab Office in New York reported to the Arab League on the rift between the Arab Office and Jewish organizations. The report states, according to the Voice, that these organizations are pressuring the United States government to prevent further distribution of an Arab League pamphlet on Israel espionage in Egypt, a pamphlet that has made a deep impression upon Americans.

Not only does the Voice of the Arabs keep the Arab world informed on the battle against American Zionism, it also is featuring a series of talks on "International Zionism." Although the Arab stand, on the diplomatic level, is that they oppose Zionism because of its political intrusions into *their* world, and not on any racist or religious grounds, the following excerpts from yesterday's talk should demonstrate just how broadly they mean the term "Zionist" to be really taken:

"Zionism cannot pursue an honest course. Should it do so it would contradict its faith that Israel has a God of its own that cannot be shared by other peoples. The Zionists who claim that God is theirs alone and that they are his chosen people do not permit anybody to share this monopoly with them. The Zionists never preach their re-

III Cross-Currents in the Middle East

ligion as others of different religions do. All they can do is to destroy other people's faith, ethics and teachings.

"Zionism has taken part in every movement of destruction; the last of these movements in which it has participated is the movement of Communism. A Zionist may be a millionaire, but nevertheless he encourages the spread of Communism and at the same time finances it with money and propaganda."

The speaker then went on to identify leaders of the Russian Revolution by their "Zionist" names: Zinoviev was really Hirsch Apfelbaum, Yagoda was really Yahuda, etc. Anyone who has read Conde McGinley's forays into political history will find all this pretty familiar stuff.

That may be merely one of those coincidences where "great minds" move in the same channel. Little was left to coincidence, however, when the Voice of the Arabs quoted from Mrs. Van Hyning's *Women's Voice* nine days ago.

In the course of some remarks "proving" that "the West does not like Israel nor does it show any kindness toward the Jews, merely because they are Jews" but "supports Israel because Zionism has succeeded in convincing [it] that to support Israel is in itself to support its own interests," the speaker, Ahmad Said, documented his thesis with the words of "the great author [Milner]." Here are some excerpts:

"The United States is a land for Jews in which they can tell lies and loot as they like. . . . When the Jews co-operate with the communists, the Americans only blame themselves because they have not taught those immigrants patriotism. The Jews have never felt love for the homeland except in connection with Germany—Germany which suffered for five hundred years from the crimes of the Jews. . . . The Jews have given the secret of the atom bomb to Russia. The Jews sacrificed for this purpose the two-member Jewish Rosenberg family. . . . This state of affairs cannot be tolerated any longer. . . ."

The speaker also quoted a resident in South Africa about the "efforts of international Zionism to bring about the realization of the domination of the world by the Jews." And among the "treacherous Jews" cited as participants in this plot was Alger Hiss.

It would defeat the efforts of any semantics expert, I am sure, to differentiate between anti-Zionism and old reliable anti-Semitism in the quoted broadcasts; even if the Arabs, being Semitic, cannot possibly be anti-Semitic. We know *that* semantic bit of sleight of hand.

Also, it would interest me very much to discover through what channels the Arabs get their foreign-published anti-Jewish literature. *Women's Voice* is hardly a publication one runs across casually. Who collects this stuff and sends it from the States?

JULY 1, 1955
Library to Research

The "great author" quoted on the Voice of the Arabs is Eustace Mullins (not "Milner"), the gutter anti-Semite whose writings have been published by only the lowest hate sheets in the country. The quotes were taken from a Mullins article entitled "Why Do the Jews Hate America?" which appeared in the March 1955 issue of *Women's Voice*.

JULY 1, 1955
AF to BRE

In a sense it hardly matters who is providing the Arab radio with its supply of American anti-Semitic material. The significant thing is the rapport between the Arab propagandists and our domestic hate peddlers. And the consistency with which they echo and quote each other makes that rapport obvious, even if we had no other evidence of it. Which, in any case, we do. Nor does the Arab world even need the American literature; Rahim's office seems to be supplying them with summaries of the stuff.

We have here a report from our Middle Eastern Correspondent that should interest you. It will make the above remarks abundantly clear.

Kamil Abdul Rahim's report to the Arab League headquarters in Cairo, which has been given the radio coverage I already informed you of, has now been reproduced in the press. The Egyptian newspaper *Al Gomhouria,* organ of the army, ran it June 26. Here are some excerpts:

> The revelations of the scandals of espionage in the U.S. which allowed the Russians to obtain the atom secrets increased tremendously the horrified feelings of the people against them when it was revealed that the majority of the spies who engaged themselves in such operations were Jews.
>
> From that day on, the idea of associating Judaism and communism started in America. The series of campaigns, started in order to fight McCarthy in his struggle against communism, increased this feeling, since it appeared to public opinion that those suspected of communism were Jews to the extent of 90%. The general statistic proved that the average American believes that the Jew is a clever man but sly and unreliable in his general attitude. . . .
>
> The Jews have a strength in American life because of their great influence in government circles and among the very wealthy . . . and it is known that those who have influence in the U.S. fear the Jews and try always to be nice to them in order not to provoke their fury and not to face their terrible revenges. . . .
>
> Among the plans which the Jews use in order to strengthen themselves is to obtain unity with other minorities like the Negroes, making them believe that they are persecuted. They have actually succeeded in winning many of them to their side, although the statistics prove that the majority hate the Jews, distrust them and try to avoid them.

JULY 6, 1955
AF to BRE

Just in case you haven't had enough, please be informed that four days ago Dr. Ezzat Tannous wrote a letter to James Madole of the National Renaissance Party in which, wishing the petty Fuehrer of the NRP "good luck," he expressed the hope that they could get together soon.

Apparently Madole has been furnishing Tannous with material, for the good doctor writes Madole that he has "received last week the interesting package of informative documents you were kind enough to send me and I am reading them with great care and interest. Since I am leaving soon for a short trip to Beirut, Lebanon, I will not be able to see you before my departure but I do hope sincerely to do so, upon my return. There are many problems which I would like very much to talk about with you."

AUGUST 5, 1955
Library to AF

The cultural exchange between the Arab countries of the Middle East and the United States, so devoutly championed by AFME and the Arab Information Center, is going strong. It may be true that the cultural ideas being exchanged have either a strong family resemblance or are identical, but at least one can say that they're getting around. And so are the cultured types who are expounding them.

You may recall that the Rev. Mr. Winrod had a brief contact with Rahim three years ago when Rahim was Egyptian ambassador. You certainly remember the directives to Arab students in the United States that Rahim's Arab Information Center put out this year: one of the cultural arguments advised for the students was the affinity between Islam and Christianity. Well, this idea has gotten back to the Middle East; and the Rev. Mr. Winrod with it.

The Beirut *Daily Star,* leading English-language newspaper in Lebanon and Syria, on July 29 carried a story on a talk made by Winrod during a tour of the Middle East countries, about which "he is writing reports for 23 American journals and newspapers." Winrod is described as "active in American politics having once been a candidate for the United States Senate. He is known to have powerful contacts in the Government of Washington, D.C. . . . [and] is internationally famous as a radio speaker, with a daily broadcast in America that enjoys a listening audience of over six million."

The dispatch then prints in full "a talk he recently gave over the Jordanian Jerusalem Radio . . ." in the course of which he had occasion to quote—himself. "Bear in mind," he cautioned his listeners, "that I was speaking as a Christian leader, addressing my remarks to a radio

III Cross-Currents in the Middle East

listening audience in the Western world." Here is the substance, with quotes, of his self-citation:

"'Every religion on the face of the earth is today threatened by the forces of international atheism. . . . International atheism makes no discrimination between the mosque of the Moslems and the church of the Christians. It is motivated by blind demoniac hatred for all religion. . . . Atheism has taken the initiative. Religion now assume [sic] the aggressive.'"

Winrod then took a short time (before further defining the atheism that apparently does not attack synagogues) to put aside the differences between Moslem and Christian beliefs as unimportant in view of the "basic fundamentals on which agreement exists. . . ." And he commended "the Moslems for standing like a dike . . ." without which "atheism would have swept across the Middle East, the Mediterranean and into Africa."

So far, except for the oversight of one of the Western world's important religions, his talk was not much more than artful hogwash with a thin flavoring of comparative theology. Even his little omission might have been put down to diplomatic tact. And his geographical description of the possible course of "atheism" appears to threaten Israel as well as the rest. But he did not leave his audience with an undiplomatic doubt about the extent of his sympathies or the nature of what he considered his foes and theirs.

"Finally, on this subject, let me say that both Moslem and Christian face the same enemy, atheism, Communism and Zionism . . ." was Winrod's eventual clarification. And surely we know enough by now about "Zionism," as used in similar contexts, to know exactly how the word was understood by Winrod's public.

The central purpose unifying the divergent countries of the Arab League is a determination to destroy Israel. A major task assigned to Kamil Abdul Rahim, director of their Information Center in the United States, is to help them achieve that goal. His plans for the Arab Information Center are ambitious; the Center can be invaluable in co-ordinating the lobbying of the Arab states at the UN and in Washington. Every public relations medium must be exploited—press, pub-

lications, radio, TV, and the lecturer's platform. Arab exchange students must be utilized. The American Friends of the Middle East must be used. And, of course, as we have now seen beyond a shadow of doubt, the unsavory assortment of American anti-Semites must be contacted, cultivated, and traded with.

Expansion of Arab Center activities will intensify but not change the basic propaganda themes: despite the Arab-Czech arms deal of September 1955, Arab countries will be painted in the United States as an anti-communist bastion; increased shipments of arms from the Soviet world to the Arabs will be justified as necessary to safeguard the Middle East against Israeli aggression; crocodile tears will be shed over the truly tragic plight of the Arab refugees who will be portrayed as victims of Israeli barbarism; Zionism will be simultaneously branded as a handmaiden of Western imperialism and Soviet communism; and, of course, the illusion of the Arab states as defenders of Christian holy places will not be neglected. (Arab propaganda prepared for home consumption in the Middle East will continue to be substantially different from the themes utilized by Kamil Abdul Rahim in the United States. For Middle East purposes there is already a soft-pedaling of anti-communist propaganda and an increase to a fever pitch of anti-Western invective. Rahim is only too acutely aware of the severe contradictions between the Arab propaganda line at home and the one he utilizes in the U.S. This does not make his job impossible, simply more difficult.)

Already being distributed in this country is an illustrated booklet called Jewish Atrocities in the Holy Land. It was published in Cairo by the Arab League Information Bureau; it deals with Zionist "crimes" of course, not Jewish. We have seen other similar booklets distributed, we have seen some of the people and organizations that distributed them. There will be more of the same.

The work of Arab exchange students is already fully under way. On August 8, 1955, the Cairo radio reported that the Arab League had "mobilized the efforts of Arab students studying abroad, particularly in the United States. . . . It has distributed pamphlets among them and has furnished them with information required to combat Zionism. It has also asked them to perform the duty of making propaganda in favor of their countries through speeches and articles in and outside of their universities."

One can also make a safe guess that the real position of the Arab League—no peace with Israel—will seldom be admitted by the Arabs in the United States, and that Rahim will continue to disclaim any use of American anti-Semites. It is also fairly certain that his anti-Zionist information will, in its general orientation, remain remarkably similar to what has long been known as anti-Semitic propaganda.

It is also certain that, in keeping with all its aims, the Arab Information Center will continue to spread divisive confusion in the United States wherever it can. If nothing else, this was foreshadowed at a conference held last November by Rahim and the Arab UN delegates.

Rahim told the Arab diplomats that there is an "absolute" need for a "real concerted effort" on the question of Israel. He described Israel as the "real danger and the real enemy." But he also stressed the importance of avoiding any impression that the Center is only concerned with that problem.

Rahim also said he will not permit his office to become involved in charges of anti-Semitism. Accordingly, use of the word "Jew" or overt anti-Semitism of any kind should be barred. However, Rahim maintains that you can attack Jews without resorting to open anti-Semitism because in the United States Zionists and Jews often get mixed up in the public mind. "I know this and experienced it," he said, indicating plainly that he intended to exploit this confusion. Part of his plan, he says, will be to fight Zionist pressure on U.S. public opinion, a pressure which he contends is "actually promoted by Jewish interests." Both the "Zionist pressure" and the "Jewish interests," he said, are his targets.

Rahim has been carefully exploiting the confusion. On September 5, 1955, speaking in Madison, Wisconsin, at the open session of the fourth annual convention of the Organization of Arab Students in the U.S., he said the Arab states have three basic political problems: to consolidate their newly won independence, to help Arabs in North Africa and Southern Yemen win independence, and to combat "the Zionist menace."

"Vociferous enemies of the Arab world," he said, "well organized and in virtual control of many an instrument of communication in this land, have made it their job to discredit your civilization, to distort the truths about your situations, to misrepresent your problems and in every possible way to poison the minds of the noble American people against you. Whether we like it or not, a clever and organized and vicious propaganda machine is daily grinding out lies and disseminating half truths about us. But . . . I can honestly assure you that the situation is not hopeless and that Zionist propaganda, regardless of the unlimited funds at its disposal and the other advantages which it enjoys, will not in the end succeed in blinding the eyes and minds of a people as essentially fair-minded and open-minded as the American people."

6 The Touchstone

Thus, to attack the American Jewish community, the magic word is "Zionist." Such tactics have long been standard practice among the country's top anti-Semites.

This basic purpose of the Arab propaganda project, conceived and directed by agents of a foreign power, is aimed at many Americans who are not at all concerned with Middle East politics; and can only lead to increased tension within our borders at a time when the nation can ill afford it. There is an ample supply of native hatemongers bedeviling American minorities and seeking to divide us without foreign importations. In ultimate terms, the Arab League propaganda objective can be as destructive here as a fifth column.

A Final Word

And so our book ends—but not the story. In the struggle of civilized people to obliterate prejudice and bigotry the end is not yet in sight. The story will continue to develop from day to day so long as men are willing to permit their bitter and illogical hatreds to color their attitudes and actions.

Our book, reaching as it does into three major regions of the world, is rooted in great political issues which have arisen in each of these places. For Germany a complex question is clearly evident: what are the most effective antidotes to the fascist infection that remains as a potential threat in this re-created democracy? On this question there is great room for argument. With respect to the Middle East the problem is equally complicated: how best can permanent peace be brought to that war-fevered area? On this problem, too, there is great room for argument. Here at home the issue is no less difficult: how do we offset the menace of communist conspiracy and the dangers of domestic hatemongering without limiting our basic constitutional liberties? Again, there is much room for argument.

But as much latitude as there may be for legitimate controversy in all of these issues, we must never agree that there is sufficient room for the injection of religious or racial bigotry. Nor should we permit room

A Final Word

for the injection of spurious argumentation which, while seemingly genuine, is actually based in or stimulated by hatred.

There are men who will abuse the normal give-and-take processes that are pursued in the shaping of public opinion in a democracy. Complex political issues which cause great cleavages among the people will be the opportunities for these men to poison healthy public debate and discussion. But their malfeasances will be only interruptions—nothing more. So long as other men, men of good-will, remain alert and report these malignant activities to the general community, and help to create effective countermeasures, the forces of disruption can never stifle our democratic freedoms. This neutralizing task, however, will always be an unfinished business.

Not long ago, U. S. Senator Clifford Case of New Jersey made our point in these words: "Freedom is not something that can be achieved once and for all time. It is a continuing process, a process that survives only as it is lived and practiced. In this sense, freedom is an objective that can never be won. It can only be lost."

The good sense of the American people will, we have faith, always prevent cross-currents of religious prejudice from becoming violent rip tides capable of capsizing the vessel of state.